100 STORY POEMS

Henry C Pitz

100 STORY POEMS

Selected by

ELINOR PARKER

ILLUSTRATED BY HENRY C. PITZ

THOMAS Y. CROWELL COMPANY
New York

For permission to reprint the copyrighted poems in this anthology, acknowledgment is extended to the following:

Brandt & Brandt for "Ballad of William Sycamore" from *Selected Works of Stephen Vincent Benét*, published by Rinehart & Company, Inc., copyright 1922 by Stephen Vincent Benét.

Dodd, Mead & Company for "Lepanto" from *The Collected Poems of G. K. Chesterton*, reprinted by permission of Dodd, Mead & Company, Inc., copyright 1932 by Dodd, Mead & Company, Inc.

Doubleday & Company, Inc. for "Eddi's Service" from *Rewards and Fairies* by Rudyard Kipling, copyright 1910 by Rudyard Kipling, reprinted by permission of Mrs. George Bambridge and Doubleday & Company, Inc.

Doubleday & Company, Inc. for "Save the Tiger" from *Laughing Ann* by A. P. Herbert, copyright 1926 by Doubleday & Company, Inc. reprinted by permission of the author and the Proprietors of *Punch*.

Harcourt, Brace and Company, Inc. for "Growltiger's Last Stand" from *Old Possum's Book of Practical Cats* by T. S. Eliot, copyright 1939 by T. S. Eliot, reprinted by permission of Harcourt, Brace and Company, Inc.

Henry Holt and Company, Inc. for "Berries" from *Collected Poems, 1901–1918* by Walter de la Mare, copyright 1920 by Henry Holt and Company, Inc., copyright 1948 by Walter de la Mare, used by permission of the publishers.

Houghton Mifflin Company for "The Enchanted Shirt" from *Pike County Ballads* by John Hay.

Alfred A. Knopf for "Jim" from *Cautionary Verses* by Hilaire Belloc, reprinted by permission of Alfred A. Knopf, Inc., copyright 1931 by Hilaire Belloc.

Alfred A. Knopf for "Dunkirk" from *Dunkirk* by Robert Nathan, reprinted by permission of Alfred A. Knopf, Inc., copyright 1941, 1945 by Robert Nathan.

165430

For Charlotte Elinor Parker

CONTENTS

POEMS ABOUT HISTORY

THE SKELETON IN ARMOR

"Speak! speak! thou fearful guest!
    Who, with thy hollow breast
Still in rude armor drest,
    Comest to daunt me!
Wrapt not in Eastern balms,
But with thy fleshless palms
Stretched, as if asking alms,
    Why dost thou haunt me?"

Then, from those cavernous eyes
Pale flashes seemed to rise,
As when the Northern skies
    Gleam in December;
And, like the water's flow
Under December's snow,
Came a dull voice of woe
    From the heart's chamber.

"I was a Viking old!
My deeds, though manifold,
No Skald in song has told
    No Saga taught thee!
Take heed, that in thy verse
Thou dost the tale rehearse,

Else dread a dead man's curse;
    For this I sought thee.

"Far in the Northern Land,
By the wild Baltic's strand,
I, with my childish hand,
    Tamed the gerfalcon;
And, with my skates fast-bound,
Skimmed the half-frozen Sound,
That the poor whimpering hound
    Trembled to walk on.

"Oft to his frozen lair
Tracked I the grisly bear,
While from my path the hare
    Fled like a shadow;
Oft through the forest dark
Followed the were-wolf's bark,
Until the soaring lark
    Sang from the meadow.

"But when I older grew,
Joining a corsair's crew,
O'er the dark sea I flew
    With the marauders.
Wild was the life we led;
Many the souls that sped,
Many the hearts that bled,
    By our stern orders.

[3]

"Many a wassail-bout
Wore the long Winter out;
Often our midnight shout
  Set the cocks crowing,
As we the Berserk's tale
Measured in cups of ale,
Draining the oaken pail,
  Filled to o'erflowing.

"Once as I told in glee
Tales of the stormy sea,
Soft eyes did gaze on me,
  Burning yet tender;
And as the white stars shine
On the dark Norway pine,
On that dark heart of mine
  Fell their soft splendor.

"I wooed the blue-eyed maid,
Yielding, yet half afraid,
And in the forest's shade
  Our vows were plighted.
Under its loosened vest
  Fluttered her little breast,
Like birds within their nest
  By the hawk frighted.

"Bright in her father's hall
Shields gleamed upon the wall,

[4]

Loud sang the minstrels all,
  Chanting his glory;
When of old Hildebrand
I asked his daughter's hand,
Mute did the minstrels stand
  To hear my story.

"While the brown ale he quaffed,
Loud then the champion laughed,
And as the wind-gusts waft
  The sea-foam brightly,
So the loud laugh of scorn,
Out of those lips unshorn,
From the deep drinking-horn
  Blew the foam lightly.

"She was a Prince's child,
I but a Viking wild,
And though she blushed and smiled,
  I was discarded!
Should not the dove so white
Follow the sea-mew's flight,
Why did they leave that night
  Her nest unguarded?

"Scarce had I put to sea,
Bearing the maid with me,
Fairest of all was she
  Among the Norsemen!

When on the white sea-strand,
Waving his arméd hand,
Saw we old Hildebrand,
    With twenty horsemen.

"Then launched they to the blast,
Bent like a reed each mast,
Yet we were gaining fast,
    When the wind failed us;
And with a sudden flaw
Came round the gusty Skaw,
So that our foe we saw
    Laugh as he failed us.

"And as to catch the gale
Round veered the flapping sail,
" 'Death!' was the helmsman's hail,
    " 'Death without quarter!'
Mid-ships with iron keel
Struck we her ribs of steel;
Down her black hulk did reel
    Through the black water!

"As with his wings aslant,
Sails the fierce cormorant,
Seeking some rocky haunt,
    With his prey laden,—
So toward the open main,
Beating to sea again,

Through the wild hurricane,
   Bore I the maiden.

"Three weeks we westward bore,
And when the storm was o'er,
Cloud-like we saw the shore
   Stretching to leeward;
There for my lady's bower,
Built I the lofty tower
Which, to this very hour,
   Stands looking seaward.

"There lived we many years;
Time dried the maiden's tears;
She had forgot her fears,
   She was a mother;
Death closed her mild blue eyes,
Under that tower she lies!
Ne'er shall the sun arise
   On such another!

"Still grew my bosom then,
Still as a stagnant fen!
Hateful to me were men,
   The sunlight was hateful!
In the vast forest here,
Clad in my warlike gear,
Fell I upon my spear,
   Oh, death was grateful!

"Thus, seamed with many scars,
Bursting these prisons bars,
Up to its native stars
  My soul ascended!
There from the flowing bowl
Deep drinks the warrior's soul,
Skoal! to the Northland! *Skoal!*"
  Thus the tale ended.

HENRY WADSWORTH LONGFELLOW

COLUMBUS

Behind him lay the gray Azores,
Behind the Gates of Hercules;
Before him not the ghost of shores,
Before him only shoreless seas.
The good mate said: "Now we must pray,
For lo! the very stars are gone.
Brave Admiral, speak, what shall I say?"
"Why, say, 'Sail on! sail on! and on!' "

"My men grow mutinous day by day;
My men grow ghastly wan and weak."
The stout mate thought of home; a spray
Of salt wave washed his swarthy cheek.
"What shall I say, brave Admiral, say,
If we sight naught but seas at dawn?"
"Why, you shall say at break of day,
'Sail on! sail on! and on!' "

They sailed and sailed, as wind might blow,
Until at last the blanched mate said:
"Why, now not even God would know
Should I and all my men fall dead.
These very winds forget their way,
For God from these dread seas is gone.

Now speak, brave Admiral, speak and say"—
He said, "Sail on! sail on! and on!"

They sailed. They sailed. Then spake the mate:
"This mad sea shows his teeth tonight.
He curls his lip, he lies in wait,
With lifted teeth, as if to bite!
Brave Admiral, say but one good word:
What shall we do when hope is gone?"
The words leapt like a leaping sword:
"Sail on! sail on! sail on! and on!"

Then pale and worn, he kept his deck,
And peered through darkness. Ah, that night
Of all dark nights! And then a speck—
A light! a light! at last a light!
It grew, a starlit flag unfurled!
It grew to be Time's burst of dawn.
He gained a world; he gave that world
Its grandest lesson: "On! sail on!"

JOAQUIN MILLER

LANDING OF THE PILGRIM FATHERS

The breaking waves dashed high
On a stern and rock-bound coast;
And the woods against a stormy sky,
Their giant branches tossed;
And the heavy night hung dark
The hills and waters o'er—
When a band of exiles moored their bark
On a wild New England shore.

Not as the conqueror comes,
They, the true-hearted, came;—
Not with the roll of stirring drums,
And the trumpets that sing of fame;—
Not as the flying come,
In silence and in fear;
They shook the depths of the desert's gloom
With their hymns of lofty cheer.

Amidst the storm they sang,
And the stars heard, and the sea!
And the sounding aisles of the dim woods rang
To the anthem of the free;
The ocean eagle soared
From his nest by the white wave's foam,

And the rocking pines of the forest roared:—
This was their welcome home!

There were men with hoary hair
Amidst that pilgrim band;
Why had they come to wither there,
Away from their childhood's land?
There was woman's fearless eye,
Lit by her deep love's truth;
There was manhood's brow serenely high,
And the fiery heart of youth.

What sought they thus afar?
Bright jewels of the mine?
The wealth of seas? the spoils of war?
They sought a faith's pure shrine!
Ay, call it holy ground,
The soil where first they trod!
They left unstained what there they found—
Freedom to worship God!

FELICIA DOROTHEA HEMANS

PAUL REVERE'S RIDE

Listen, my children, and you shall hear
Of the midnight ride of Paul Revere,
On the eighteenth of April, in Seventy-five;
Hardly a man is now alive
Who remembers that famous day and year.
He said to his friend, "If the British march
By land or sea from the town tonight,
Hang a lantern aloft in the belfry arch
Of the North Church tower as a signal light,—
One, if by land, and two, if by sea;
And I on the opposite shore will be,
Ready to ride and spread the alarm
Through every Middlesex village and farm,
For the country folk to be up and to arm."

Then he said, "Good night!" and with muffled oar
Silently rowed to the Charlestown shore,
Just as the moon rose over the bay,
Where swinging wide at her moorings lay
The *Somerset*, British man-of-war;
A phantom ship, with each mast and spar
Across the moon like a prison bar,
And a huge black hulk, that was magnified
By its own reflection in the tide.

Meanwhile, his friend through alley and street
Wanders and watches, with eager ears,
Till in the silence around him he hears
The muster of men at the barrack door,
The sound of arms, and the tramp of feet,
And the measured tread of the grenadiers,
Marching down to their boats on the shore.

Then he climbed the tower of the Old North Church,
By the wooden stairs, with stealthy tread,
To the belfry-chamber overhead,
And startled the pigeons from their perch
On the somber rafters, that round him made
Masses and moving shapes of shade,—
By the trembling ladder, steep and tall,
To the highest window in the wall,
Where he paused to listen and look down
A moment on the roofs of the town
And the moonlight flowing over all.

Beneath in the churchyard, lay the dead,
In their night-encampment on the hill,
Wrapped in silence so deep and still
That he could hear, like a sentinel's tread,
The watchful night-wind, as it went
Creeping along from tent to tent,
And seeming to whisper, "All is well!"
A moment only he feels the spell
Of the place and the hour, and the secret dread

Of the lonely belfry and the dead;
For suddenly all his thoughts are bent
On a shadowy something far away,
Where the river widens to meet the bay,—
A line of black that bends and floats
On the rising tide, like a bridge of boats.

Meanwhile, impatient to mount and ride,
Booted and spurred, with a heavy stride
On the opposite shore walked Paul Revere.
Now he patted his horse's side,
Now gazed at the landscape far and near,
Then, impetuous, stamped the earth,
And turned and tightened his saddle girth;
But mostly he watched with eager search
The belfry tower of the Old North Church,
Lonely and spectral and somber and still.
And lo! as he looks, on the belfry height
A glimmer, and then a gleam of light!
He springs to the saddle, the bridle he turns,
But lingers and gazes, till full on his sight
A second lamp in the belfry burns!

A hurry of hoofs in a village street,
A shape in the moonlight, a bulk in the dark,
And beneath, from the pebbles, in passing, a spark
Struck out by a steed flying fearless and fleet;
That was all! And yet, through the gloom and the light,
The fate of a nation was riding that night;

And the spark struck out by that steed, in his flight,
Kindled the land into flame with its heat.
He has left the village and mounted the steep,
And beneath him, tranquil and broad and deep,
Is the Mystic, meeting the ocean tides;
And under the alders that skirt its edge,
Now soft on the sand, now loud on the ledge,
Is heard the tramp of his steed as he rides.

It was twelve by the village clock,
When he crossed the bridge into Medford town.
He heard the crowing of the cock,
And the barking of the farmer's dog,
And he felt the damp of the river fog,
That rises after the sun goes down.

It was one by the village clock,
When he galloped into Lexington.
He saw the gilded weathercock
Swim in the moonlight as he passed,
And the meeting-house windows, blank and bare,
Gaze at him with a spectral glare,
As if they already stood aghast
At the bloody work they would look upon.

It was two by the village clock,
When he came to the bridge in Concord town.
He heard the bleating of the flock,
And the twitter of birds among the trees,

And felt the breath of the morning breeze
Blowing over the meadows brown.
And one was safe and asleep in his bed
Who at the bridge would be first to fall,
Who that day would be lying dead,
Pierced by a British musket-ball.

You know the rest. In books you have read,
How the British Regulars fired and fled,—
How the farmers gave them ball for ball,
From behind each fence and farmyard wall,
Chasing the redcoats down the lane,
Then crossing the fields to emerge again
Under the trees at the turn of the road,
And only pausing to fire and load.

So through the night rode Paul Revere;
And so through the night went his cry of alarm
To every Middlesex village and farm,—
A cry of defiance, and not of fear,
A voice in the darkness, a knock at the door,
And a word that shall echo for evermore!
For, borne on the night-wind of the Past,
Through all our history, to the last,
In the hour of darkness and peril and need,
The people will waken and listen to hear
The hurrying hoof-beats of that steed,
And the midnight message of Paul Revere.

HENRY WADSWORTH LONGFELLOW

DEATH AND GENERAL PUTNAM

His iron arm had spent its force,
No longer might he rein a horse;
Lone, beside the dying blaze
Dreaming dreams of younger days
   Sat old Israel Putnam.

Twice he heard, then three times more
A knock upon the open door,
A knock he could not fail to know,
That old man in the ember-glow.
   "Come," said General Putnam.

The door swung wide; in cloak and hood
Lean and tall the pilgrim stood
And spoke in tones none else might hear,
"Once more I come to bring you Fear!"
   "Fear?" said General Putnam.

"You know not Fear? And yet this face
Your eyes have seen in many a place
Since first in stony Pomfret, when

You dragged the mad wolf from her den."
  "Yes," said General Putnam.

"Was I not close, when, stripped and bound
With blazing fagots heaped around
You heard the Huron war cry shrill?
Was I not close at Bunker Hill?"
  "Close," said General Putnam.

"Am I not that which strong men dread
On stricken field or fevered bed
On gloomy trail and stormy sea,
And dare you name my name to me?"
  "Death," said General Putnam.

"We have been comrades, you and I,
In chase and war beneath this sky;
And now, whatever Fate may send,
Old comrade, can you call me friend?"
  "Friend!" said General Putnam.

Then up he rose, and forth they went
Away from battleground, fortress, tent,
Mountain, wilderness, field and farm,
Death and the General, arm-in-arm,
  Death and General Putnam.
                    ARTHUR GUITERMAN

DANIEL BOONE

Daniel Boone at twenty-one
Came with his tomahawk, knife, and gun
Home from the French and Indian War
To North Carolina and the Yadkin shore.
He married his maid with a golden band,
Builded his house and cleared his land;
But the deep woods claimed their son again
And he turned his face from the homes of men.
Over the Blue Ridge, dark and lone,
The Mountains of Iron, the Hills of Stone,
Braving the Shawnee's jealous wrath,
He made his way on the Warrior's Path.
Alone he trod the shadowed trails;
But he was lord of a thousand vales
As he roved Kentucky, far and near,
Hunting the buffalo, elk, and deer.
What joy to see, what joy to win
So fair a land for his kith and kin,
Of streams unstained and woods unhewn!
"Elbow room!" laughed Daniel Boone.

"Daniel Boone" from *I Sing the Pioneer* by Arthur Guiterman, published and copyright, 1926, E. P. Dutton & Company, Inc., New York.

On the Wilderness Road that his axmen made
The settlers flocked to the first stockade;
The deerskin shirts and the coonskin caps
Filed through the glens and the mountain gaps;
And hearts were high in the fateful spring
When the land said "Nay!" to the stubborn king.
While the men of the East of farm and town
Strove with the troops of the British Crown,
Daniel Boone from a surge of hate
Guarded a nation's westward gate.
Down in the fort in a wave of flame
The Shawnee horde and the Mingo came,
And the stout logs shook in a storm of lead;
But Boone stood firm and the savage fled.
Peace! And the settlers flocked anew,
The farm lands spread, the town lands grew;
But Daniel Boone was ill at ease
When he saw the smoke in his forest trees.
"There'll be no game in the country soon.
Elbow room!" cried Daniel Boone.

Straight as a pine at sixty-five—
Time enough for a man to thrive—
He launched his bateau on Ohio's breast
And his heart was glad as he oared it west;
There was kindly folk and his own true blood
Where great Missouri rolls his flood;
New woods, new streams, and room to spare,

And Daniel Boone found comfort there.
Yet far he ranged toward the sunset still,
Where the Kansas runs and the Smoky Hill,
And the prairies toss, by the south wind blown;
And he killed his bear on the Yellowstone.
But ever he dreamed of new domains
With vaster woods and wider plains;
Ever he dreamed of a world-to-be
Where there are no bounds and the soul is free.
At fourscore-five, still stout and hale,
He heard a call to a farther trail;
So he turned his face where the stars are strewn;
"Elbow room!" sighed Daniel Boone.

Down the Milky Way in its banks of blue
Far he has paddled his white canoe
To the splendid quest of the tameless soul—
He has reached the goal where there is no goal.
Now he rides and rides an endless trail
On the hippogriff of the flaming tail
Or the horse of the stars with the golden mane,
As he rode the first of the blue-grass strain.
The joy that lies in the search he seeks
On breathless hills with crystal peaks;
He makes his camp on heights untrod,
The steps of the shrine, alone with God.
Through the woods of the vast, on the plains of space
He hunts the pride of the mammoth race
And the dinosaur of the triple horn,

The manticore and the unicorn,
As once by the broad Missouri's flow
He followed the elk and the buffalo.
East of the sun and west of the moon,
"Elbow room!" laughs Daniel Boone.

ARTHUR GUITERMAN

BARBARA FRIETCHIE

Up from the meadows rich with corn,
Clear in the cool September morn,

The clustered spires of Frederick stand
Green-walled by the hills of Maryland,

Round about them orchards sweep,
Apple and peach-tree fruited deep,

Fair as a garden of the Lord
To the eyes of the famished rebel horde,

On that pleasant morn of the early fall
When Lee marched over the mountain wall;

Over the mountains winding down,
Horse and foot, into Frederick town.

Forty flags with their silver stars,
Forty flags with their crimson bars,

Flapped in the morning wind: the sun
Of noon looked down, and saw not one.

Up rose old Barbara Frietchie then,
Bowed with her fourscore years and ten;

Bravest of all in Frederick town,
She took up the flag the men hauled down;

In her attic window the staff she set,
To show that one heart was loyal yet.

Up the street came the rebel tread,
Stonewall Jackson riding ahead.

Under his slouched hat left and right
He glanced; the old flag met his sight.

"Halt!"—the dust-brown ranks stood fast.
"Fire!"—out blazed the rifle blast.

It shivered the window, pane and sash;
It rent the banner with seam and gash.

Quick, as it fell, from the broken staff
Dame Barbara snatched the silken scarf.

She leaned far out on the window-sill,
And shook it forth with a royal will.

"Shoot, if you must, this old grey head,
But spare your country's flag," she said.

A shade of sadness, a blush of shame,
Over the face of the leader came;

The nobler nature within him stirred
To life at that woman's deed and word;

"Who touches a hair of yon grey head
Dies like a dog! March on!" he said.

All day long through Frederick street
Sounded the tread of marching feet:

All day long that free flag tost
Over the heads of the rebel host.

Ever its torn folds rose and fell
On the loyal winds that loved it well;

And through the hill-gaps sunset light
Shone over it with a warm good-night.

Barbara Frietchie's work is o'er,
And the rebel rides on his raids no more.

Honor to her! and let a tear
Fall, for her sake, on Stonewall's bier.

Over Barbara Frietchie's grave,
Flag of freedom and union, wave!

Peace, and order, and beauty draw
Round thy symbol of light and law;

And ever the stars above look down
On thy stars below in Frederick town!

JOHN GREENLEAF WHITTIER

SHERIDAN'S RIDE

Up from the South at break of day,
Bringing to Winchester fresh dismay,
The affrighted air with a shudder bore,
Like a herald in haste, to the chieftain's door,
The terrible grumble, and rumble, and roar,
Telling the battle was on once more,
And Sheridan twenty miles away.

And wider still those billows of war
Thundered along the horizon's bar;
And louder yet into Winchester rolled
The roar of that red sea uncontrolled,
Making the blood of the listener cold,
As he thought of the stake in that fiery fray,
With Sheridan twenty miles away.

But there is a road from Winchester town,
A good, broad highway leading down;
And there, through the flush of the morning light,
A steed as black as the steeds of night
Was seen to pass, as with eagle flight;
As if he knew the terrible need,
He stretched away with the utmost speed;

Hills rose and fell; but his heart was gay,
With Sheridan fifteen miles away.

Still sprung from those swift hoofs, thundering South,
The dust, like smoke from the cannon's mouth;
Or the trail of a comet, sweeping faster and faster,
Foreboding to traitors the doom of disaster,
The heart of the steed and the heart of the master
Were beating like prisoners assaulting their walls,
Impatient to be where the battlefield calls;
Every nerve of the charger was strained to full play,
With Sheridan only ten miles away.

Under his spurning feet the road
Like an arrowy Alpine river flowed,
And the landscape sped away behind
Like an ocean flying before the wind,
And the steed, like a barque fed with furnace ire,
Swept on, with his wild eye full of fire.
But lo! he is nearing his heart's desire;
He is snuffing the smoke of the roaring fray,
With Sheridan only five miles away.

The first that the general saw were the groups
Of stragglers, and then the retreating troops;
What was done? What to do? A glance told him both,
Then striking his spurs, with a terrible oath,
He dashed down the line 'mid a storm of huzzas,
And the wave of retreat checked its course there, because

The sight of the master compelled it to pause.
With foam and with dust the black charger was gray;
By the flash of his eye and the red nostril's play,
He seemed to the whole great army to say,
"I have brought you Sheridan all the way
From Winchester down to save the day!"

Hurrah! Hurrah for Sheridan!
Hurrah! Hurrah for horse and man!
And when their statues are placed on high,
Under the dome of the Union sky,
The American soldier's Temple of Fame;
There with the glorious general's name,
Be it said, in letters both bold and bright,
"Here is the steed that saved the day,
By carrying Sheridan into the fight,
From Winchester, twenty miles away!"

THOMAS BUCHANAN READ

THE WHITE SHIP

By none but me can the tale be told,
The butcher of Rouen, poor Berold.
(*Lands are swayed by a King on a throne.*)
'Twas a royal train put forth to sea
Yet the tale can be told by none but me.
(*The sea hath no King but God alone.*)

King Henry held it as life's whole gain
That after his death his son should reign.

'Twas so in my youth I heard men say,
And my old age calls it back today.

King Henry of England's realm was he,
And Henry Duke of Normandy.

The times had changed when on either coast
"Clerkly Harry" was all his boast.

Of ruthless strokes full many a one
He had struck to crown himself and his son;
And his elder brother's eyes were gone.

And when to the chase his court would crowd,
The poor flung ploughshares on his road,
And shrieked: 'Our cry is from King to God!'

But all the chiefs of the English land
Had knelt and kissed the Prince's hand.

And next with his son he sailed to France
To claim the Norman allegiance:

And every baron in Normandy
Had taken the oath of fealty.

'Twas sworn and sealed, and the day had come
When the King and the Prince might journey home:

For Christmas cheer is to home hearts dear,
And Christmas now was drawing near.

Stout Fitz-Stephen came to the King,—
A pilot famous in seafaring;

And he held to the King, in all men's sight,
A mark of gold for his tribute's right.

"Liege Lord! my father guided the ship
From whose boat your father's foot did slip
When he caught the English soil in his grip,

"And cried: 'By this clasp I claim command
O'er every rood of English land!'

"He was borne to the realm you rule o'er now
In that ship with the archer carved at her prow:

"And thither I'll bear, an it be my due,
Your father's son and his grandson too.

"The famed White Ship is mine in the bay,
From Harfleur's harbor she sails today,

"With masts fair-pennoned as Norman spears
And with fifty well-tried mariners."

Quoth the King: "My ships are chosen each one,
But I'll not say nay to Stephen's son.

"My son and daughter and fellowship
Shall cross the water in the White Ship."

The King set sail with the eve's south wind,
And soon he left that coast behind.

The Prince and all his, a princely show,
Remained in the good White Ship to go.

With noble knights and with ladies fair,
With courtiers and sailors gathered there,
Three hundred living souls we were:

And I Berold was the meanest hind
In all that train to the Prince assign'd.

The Prince was a lawless shameless youth;
From his father's loins he sprang without ruth:

Eighteen years till then he had seen,
And the devil's dues in him were eighteen.

And now he cried: "Bring wine from below;
Let the sailors revel ere yet they row:

"Our speed shall o'ertake my father's flight
Though we sail from the harbor at midnight."

The rowers made good cheer without check;
The lords and ladies obeyed his beck;
The night was light, and they danced on the deck.

But at midnight's stroke they cleared the bay,
And the White Ship furrowed the water-way.

The sails were set, and the oars kept tune
To the double flight of the ship and the moon:

Swifter and swifter the White Ship sped
Till she flew as the spirit flies from the dead:

As white as a lily glimmered she
Like a ship's fair ghost upon the sea.

And the Prince cried, "Friends, 'tis the hour to sing!
Is a songbird's course so swift on the wing?"

[34]

And under the winter stars' still throng,
From brown throats, white throats, merry and strong,
The knights and the ladies raised a song.

A song,—nay, a shriek that rent the sky,
That leaped o'er the deep!—the grievous cry
Of three hundred living that now must die.

An instant shriek that sprang to the shock
As the ship's keel felt the sunken rock.

'Tis said that afar—a shrill strange sigh—
The King's ships heard it and knew not why.

Pale Fitz-Stephen stood by the helm
'Mid all those folks that the waves must whelm.

A great King's heir for the waves to whelm,
And the helpless pilot pale at the helm!

The ship was eager and sucked athirst,
By the stealthy stab of the sharp reef pierc'd:

And like the moil round a sinking cup,
The waters against her crowded up.

A moment the pilot's senses spin,—
The next he snatched the Prince 'mid the din,
Cut the boat loose, and the youth leaped in.

A few friends leaped with him, standing near,
"Row! the sea's smooth and the night is clear!"

"What! none to be saved but these and I?"
"Row, row as you'd live! All here must die!"

Out of the churn of the choking ship,
Which the gulf grapples and the waves strip,
They struck with the strained oars' flash and dip.

'Twas then o'er the splitting bulwarks' brim
The Prince's sister screamed to him.

He gazed aloft, still rowing apace,
And through the whirled surf he knew her face.

To the toppling decks clave one and all
As a fly cleaves to a chamber-wall.

I Berold was clinging anear;
I prayed for myself and quaked with fear,
But I saw his eyes as he looked at her.

He knew her face and he heard her cry,
And he said, "Put back! she must not die!"

And back with the current's force they reel
Like a leaf that's drawn to a water-wheel.

'Neath the ship's travail they scarce might float,
But he rose and stood in the rocking boat.

Low the poor ship leaned on the tide:
O'er the naked keel as she best might slide,
The sister toiled to the brother's side.

He stretched an oar to her from below,
And stiffened his arms to clutch her so.

But now from the ship some spied the boat,
And "Saved!" was the cry from many a throat.

And down to the boat they leaped and fell:
It turned as a bucket turns in a well,
And nothing was there but the surge and the swell.

The Prince that was and the King to come,
There in an instant gone to his doom,

Despite of all England's bended knee
And mauger the Norman fealty!

He was a Prince of lust and pride;
He showed no grace till the hour he died.

When he should be King, he oft would vow,
He'd yoke the peasant to his own plough.
O'er him the ships score their furrows now.

God only knows where his soul did wake,
But I saw him die for his sister's sake.

By none but me can the tale be told,
The butcher of Rouen, poor Berold.
(*Lands are swayed by a King on a throne.*)
'Twas a royal train put forth to sea,
Yet the tale can be told by none but me.
(*The sea hath no King but God alone.*)

And now the end came o'er the waters' womb
Like the last great Day that's yet to come.

With prayers in vain and curses in vain,
The White Ship sundered on the mid-main:

And what were men and what was a ship
Were toys and splinters in the sea's grip.

I Berold was down in the sea;
And passing strange though the thing may be,
Of dreams then known I remember me.

Blithe is the shout on Harfleur's strand
When morning lights the sails to land:

And blithe is Honfleur's echoing gloam
When mothers call the children home:

And high do the bells of Rouen beat
When the Body of Christ goes down the street.

These things and the like were heard and shown
In a moment's trance 'neath the sea alone;

And when I rose, 'twas the sea did seem,
And not these things, to be all a dream.

The ship was gone and the crowd was gone,
And the deep shuddered and the moon shone,

And in a strait grasp my arms did span
The mainyard rent from the mast where it ran;
And on it with me was another man.

Where lands were none 'neath the dim sea-sky,
We told our names, that man and I,

"O I am Godefroy de l'Aigle hight,
And son I am to a belted knight."

"And I am Berold the butcher's son
Who slays the beasts in Rouen town."

Then cried we upon God's name, as we
Did drift on the bitter winter sea.

But lo! a third man rose o'er the wave,
And we said, "Thank God! us three may He save!"

He clutched to the yard with panting stare,
And we looked and knew Fitz-Stephen there.

He clung, and "What of the Prince?" quoth he,
"Lost, lost!" we cried. He cried, "Woe on me!"
And loosed his hold and sank through the sea.

And soul with soul again in that space
We two were together face to face:

And each knew each, as the moments sped,
Less for one living than for one dead:

And every still star overhead
Seemed an eye that knew we were but dead.

And the hours passed; till the noble's son
Sighed, "God be thy help! my strength's foredone!

"O farewell, friend, for I can no more!"
"Christ take thee!" I moaned; and his life was o'er.

Three hundred souls were all lost but one,
And I drifted over the sea alone.

At last the morning rose on the sea
Like an angel's wing that beat towards me.

[40]

Sore numbed I was in my sheepskin coat;
Half dead I hung, and might nothing note,
Till I woke sun-warmed in a fisher-boat.

The sun was high o'er the eastern brim
As I praised God and gave thanks to Him.

That day I told my tale to a priest,
Who charged me, till the shrift were releas'd,
That I should keep it in mine own breast.

And with the priest I thence did fare
To King Henry's court at Winchester.

We spoke with the King's high chamberlain,
And he wept and mourned again and again,
As if his own son had been slain:

And round us ever there crowded fast
Great men with faces all aghast:

And who so bold that might tell the thing
Which now they knew to their lord the King?
Much woe I learnt in their communing.

The King had watched with a heart sore stirred
For two whole days, and this was the third:

And still to all his court would he say,
"What keeps my son so long away?"

[41]

And they said: "The ports lie far and wide
That skirt the swell of the English tide;

"And England's cliffs are not more white
Than her women are, and scarce so light
Her skies as their eyes are blue and bright;

"And in some port that he reached from France
The Prince has lingered for his pleasáunce."

But once the King asked: "What distant cry
Was that we heard 'twixt the sea and sky?"

And one said: "With suchlike shouts, pardie!
Do the fishers fling their nets at sea."

And one: "Who knows not the shrieking quest
When the sea-mew misses its young from the nest?"

'Twas thus till now they had soothed his dread,
Albeit they knew not what they said:

But who should speak today of the thing
That all knew there except the King?

Then pondering much they found a way,
And met round the King's high seat that day:

And the King sat with a heart sore stirred,
And seldom he spoke and seldom heard.

[42]

'Twas then through the hall the King was 'ware
Of a little boy with golden hair,

As bright as the golden poppy is
That the beach breeds for the surf to kiss:

Yet pale his cheek as the thorn in Spring,
And his garb black like the raven's wing.

Nothing heard but his foot through the hall,
For now the lords were silent all.

And the King wondered, and said, "Alack!
Who sends me a fair boy dressed in black?

"Why, sweet heart, do you pace through the hall
As though my court were a funeral?"

Then lowly knelt the child at the dais,
And looked up weeping in the King's face.

"O wherefore black, O King, ye may say,
For white is the hue of death today.

"Your son and all his fellowship
Lie low in the sea with the White Ship."

King Henry fell as a man struck dead;
And speechless still he stared from his bed
When to him next day my rede I read.

[43]

There's many an hour must needs beguile
A King's high heart that he should smile,—

Full many a lordly hour, full fain
Of his realm's rule and pride of his reign:—

But this King never smiled again.

By none but me can the tale be told,
The butcher of Rouen, poor Berold.
(*Lands are swayed by a King on a throne.*)
'Twas a royal train put forth to sea,
Yet the tale can be told by none but me.
(*The sea hath no King but God alone.*)

DANTE GABRIEL ROSSETTI

AGINCOURT

Fair stood the wind for France
When we our sails advance,
Nor now to prove our chance
    Longer will tarry;
But putting to the main,
At Caux, the mouth of Seine,
With all his martial train
    Landed King Harry.

And taking many a fort,
Furnish'd in warlike sort,
Marcheth tow'rds Agincourt
    In happy hour;
Skirmishing day by day
With those that stopp'd his way,
Where the French gen'ral lay
    With all his power.

Which, in his height of pride,
King Henry to deride,
His ransom to provide
    Unto him sending;
Which he neglects the while
As from a nation vile,

Yet with an angry smile
    Their fall portending.

And turning to his men,
Quoth our brave Henry then,
"Though they to one be ten
    Be not amazéd:
Yet have we well begun;
Battles so bravely won
Have ever to the sun
    By fame been raiséd.

"And for myself (quoth he):
This my full rest shall be:
England ne'er mourn for me
    Nor more esteem me:
Victor I will remain
Or on this earth lie slain,
Never shall she sustain
    Loss to redeem me.

"Poitiers and Cressy tell,
When most their pride did **swell,**
Under our swords they fell:
    No less our skill is
Than when our grandsire **great,**
Claiming the regal seat,
With many a warlike feat
    Lopp'd the French lilies."

[46]

The Duke of York so dread
The eager vaward led;
With the main Henry sped
    Among his henchmen.
Excester had the rear,
A braver man not there;
O Lord, how hot they were
    On the false Frenchmen!

They now to fight are gone,
Armor on armor shone,
Drum now to drum did groan,
    To hear was wonder;
That with the cries they make
The very earth did shake:
Trumpet to trumpet spake,
    Thunder to thunder.

Well it thine age became,
O noble Erpingham,
Which didst the signal aim
    To our hid forces!
When from a meadow by,
Like a storm suddenly
The English archery
    Stuck the French horses.

With Spanish yew so strong,
Arrows a cloth-yard long

[47]

That like to serpents stung,
    Piercing the weather;
None from his fellow starts,
But playing manly parts,
And like true English hearts
    Stuck close together.

When down their bows they threw,
And forth their bilbos drew,
And on the French they flew,
    Not one was tardy;
Arms were from shoulder sent,
Scalps to the teeth were rent,
Down the French peasants went—
    Our men were hardy!

This while our noble king,
His broadsword brandishing,
Down the French host did ding
    As to o'erwhelm it;
And many a deep wound lent,
His arms with blood besprent,
And many a cruel dent
    Bruiséd his helmet.

Gloster, that duke so good,
Next of the royal blood,
For famous England stood
    With his brave brother;

Clarence, in steel so bright,
Though but a maiden knight,
Yet in that furious fight
　　Scarce such another.

Warwick in blood did wade,
Oxford the foe invade,
And cruel slaughter made
　　Still as they ran up;
Suffolk his axe did ply,
Beaumont and Willoughby
Bare them right doughtily,
　　Ferrers and Fanhope.

Upon Saint Crispin's Day
Fought was this noble fray,
Which fame did not delay
　　To England to carry.
O when shall English men
With such acts fill a pen?
Or England breed again
　　Such a King Harry?

　　　　　　　　MICHAEL DRAYTON

DRAKE'S DRUM

Drake he's in his hammock an' a thousand mile away,
  (Capten, art tha sleepin' there below?),
Slung atween the round shot in Nombre Dios Bay,
  An' dreamin' arl the time o' Plymouth Hoe.
Yarnder lumes the Island, yarnder lie the ships,
  Wi' sailor lads a-dancin' heel-an'-toe,
An' the shore-lights flashin', an' the night-tide dashin',
  He sees et arl so plainly as he saw et long ago.

Drake he was a Devon man, an' ruled the Devon seas,
  (Capten, art tha sleepin' there below?),
Rovin' tho' his death fell, he went wi' heart at ease,
  An' dreamin' arl the time o' Plymouth Hoe.
"Take my drum to England, hang et by the shore,
  Strike et when your powder's runnin' low;
If the Dons sight Devon, I'll quit the port o' Heaven,
  An' drum them up the Channel as we drumm'd them long
    ago."

Drake he's in his hammock till the great Armadas come,
  (Capten, art tha sleepin' there below?),
Slung atween the round shot, listenin' for the drum,
  An' dreamin' arl the time o' Plymouth Hoe.
Call him on the deep sea, call him up the Sound,

Call him when ye sail to meet the foe;
Where the old trade's plyin' an' the old flag flyin'
They shall find him ware an' wakin', as they found him
long ago!

HENRY NEWBOLT

THE BATTLE OF BLENHEIM

I

It was a summer's evening,—
  Old Kaspar's work was done,
And he before his cottage door
  Was sitting in the sun;
And by him sported on the green
His little grandchild Wilhelmine.

II

She saw her brother Peterkin
  Roll something large and round,
Which he beside the rivulet,
  In playing there, had found;
He came to ask what he had found
That was so large and smooth and round.

III

Old Kaspar took it from the boy,
  Who stood expectant by;
And then the old man shook his head,
  And, with a natural sigh,—
" 'Tis some poor fellow's skull," said he,
"Who fell in the great victory.

IV

"I find them in the garden,
  For there's many hereabout;
And often, when I go to plough,
  The ploughshare turns them out;
For many thousand men," said he,
"Were slain in the great victory."

V

"Now tell us what 'twas all about,"
  Young Peterkin he cries;
And little Wilhelmine looks up
  With wonder-waiting eyes,—
"Now tell us all about the war,
And what they fought each other for."

VI

"It was the English," Kaspar cried,
  "Who put the French to rout;
But what they fought each other for
  I could not well make out;
But everybody said," quoth he,
" 'Twas a famous victory.

VII

"My father lived at Blenheim then,
  Yon little stream hard by;
They burnt his dwelling to the ground,
  And he was forced to fly;

[53]

So with his wife and child he fled,
Nor had he where to rest his head.

VIII

"With fire and sword the country round
   Was wasted far and wide;
And many a childing mother there,
   And new-born baby died;
But things like that, you know, must be
At every famous victory.

IX

"They say it was a shocking sight
   After the field was won,—
For many thousand bodies here
   Lay rotting in the sun;
But things like that, you know, must be
After a famous victory.

X

"Great praise the Duke of Marlborough won,
   And our Good Prince Eugene."
"Why, 'twas a very wicked thing!"
   Said little Wilhelmine.
"Nay, nay, my little girl!" quoth he,
"It was a famous victory.

XI

"And everybody praised the Duke
   Who this great fight did win."

"But what good came of it at last,"
  Quoth little Peterkin.
"Why, that I cannot tell," said he;
"But 'twas a famous victory."

ROBERT SOUTHEY

MOY CASTLE

There are seven men in Moy Castle
   And merry men this night;
There are seven men in Moy Castle
   Whose hearts are gay and light.

Prince Charlie came to Moy Castle
   And asked for shelter there,
And down came Lady M'Intosh,
   As proud as she was fair.

"I'm a hunted man, Lady M'Intosh—
   A price is on my head!
If Lord Loudon knew thou'dst sheltered me,
   Both thou and I were sped."

"Come in! come in, my prince!" said she,
   And opened wide the gate;
"To die with Prince Charlie Stuart,
   I ask no better fate."

She's called her seven trusty men,
   The blacksmith at their head:
"Ye shall keep watch in the castle wood,
   To save our prince from dread."

The lady has led the prince away,
   To make him royal cheer;
The seven men of M'Intosh
   Have sought the forest drear.

And there they looked and listened,
   Listened and looked amain;
And they heard the sound of the falling leaves,
   And the soft sound of the rain.

The blacksmith knelt beside an oak,
   And laid his ear to the ground,
And under the noises of the wood
   He heard a distant sound.

He heard the sound of many feet,
   Warily treading the heather—
He heard the sound of many men
   Marching softly together.

"There's no time now to warn the prince,
   The castle guards are few;
'Tis wit will win the play tonight,
   And what we here can do."

He's gi'en the word to his six brethren,
   And through the wood they're gone;
The seven men of M'Intosh
   Each stood by himself alone.

"And he who has the pipes at his back,
  His best now let him play;
And he who has no pipes at his back,
  His best word let him say."

It was five hundred Englishmen
  Were treading the purple heather,
Five hundred of Lord Loudon's men
  Marching softly together.

"There's none tonight in Moy Castle
  But servants poor and old;
If we bring the prince to Loudon's lord,
  He'll fill our hands with gold."

They came lightly on their way,
  Had never a thought of ill,
When suddenly from the darksome wood
  Broke out a whistle shrill.

And straight the wood was filled with cries,
  With shouts of angry men,
And the angry skirl of the bagpipes
  Came answering the shouts again.

The Englishmen looked and listened,
  Listened and looked amain,
And nought could they see through the murk night,
  But the pipes shrieked out again.

[58]

"Hark to the slogan of Lochiel,
  To Keppoch's gathering cry!
Hark to the rising swell that tells
  Clanranald's men are nigh!

"Now woe to the men that told us
  Lochiel was far away!
The whole of the Highland army
  Is waiting to bar our way

"It's little we'll see of Charlie Stuart
  And little of Loudon's gold,
And but we're away from this armed wood,
  Our lives have but little hold."

It was five hundred Englishmen,
  They turned their faces and ran,
And well for him with the swiftest foot,
  For he was the lucky man.

And woe to him that was lame or slow,
  For they trampled him on the heather!
And back to the place from whence they came
  They're hirpling all together.

Lord Loudon's men, they are gone full far,
  Over the brow of the hill;
The seven men of M'Intosh,
  Their pipes are crying still.

They leaned them to a tree and laughed,
  'Twould do you good to hear,
And they are away to Moy Castle
  To tell their lady dear.

And who but Lady M'Intosh
  Would praise her men so bold?
And who but Prince Charlie Stuart
  Would count the good French gold?

There are seven men in Moy Castle
  Are joyful men this night;
There are seven men in Moy Castle
  Whose hearts will aye be light.

TRADITIONAL: SCOTS

BURIAL OF SIR JOHN MOORE

Not a drum was heard, not a funeral note,
   As his corse to the rampart we hurried;
Not a soldier discharged his farewell shot
   O'er the grave where our hero we buried.

We buried him darkly, at dead of night,
   The sods with our bayonets turning;
By the struggling moonbeams' misty light,
   And the lantern dimly burning.

No useless coffin inclosed his breast,
   Not in sheet nor in shroud we wound him;
But he lay, like a warrior taking his rest,
   With his martial cloak around him.

Few and short were the prayers we said,
   And we spoke not a word of sorrow;
But we steadfastly gazed on the face that was dead,
   And we bitterly thought of the morrow.

We thought, as we hollowed his narrow bed,
   And smoothed down his lonely pillow,
That the foe and the stranger would tread o'er his head,
   And we far away on the billow!

Lightly they'll talk of the spirit that's gone,
   And o'er his cold ashes upbraid him;
But little he'll reck, if they let him sleep on,
   In the grave where a Briton has laid him!

But half of our heavy task was done,
   When the clock struck the hour for retiring,
And we heard the distant and random gun
   That the foe was sullenly firing.

Slowly and sadly we laid him down,
   From the field of his fame fresh and gory!
We carved not a line, we raised not a stone,
   But we left him alone with his glory.

CHARLES WOLFE

THE EVE OF WATERLOO

There was a sound of revelry by night,
    And Belgium's capital had gather'd then
Her Beauty and her Chivalry, and bright
    The lamps shone o'er fair women and brave men.
A thousand hearts beat happily; and when
    Music arose with its voluptuous swell,
Soft eyes look'd love to eyes which spake again,
    And all went merry as a marriage-bell;
But hush! hark! a deep sound strikes like a rising knell!

Did ye not hear it?— No; 'twas but the wind,
    Or the car rattling o'er the stony street;
On with the dance! let joy be unconfined;
    No sleep till morn, when Youth and Pleasure meet
To chase the glowing hours with flying feet.
    But hark!—that heavy sound breaks in once more,
As if the clouds its echo would repeat;
    And nearer, clearer, deadlier than before!
Arm! arm! it is—it is—the cannon's opening roar!

Within a window'd niche of that high hall
    Sate Brunswick's fated chieftain; he did hear
That sound, the first amid the festival,
    And caught its tone with Death's prophetic ear;

[63]

And when they smiled because he deem'd it near,
   His heart more truly knew that peal too well
Which stretched his father on a bloody bier,
   And rous'd the vengeance blood alone could quell:
He rush'd into the field, and, foremost fighting, fell.

Ah! then and there was hurrying to and fro,
   And gathering tears and tremblings of distress,
And cheeks all pale, which but an hour ago
   Blush'd at the praise of their own loveliness;
And there were sudden partings, such as press
   The life from out young hearts, and choking sighs
Which ne'er might be repeated: who would guess
   If ever more should meet those mutual eyes,
Since upon night so sweet such awful morn could rise!

And there was mounting in hot haste: the steed,
   The mustering squadron, and the clattering car,
Went pouring forward with impetuous speed,
   And swiftly forming in the ranks of war;
And the deep thunder peal on peal afar;
   And near, the beat of the alarming drum
Rous'd up the soldier ere the morning star;
   While throng'd the citizens with terror dumb,
Or whispering with white lips—"The foe! they come! they
     come!"

And wild and high the "Camerons' gathering" rose,
   The war-note of Lochiel, which Albyn's hills

[64]

Have heard, and heard, too, have her Saxon foes:
　　How in the noon of night that pibroch thrills
Savage and shrill! But with the breath which fills
　　Their mountain-pipe, so fill the mountaineers
With the fierce native daring which instils
　　The stirring memory of a thousand years,
And Evan's, Donald's fame rings in each clansman's ears!

And Ardennes waves above them her green leaves,
　　Dewy with Nature's tear-drops, as they pass,
Grieving, if aught inanimate e'er grieves,
　　Over the unreturning brave,—alas!
Ere evening to be trodden like the grass
　　Which now beneath them, but above shall grow
In its next verdure, when this fiery mass
　　Of living valor, rolling on the foe,
And burning with high hope, shall moulder cold and low.

Last noon beheld them full of lusty life,
　　Last eve in Beauty's circle proudly gay,
The midnight brought the signal-sound of strife,
　　The morn the marshaling in arms,—the day
Battle's magnificently stern array!
　　The thunder-clouds close o'er it, which when rent
The earth is cover'd thick with other clay,
　　Which her own clay shall cover, heap'd and pent,
Rider and horse,—friend, foe,—in one red burial blent!

LORD BYRON

[65]

THE CHARGE OF
THE LIGHT BRIGADE

Half a league, half a league,
Half a league onward,
All in the valley of Death
    Rode the six hundred.
"Forward, the Light Brigade!
Charge for the guns!" he said.
Into the valley of Death
    Rode the six hundred.

"Forward, the Light Brigade!"
Was there a man dismayed?
Not though the soldier knew
    Someone had blundered.
Theirs not to make reply,
Theirs not to reason why,
Theirs but to do and die.
Into the valley of Death
    Rode the six hundred.

Cannon to right of them,
Cannon to left of them,
Cannon in front of them
    Volleyed and thundered;
Stormed at with shot and shell,

Boldly they rode and well,
Into the jaws of Death,
Into the mouth of Hell
    Rode the six hundred.

Flashed all their sabers bare,
Flashed as they turned in air
Sabring the gunners there,
Charging an army, while
    All the world wondered:
Plunged in the battery-smoke
Right through the line they broke;
Cossack and Russian
Reeled from the saber-stroke
    Shattered and sundered.
Then they rode back, but not,
    Not the six hundred.

Cannon to right of them,
Cannon to left of them,
Cannon behind them
    Volleyed and thundered;
Stormed at with shot and shell,
While horse and hero fell,
They that had fought so well
Came through the jaws of Death,
Back from the mouth of Hell,
All that was left of them,
    Left of six hundred.

When can their glory fade?
O the wild charge they made!
    All the world wondered.
Honor the charge they made!
Honor the Light Brigade,
    Noble six hundred!

ALFRED TENNYSON

DUNKIRK

Will came back from school that day,
And he had little to say.
But he stood a long time looking down
To where the gray-green Channel water
Slapped at the foot of the little town,
And to where his boat, the Sarah P,
Bobbed at the tide on an even keel,
With her one old sail, patched at the leech,
Furled like a slattern down at heel.

He stood for a while above the beach,
He saw how the wind and current caught her;
He looked a long time out to sea.
There was steady wind, and the sky was pale,
And a haze in the east that looked like smoke.

Will went back to the house to dress.
He was half way through, when his sister Bess
Who was near fourteen, and younger than he
By just two years, came home from play.
She asked him, "Where are you going, Will?"
He said, "For a good long sail."
"Can I come along?"
                    "No, Bess," he spoke.

"I may be gone for a night and a day."
Bess looked at him. She kept very still.
She had heard the news of the Flanders rout,
How the English were trapped above Dunkirk,
And the fleet had gone to get them out—
But everyone thought it wouldn't work.
There was too much fear, there was too much doubt.

She looked at him, and he looked at her.
They were English children, born and bred.
He frowned her down, but she wouldn't stir.
She shook her proud young head.
"You'll need a crew," she said.

They raised the sail on the Sarah P,
Like a penoncel on a young knight's lance,
And headed the Sarah out to sea,
To bring their soldiers home from France.

There was no command, there was no set plan,
But six hundred boats went out with them
On the gray-green waters, sailing fast,
River excursion and fisherman,
Tug and schooner and racing M,
And the little boats came following last.

From every harbor and town they went
Who had sailed their craft in the sun and rain,
From the South Downs, from the cliffs of Kent,

From the village street, from the country lane.
There are twenty miles of rolling sea
From coast to coast, by the seagull's flight,
But the tides were fair and the wind was free,
And they raised Dunkirk by the fall of night.

They raised Dunkirk with its harbor torn
By the blasted stern and the sunken prow;
They had raced for fun on an English tide,
They were English children bred and born,
And whether thcy lived, or whether they died,
They raced for England now.

Bess was as white as the Sarah's sail,
She set her teeth and smiled at Will.
He held his course for the smoky veil
Where the harbor narrowed thin and long.
The British ships were firing strong.

He took the Sarah into his hands,
He drove her in through fire and death
To the wet men waiting on the sands.
He got his load and he got his breath,
And she came about, and the wind fought her.

He shut his eyes and he tried to pray.
He saw his England where she lay,
The wind's green home, the sea's proud daughter,
Still in the moonlight, dreaming deep,

The English cliffs and the English loam—
He had fourteen men to get away,
And the moon was clear, and the night like day
For planes to see where the white sails creep
Over the black water.

He closed his eyes and he prayed for her,
For England's hope and for England's fate;
He prayed to the men who had made her great,
Who had built her land of forest and park,
Who had made the seas an English lake;
He prayed for a fog to bring the dark;
He prayed to get home for England's sake.
And the fog came down on the rolling sea,
And covered the ships with English mist.
And diving planes were baffled and blind.

For Nelson was there in the Victory,
With his one good eye, and his sullen twist,
And guns were out on The Golden Hind,
Their shot flashed over the Sarah P.
He could hear them cheer as he came about.

By burning wharves, by battered slips,
Galleon, frigate, and brigantine,
The old dead Captains fought their ships.
And the great dead Admirals led the line.
It was England's night, it was England's sea.

The fog rolled over the harbor key.
Bess held to the stays, and conned him out.

And through the dark, while the Sarah's wake
Hissed behind him, and vanished in foam,
There at his side sat Francis Drake,
And held him true, and steered him home.

ROBERT NATHAN

HORATIUS

Lars Porsena of Clusium
  By the Nine Gods he swore
That the great house of Tarquin
  Should suffer wrong no more.
By the Nine Gods he swore it,
  And named a trysting day,
And bade his messengers ride forth,
East and west and south and north,
  To summon his array.

East and west and south and north
  The messengers ride fast,
And tower and town and cottage
  Have heard the trumpet's blast.
Shame on the false Etruscan
  Who lingers in his home
When Porsena of Clusium
  Is on his march for Rome.

The horsemen and the footmen
  Are pouring in amain,
From many a stately market-place,
  From many a fruitful plain;
From many a lonely hamlet,

Which, hid by beech and pine,
Like an eagle's nest, hangs on the crest
  Of purple Apennine;

From lordly Volaterrae,
  Where scowls the far-famed hold
Piled by the hands of giants
  For godlike kings of old;
From seagirt Populonia,
  Whose sentinels descry
Sardinia's snowy mountain tops
  Fringing the southern sky;

From the proud mart of Pisae,
  Queen of the western waves,
Where ride Massilia's triremes
  Heavy with fair-haired slaves;
From where sweet Clanis wanders
  Through corn and vines and flowers;
From where Cortona lifts to heaven
  Her diadem of towers.

Tall are the oaks whose acorns
  Drop in dark Auser's rill;
Fat are the stags that champ the boughs
  Of the Ciminian hill;
Beyond all streams Clitumnus
  Is to the herdsman dear;
Best of all pools the fowler loves
  The great Volsinian mere.

[75]

But now no stroke of woodman
  Is heard by Auser's rill;
No hunter tracks the stag's green path
  Up the Ciminian hill;
Unwatched along Clitumnus
  Grazes the milk-white steer;
Unharmed the water fowl may dip
  In the Volsinian mere.

The harvests of Arretium,
  This year, old men shall reap;
This year, young boys in Umbro
  Shall plunge the struggling sheep;
And in the vats of Luna,
  This year, the must shall foam
Round the white feet of laughing girls
  Whose sires have marched to Rome.

There be thirty chosen prophets,
  The wisest of the land,
Who always by Lars Porsena
  Both morn and evening stand:
Evening and morn the Thirty
  Have turned the verses o'er,
Traced from the right on linen white
  By mighty seers of yore.

And with one voice the Thirty
  Have their glad answer given:

"Go forth, go forth, Lars Porsena;
  Go forth, beloved of Heaven;
Go, and return in glory
  To Clusium's royal dome;
And hang round Nurscia's altars
  The golden shields of Rome."

And now hath every city
  Sent up her tale of men;
The foot are fourscore thousand,
  The horse are thousands ten.
Before the gates of Sutrium
  Is met the great array.
A proud man was Lars Porsena
  Upon the trysting day.

For all the Etruscan armies
  Were ranged beneath his eye,
And many a banished Roman,
  And many a stout ally;
And with a mighty following
  To join the muster came
The Tusculan Mamilius
  Prince of the Latian name.

But by the yellow Tiber
  Was tumult and affright:
From all the spacious champaign
  To Rome men took their flight.

A mile around the city,
  The throng stopped up the ways;
A fearful sight it was to see
  Through two long nights and days.

For aged folk on crutches,
  And women great with child,
And mothers sobbing over babes
  That clung to them and smiled.
And sick men borne in litters
  High on the necks of slaves,
And troops of sun-burned husbandmen
  With reaping-hooks and staves.

And droves of mules and asses
  Laden with skins of wine,
And endless flocks of goats and sheep,
  And endless herds of kine,
And endless trains of wagons
  That creaked beneath the weight
Of corn-sacks and of household goods,
  Choked every roaring gate.

Now from the rock Tarpeian,
  Could the wan burgher spy
The line of blazing villages
  Red in the midnight sky.
The Fathers of the City
  They sat all night and day,

For every hour some horseman came
  With tidings of dismay.

To eastward and to westward
  Have spread the Tuscan bands;
Nor house, nor fence, nor dovecot
  In Crustumerium stands.
Verbenna down to Ostia
  Hath wasted all the plain;
Astur hath stormed Janiculum,
  And the stout guards are slain.

I wis, in all the Senate,
  There was no heart so bold,
But sore it ached, and fast it beat,
  When that ill news was told.
Forthwith up rose the Consul,
  Up rose the Fathers all;
In haste they girded up their gowns,
  And hied them to the wall.

They held a council standing
  Before the River-Gate;
Short time there was, ye well may guess,
  For musing or debate.
Out spake the Consul roundly:
  "The bridge must straight go down;
For since Janiculum is lost,
  Nought else can save the town."

Just then a scout came flying,
  All wild with haste and fear:
"To arms! to arms! Sir Consul:
  Lars Porsena is here."
On the low hills to westward
  The Consul fixed his eye,
And saw the swarthy storm of dust
  Rise fast along the sky.

And nearer fast and nearer
  Doth the red whirlwind come;
And louder still and still more loud,
From underneath that rolling cloud,
Is heard the trumpet's war-note proud,
  The trampling and the hum.
And plainly and more plainly
  Now through the gloom appears,
Far to left and far to right,
In broken gleams of dark-blue light,
The long array of helmets bright,
  The long array of spears.

And plainly and more plainly,
  Above that glimmering line,
Now might ye see the banners
  Of twelve fair cities shine;
But the banner of proud Clusium
  Was highest of them all,
The terror of the Umbrian,
  The terror of the Gaul.

And plainly and more plainly
   Now might the burghers know,
By port and vest, by horse and crest,
   Each warlike Lucumo.
There Cilnius of Arretium
   On his fleet roan was seen;
And Astur of the fourfold shield,
Girt with the brand none else may wield,
Tolumnius with the belt of gold,
And dark Verbenna from the hold
   By reedy Thrasymene.

Fast by the royal standard,
   O'erlooking all the war,
Lars Porsena of Clusium
   Sat in his ivory car.
By the right wheel rode Mamilius,
   Prince of the Latian name;
And by the left false Sextus,
   That wrought the deed of shame.

But when the face of Sextus
   Was seen among the foes,
A yell that rent the firmament
   From all the town arose.
On the house-tops was no woman
   But spat towards him and hissed,
No child but screamed out curses,
   And shook its little fist.

But the Consul's brow was sad,
  And the Consul's speech was low,
And darkly looked he at the wall,
  And darkly at the foe.
"Their van will be upon us
  Before the bridge goes down;
And if they once may win the bridge,
  What hope to save the town?"

Then out spake brave Horatius,
  The Captain of the Gate:
"To every man upon this earth
  Death cometh soon or late,
And how can man die better
  Than facing fearful odds,
For the ashes of his fathers,
  And the temples of his Gods,

"And for the tender mother
  Who dandled him to rest,
And for the wife who nurses
  His baby at her breast,
And for the holy maidens
  Who feed the eternal flame,
To save them from false Sextus
  That wrought the deed of shame?

"Hew down the bridge, Sir Consul,
  With all the speed ye may;

I, with two more to help me,
　　Will hold the foe in play.
In yon straight path a thousand
　　May well be stopped by three.
Now who will stand on either hand,
　　And keep the bridge with me?"

Then out spoke Spurius Lartius;
　　A Ramnian proud was he:
"Lo, I will stand at thy right hand,
　　And keep the bridge with thee."
And out spoke strong Herminius;
　　Of Titian blood was he:
"I will abide on thy left side,
　　And keep the bridge with thee."

"Horatius," quoth the Consul,
　　"As thou sayest, so let it be."
And straight against that great array
　　Forth went the dauntless Three.
For Romans in Rome's quarrel
　　Spared neither land nor gold,
Nor son nor wife, nor limb nor life,
　　In the brave days of old.

Then none was for a party;
　　Then all were for the state;
Then the great man helped the poor,
　　And the poor man loved the great;

Then lands were fairly portioned;
   Then spoils were fairly sold;
The Romans were like brothers
   In the brave days of old.

Now Roman is to Roman
   More hateful than a foe,
And the Tribunes beard the high,
   And the Fathers grind the low.
As we wax hot in faction,
   In battle we wax cold;
Wherefore men fight not as they fought
   In the brave days of old.

Now while the Three were tightening
   Their harness on their backs,
The Consul was the foremost man
   To take in hand an axe;
And Fathers mixed with Commons,
   Seized hatchet, bar, and crow,
And smote upon the planks above,
   And loosed the props below.

Meanwhile the Tuscan army,
   Right glorious to behold,
Came flashing back the noonday light,
Rank behind rank, like surges bright
   Of a broad sea of gold.
Four hundred trumpets sounded
   A peel of warlike glee,

[84]

As that great host, with measured tread,
And spears advanced, and ensigns spread,
Rolled slowly towards the bridge's head,
    Where stood the dauntless Three.

The Three stood calm and silent,
    And looked upon the foes,
And a great shout of laughter
    From all the vanguard rose:
And forth three chiefs came spurring
    Before that deep array;
To earth they sprang, their swords they drew,
And lifted high their shields, and flew
    To win the narrow way;

Aunus from green Tifernum,
    Lord of the Hill of Vines;
And Seius, whose eight hundred slaves
    Sicken in Ilva's mines;
And Picus, long to Clusium
    Vassal in peace and war,
Who led to fight his Umbrian powers
From that gray crag where, girt with towers,
The fortress of Nequinum lowers
    O'er the pale waves of Nar.

Stout Lartius hurled down Aunus
    Into the stream beneath:
Herminius struck at Seius,
    And clove him to the teeth:

[85]

At Picus brave Horatius
   Darted one fiery thrust;
And the proud Umbrian's gilded arms
   Clashed in the bloody dust.

Then Ocnus of Falerii
   Rushed on the Roman Three;
And Lausulus of Urgo,
   The Rover of the sea;
And Aruns of Volsinium,
   Who slew the great wild boar,
The great wild boar that had his den
Amidst the reeds of Cosa's fen,
And wasted fields, and slaughtered men,
   Along Albinia's shore.

Herminius smote down Aruns:
   Lartius laid Ocnus low:
Right to the heart of Lausulus
   Horatius sent a blow.
"Lie there," he cried, "fell pirate!
   No more, aghast and pale,
From Ostia's walls the crowd shall mark
The track of thy destroying bark.
No more Campania's hinds shall fly
To woods and caverns when they spy
   Thy thrice accursed sail."

But now no sound of laughter
   Was heard among the foes.

A wild and wrathful clamor
  From all the vanguard rose.
Six spears' length from the entrance
  Halted that deep array,
And for a space no man came forth
  To win the narrow way.

But hark! the cry is Astur:
  And lo! the ranks divide;
And the great Lord of Luna
  Comes with his stately stride.
Upon his ample shoulders
  Clangs loud the fourfold shield,
And in his hand he shakes the brand
  Which none but he can wield.

He smiled on those bold Romans
  A smile serene and high;
He eyed the flinching Tuscans,
  And scorn was in his eye.
Quoth he: "The she-wolf's litter
  Stand savagely at bay;
But will ye dare to follow,
  If Astur clears the way?"

Then, whirling up his broadsword
  With both hands to the height,
He rushed against Horatius,
  And smote with all his might.

With shield and blade Horatius
    Right deftly turned the blow.
The blow, though turned, came yet too nigh;
It missed his helm, but gashed his thigh:
The Tuscans raised a joyful cry
    To see the red blood flow.

He reeled, and on Herminius
    He leaned one breathing-space;
Then, like a wild cat mad with wounds,
    Sprang right at Astur's face.
Through teeth, and skull, and helmet
    So fierce a thrust he sped,
The good sword stood a hand-breadth out
    Behind the Tuscan's head.

And the great Lord of Luna
    Fell at that deadly stroke
As falls on Mount Avernus
    A thunder-smitten oak.
Far o'er the crashing forest
    The giant arms lie spread;
And the pale augurs, muttering low,
    Gaze on the blasted head.

On Astur's throat Horatius
    Right firmly pressed his heel,
And thrice and four times tugged amain
    Ere he wrenched out the steel.

"And see," he cried, "the welcome,
    Fair guests, that waits you here!
What noble Lucumo comes next
    To taste our Roman cheer?"

But at this haughty challenge
    A sullen murmur ran,
Mingled of wrath, and shame, and dread,
    Along that glittering van.
There lacked not men of prowess,
    Nor men of lordly race;
For all Etruria's noblest
    Were round the fatal place.

But all Etruria's noblest
    Felt their hearts sink to see
On the earth the bloody corpses,
    In the path the dauntless Three:
And, from the ghastly entrance
    Where those bold Romans stood,
All shrank, like boys who unaware,
Ranging the woods to start a hare,
Come to the mouth of the dark lair
Where, growling low, a fierce old bear
    Lies amidst bones and blood.

Was none who would be foremost
    To lead such dire attack:

But those behind cried "Forward!"
 And those before cried "Back!"
And backward now and forward
 Wavers the deep array;
And on the tossing sea of steel,
To and fro the standards reel;
And the victorious trumpet-peal
 Dies fitfully away.

Yet one man for a moment
 Stood out before the crowd;
Well known was he to all the Three,
 And they gave him greeting loud:
"Now welcome, welcome Sextus!
 Now welcome to thy home!
Why dost thou stay, and turn away?
 Here lies the road to Rome."

Thrice looked he at the city;
 Thrice looked he at the dead;
And thrice came on in fury,
 And thrice turned back in dread:
And, white with fear and hatred,
 Scowled at the narrow way
Where, wallowing in a pool of blood,
 The bravest Tuscans lay.

But meanwhile axe and lever
 Have manfully been plied;

And now the bridge hangs tottering
  Above the boiling tide.
"Come back, come back, Horatius!"
  Loud cried the Fathers all.
"Back, Lartius! back, Herminius!
  Back, ere the ruin fall!"

Back darted Spurius Lartius;
  Herminius darted back:
And, as they passed, beneath their feet
  They felt the timbers crack.
But when they turned their faces,
  And on the farther shore
Saw brave Horatius stand alone,
  They would have crossed once more.

But with a crash like thunder
  Fell every loosened beam,
And, like a dam, the mighty wreck
  Lay right athwart the stream:
And a long shout of triumph
  Rose from the walls of Rome,
As to the highest turret-tops
  Was splashed the yellow foam.

And, like a horse unbroken
  When first he feels the rein,
The furious river struggled hard,
  And tossed his tawny mane,

And burst the curb, and bounded,
    Rejoicing to be free,
And whirling down, in fierce career,
Battlement, and plank, and pier,
    Rushed headlong to the sea.

Alone stood brave Horatius,
    But constant still in mind;
Thrice thirty thousand foes before,
    And the broad flood behind.
"Down with him!" cried false Sextus,
    With a smile on his pale face.
"Now yield thee," cried Lars Porsena,
    "Now yield thee to our grace."

Round turned he, as not deigning
    Those craven ranks to see;
Nought spake he to Lars Porsena,
    To Sextus nought spake he;
But he saw on Palatinus
    The white porch of his home;
And he spake to the noble river
    That rolls by the towers of Rome:

"O, Tiber! father Tiber!
    To whom the Romans pray,
A Roman's life, a Roman's arms,
    Take thou in charge this day!"
So he spake, and speaking sheathed
    The good sword by his side,

And with his harness on his back,
  Plunged headlong in the tide.

No sound of joy or sorrow
  Was heard from either bank:
But friends and foes in dumb surprise,
With parted lips and straining eyes,
  Stood gazing where he sank;
And when above the surges
  They saw his crest appear,
All Rome sent forth a rapturous cry,
And even the ranks of Tuscany
  Could scarce forbear to cheer.

But fiercely ran the current,
  Swollen high by months of rain;
And fast his blood was flowing;
  And he was sore in pain,
And heavy with his armor,
  And spent with changing blows:
And oft they thought him sinking,
  But still again he rose.

Never, I ween, did swimmer,
  In such an evil case,
Struggle through such a raging flood
  Safe to the landing place:
But his limbs were borne up bravely
  By the brave heart within,

And our good father Tiber
 Bore bravely up his chin.

"Curse on him!" quoth false Sextus;
 "Will not the villain drown?
But for this stay, ere close of day
 We should have sacked the town!"
"Heaven help him!" quoth Lars Porsena,
 "And bring him safe to shore;
For such a gallant feat of arms
 Was never seen before."

And now he feels the bottom;
 Now on dry earth he stands;
Now round him throng the Fathers
 To press his gory hands;
And now, with shouts and clapping,
 And noise of weeping loud,
He enters through the River-Gate,
 Borne by the joyous crowd.

They gave him of the corn-land,
 That was of public right,
As much as two strong oxen
 Could plow from morn till night;
And they made a molten image,
 And set it up on high,
And there it stands unto this day
 To witness if I lie.

[94]

It stands in the Comitium,
   Plain for all folk to see;
Horatius in his harness,
   Halting upon one knee:
And underneath is written,
   In letters all of gold,
How valiantly he kept the bridge
   In the brave days of old.

And still his name sounds stirring
   Unto the men of Rome,
As the trumpet-blast that cries to them
   To charge the Volscian home;
And wives still pray to Juno
   For boys with hearts as bold
As his who kept the bridge so well
   In the brave days of old.

And in the nights of winter,
   When the cold north winds blow,
And the long howling of the wolves
   Is heard amidst the snow;
When round the lonely cottage
   Roars loud the tempest's din,
And the good logs of Algidus
   Roar louder yet within;

When the oldest cask is opened,
   And the largest lamp is lit;

When the chestnuts glow in the embers,
  And the kid turns on the spit;
When young and old in circle
  Around the firebrands close;
When the girls are weaving baskets,
  And the lads are shaping bows;

When the goodman mends his armor,
  And trims his helmet's plume;
When the goodwife's shuttle merrily
  Goes flashing through the loom;
With weeping and with laughter
  Still is the story told,
How well Horatius kept the bridge
  In the brave days of old.

        THOMAS BABINGTON MACAULAY

LEPANTO

White founts falling in the courts of the sun,
And the Soldan of Byzantium is smiling as they run;
There is laughter like the fountains in that face of all men
   feared,
It stirs the forest darkness, the darkness of his beard,
It curls the blood-red crescent, the crescent of his lips,
For the inmost sea of all the earth is shaken with his ships.
They have dared the white republics up the capes of Italy,
They have dashed the Adriatic round the Lion of the Sea,
And the Pope has cast his arms abroad for agony and loss,
And called the kings of Christendom for swords about the
   Cross,
The cold queen of England is looking in the glass;
The shadow of the Valois is yawning at the mass;
From evening isles fantastical rings faint the Spanish gun,
And the Lord upon the Golden Horn is laughing in the sun.

Dim drums throbbing, in the hills half heard,
Where only on a nameless throne a crownless prince has
   stirred,
Where, risen from a doubtful seat and half-attainted stall,
The last knight of Europe takes weapons from the wall,
The last and lingering troubadour to whom the bird has
   sung,

That once went winging southward when all the world was
      young,
In that enormous silence, tiny and unafraid,
Comes up along a winding road the noise of the Crusade.
Strong gongs groaning as the guns boom far,
Don John of Austria is going to the war,
Stiff flags straining in the night-blasts cold
In the gloom black-purple, in the glint old-gold,
Torchlight crimson on the copper kettle-drums,
Then the tuckets, then the trumpets, then the cannon, and
      he comes.
Don John laughing in the brave beard curled,
Spurning of his stirrups like the thrones of all the world,
Holding his head up for a flag of all the free.
Love-light of Spain—hurrah!
Death-light of Africa!
Don John of Austria
Is riding to the sea.

Mahound is in his paradise above the evening star,
(*Don John of Austria is going to the war.*)
He moves a mighty turban on the timeless houri's knees,
His turban that is woven of the sunset and the seas.
He shakes the peacock gardens as he rises from his ease,
And he strides among the tree-tops and is taller than the
      trees,
And his voice through all the garden is a thunder sent to
      bring

Black Azrael and Ariel and Ammon on the wing.
Giants and the Genii,
Multiplex of wing and eye,
Whose strong obedience broke the sky
When Solomon was king.

They rush in red and purple from the red clouds of the morn,
From temples where the yellow gods shut up their eyes in
       scorn;
They rise in green robes roaring from the green hells of the
       sea
Where fallen skies and evil hues and eyeless creatures be;
On them the sea-valves cluster and the grey sea-forests curl,
Splashed with a splendid sickness, the sickness of the pearl;
They swell in sapphire smoke out of the blue cracks of the
       ground,—
They gather and they wonder and give worship to Mahound.
And he saith, "Break up the mountains where the hermit-
       folk may hide,
And sift the red and silver sands lest bone of saint abide,
And chase the Giaours flying night and day, not giving rest,
For that which was our trouble comes again out of the west.
We have set the seal of Solomon on all things under sun,
Of knowledge and of sorrow and endurance of things done,
But a noise is in the mountains, in the mountains, and I
       know
The voice that shook our palaces—four hundred years ago:
It is he that saith not 'Kismet'; it is he that knows not Fate;

It is Richard, it is Raymond, it is Godfrey in the gate!
It is he whose loss is laughter when he counts the wage
      worth,
Put down your feet upon him, that our peace be on the
      earth."
For he heard drums groaning and he heard guns jar,
(*Don John of Austria is going to the war.*)
Sudden and still—hurrah!
Bolt from Iberia!
Don John of Austria
Is gone by Alcalar.

St. Michael's on his Mountain in the sea-roads of the north
(*Don John of Austria is girt and going forth.*)
Where the grey seas glitter and the sharp tides shift
And the sea folk labor and the red sails lift.
He shakes his lance of iron and he claps his wings of stone;
The noise is gone through Normandy; the noise is gone
      alone;
The North is full of tangled things and texts and aching eyes
And dead is all the innocence of anger and surprise,
And Christian killeth Christian in a narrow dusty room,
And Christian dreadeth Christ that hath a newer face of
      doom,
And Christian hateth Mary that God kissed in Galilee,
But Don John of Austria is riding to the sea.
Don John calling through the blast and the eclipse
Crying with the trumpet, with the trumpet of his lips,
Trumpet that sayeth ha!

Domino gloria!
Don John of Austria
Is shouting to the ships.

King Philip's in his closet with the Fleece about his neck
(*Don John of Austria is armed upon the deck.*)
The walls are hung with velvet that is black and soft as sin,
And little dwarfs creep out of it and little dwarfs creep in.
He holds a crystal phial that has colors like the moon,
He touches, and it tingles, and he trembles very soon,
And his face is as a fungus of a leprous white and grey
Like plants in the high houses that are shuttered from the
        day,
And death is in the phial, and the end of noble work,
But Don John of Austria has fired upon the Turk.
Don John's hunting, and his hounds have bayed—
Booms away past Italy the rumor of his raid.
Gun upon gun, ha! ha!
Gun upon gun, hurrah!
Don John of Austria
Has loosed the cannonade.

The Pope was in his chapel before day or battle broke,
(*Don John of Austria is hidden in the smoke.*)
The hidden room in a man's house where God sits all the
        year,
The secret window whence the world looks small and very
        dear.
He sees as in a mirror on the monstrous twilight sea

The crescent of his cruel ships whose name is mystery;
They fling great shadows foe-wards, making Cross and Castle dark,
They veiled the pluméd lions on the galleys of St. Mark;
And above the ships are palaces of brown, black-bearded chiefs,
And below the ships are prisons, where with multitudinous griefs,
Christian captives sick and sunless, all a laboring race repines
Like a race in sunken cities, like a nation in the mines.
They are lost like slaves that swat, and in the skies of morning hung
The stairways of the tallest gods when tyranny was young.
They are countless, voiceless, hopeless as those fallen or fleeing on
Before the high King's horses in the granite of Babylon.
And many a one grows witless in his quiet room in hell
Where a yellow face looks inward through the lattice of his cell,
And he finds his God forgotten, and he seeks no more a sign—
(*But Don John of Austria has burst the battle-line!*)
Don John pounding from the slaughter-painted poop,
Purpling all the ocean like a bloody pirate's sloop,
Scarlet running over on the silvers and the golds,
Breaking of the hatches up and bursting of the holds,
Thronging of the thousands up that labor under sea,
White for bliss and blind for sun and stunned for liberty.

[102]

Vivat Hispania!
Domino Gloria!
Don John of Austria
Has set his people free!

Cervantes on his galley sets the sword back in the sheath
(*Don John of Austria rides homeward with a wreath.*)
And he sees across a weary land a straggling road in Spain,
Up which a lean and foolish knight forever rides in vain,
And he smiles, but not as Sultans smile, and settles back the
      blade . . .
(*But Don John of Austria rides home from the Crusade.*)
G. K. CHESTERTON

CASABIANCA

In the battle of the Nile, thirteen-year-old Casabianca, son of the Admiral of the Orient, remained at his post after the ship had taken fire and all the guns had been abandoned. He perished when the vessel exploded.

The boy stood on the burning deck,
Whence all but he had fled;
The flame that lit the battle's wreck,
Shone round him o'er the dead.

Yet beautiful and bright he stood,
As born to rule the storm;
A creature of heroic blood,
A proud though childlike form.

The flames rolled on; he would not go
Without his father's word;
That father, faint in death below,
His voice no longer heard.

He called aloud, "Say, Father, say,
If yet my task is done!"
He knew not that the chieftain lay
Unconscious of his son.

"Speak, Father!" once again he cried,
"If I may yet be gone!"
—And but the booming shots replied,
And fast the flames rolled on.

Upon his brow he felt their breath,
And in his waving hair;
And looked from that lone post of death
In still yet brave despair;

And shouted but once more aloud,
"My Father! must I stay?"
While o'er him fast, through sail and shroud,
The wreathing fires made way.

They wrapt the ship in splendor wild,
They caught the flag on high,
And streamed above the gallant child,
Like banners in the sky.

There came a burst of thunder sound;
The boy— Oh! where was *he?*
—Ask of the winds, that far around
With fragments strewed the sea;—

With shroud, and mast, and pennon fair,
That well had borne their part,—
But the noblest thing that perished there
Was that young, faithful heart.

FELICIA DOROTHEA HEMANS

INCIDENT OF THE FRENCH CAMP

You know, we French stormed Ratisbon;
    A mile or so away,
On a little mound, Napoleon
    Stood on our storming-day;
With neck out-thrust, you fancy how,
    Legs wide, arms locked behind,
As if to balance the prone brow,
    Oppressive with its mind.

Just as perhaps he mused, "My plans
    That soar, to earth may fall,
Let once my army-leader Lannes
    Waver at yonder wall,"—
Out 'twixt the battery-smokes there flew
    A rider, bound on bound
Full-galloping; nor bridle drew
    Until he reached the mound.

Then off there flung in smiling joy,
    And held himself erect
By just his horse's mane, a boy;
    You hardly could suspect—
(So tight he kept his lips compressed,
    Scarce any blood came through)

You looked twice ere you saw his breast
    Was all but shot in two.

"Well," cried he, "Emperor, by God's grace
    We've got you Ratisbon!
The marshal's in the market-place,
    And you'll be there anon
To see your flag-bird flap his vans
    Where I, to heart's desire,
Perched him!" The chief's eye flashed; his plans
    Soared up again like fire.

The chief's eye flashed; but presently
    Softened itself, as sheathes
A film the mother-eagle's eye
    When her bruised eaglet breathes;
"You're wounded!" "Nay," his soldier's pride
    Touched to the quick, he said:
"I'm killed, sire!" And his chief beside,
    Smiling the boy fell dead.

                ROBERT BROWNING

HOW THEY BROUGHT THE GOOD
NEWS FROM GHENT TO AIX

I sprang to the stirrup, and Joris and he;
I galloped, Dirck galloped, we galloped all three;
"Good speed!" cried the watch as the gate-bolts undrew,
"Speed!" echoed the wall to us galloping through.
Behind shut the postern, the lights sank to rest,
And into the midnight we galloped abreast.

Not a word to each other; we kept the great pace
Neck by neck, stride by stride, never changing our place;
I turned in my saddle and made its girths tight,
Then shortened each stirrup and set the pique right,
Rebuckled the cheek-strap, chained slacker the bit,
Nor galloped less steadily Roland a whit.

'Twas a moonset at starting; but while we drew near
Lokeren, the cocks crew and twilight dawned clear;
At Boom a great yellow star came out to see;
At Düffeld 'twas morning as plain as could be;
And from Mecheln church-steeple we heard the half
        chime,—
So Joris broke silence with "Yet there is time!"

At Aerschot up leaped of a sudden the sun,
And against him the cattle stood black every one,

To stare through the mist at us galloping past;
And I saw my stout galloper Roland at last,
With resolute shoulders, each butting away
The haze, as some bluff river headland its spray;

And his low head and crest, just one sharp ear bent back
For my voice, and the other pricked out on his track;
And one eye's black intelligence,—ever that glance
O'er its white edge at me, his own master, askance;
And the thick heavy spume-flakes, which aye and anon
His fierce lips shook upward in galloping on.

By Hasselt Dirck groaned; and cried Joris, "Stay spur!
Your Roos galloped bravely, the fault's not in her;
We'll remember at Aix," for one heard the quick wheeze
Of her chest, saw the stretched neck, and staggering knees,
And sunk tail, and horrible heave of the flank,
As down on her haunches she shuddered and sank.

So we were left galloping, Joris and I,
Past Looz and past Tongres, no cloud in the sky;
The broad sun above laughed a pitiless laugh;
'Neath our feet broke the brittle, bright stubble like chaff;
Till over by Dalhem a dome-spire sprang white,
And "Gallop," gasped Joris, "for Aix is in sight!"

"How they'll greet us!"—and all in a moment his roan
Rolled neck and croup over, lay dead as a stone;
And there was my Roland to bear the whole weight

Of the news which alone could save Aix from her fate,
With his nostrils like pits full of blood to the brim,
And with circles of red for his eye-sockets' rim.

Then I cast loose my buff-coat, each holster let fall,
Shook off both my jack-boots, let go belt and all,
Stood up in the stirrup, leaned, patted his ear,
Called my Roland his pet name, my horse without peer,—
Clapped my hands, laughed and sung, any noise, bad or
    good,
Till at length into Aix Roland galloped and stood.

And all I remember is friends flocking round,
As I sat with his head 'twixt my knees on the ground;
And no voice but was praising this Roland of mine,
As I poured down his throat our last measure of wine,
Which (the burgesses voted by common consent)
Was no more than his due who brought good news from
    Ghent.

ROBERT BROWNING

ROMANTIC POEMS

THE HIGHWAYMAN

The wind was a torrent of darkness among the gusty trees,
The moon was a ghostly galleon tossed upon cloudy seas,
The road was a ribbon of moonlight over the purple moor,
And the highwayman came riding—
    Riding—riding—
The highwayman came riding, up to the old inn-door.

He'd a French cocked-hat on his forehead, a bunch of lace
    at his chin,
A coat of claret velvet, and breeches of brown doe-skin;
They fitted with never a wrinkle: his boots were up to the
    thigh!
And he rode with a jeweled twinkle,
    His pistol butts a-twinkle,
His rapier hilt a-twinkle, under the jeweled sky.

Over the cobbles he clattered and clashed in the dark inn-
    yard,
And he tapped with his whip on the shutters, but all was
    locked and barred;
He whistled a tune to the window, and who should be wait-
    ing there

But the landlord's black-eyed daughter,
    Bess, the landlord's daughter,
Plaiting a dark-red love-knot into her long black hair.

And dark in the dark old inn-yard a stable-wicket creaked
Where Tim the ostler listened; his face was white and
        peaked;
His eyes were hollows of madness, his hair like mouldy hay
But he loved the landlord's daughter,
    The landlord's red-lipped daughter,
Dumb as a dog he listened, and he heard the robber say—

"One kiss, my bonny sweetheart, I'm after a prize tonight,
But I shall be back with the yellow gold before the morning
        light;
Yet, if they press me sharply, and harry me through the day,
Then look for me by moonlight,
    Watch for me by moonlight,
I'll come to thee by moonlight, though hell should bar the
        way."

He rose upright in the stirrups; he scarce could reach her
        hand,
But she loosened her hair i' the casement! His face burnt
        like a brand
As the black cascade of perfume came tumbling over his
        breast;
And he kissed its waves in the moonlight,
    (Oh, sweet black waves in the moonlight!)

Then he tugged at his rein in the moonlight, and galloped
    away to the West.

PART TWO

He did not come in the dawning; he did not come at noon;
And out o' the tawny sunset, before the rise o' the moon,
When the road was a gipsy's ribbon, looping the purple moor,
A red-coat troop came marching—
    Marching—marching—
King George's men came marching, up to the old inn-door.

They said no word to the landlord, they drank his ale instead,
But they gagged his daughter and bound her to the foot of
    her narrow bed;
Two of them knelt at her casement, with muskets at their
    side!
There was death at every window;
    And hell at one dark window;
For Bess could see, through her casement, the road that *he*
    would ride.

They had tied her up to attention, with many a sniggering
    jest;
They had bound a musket beside her, with the barrel beneath
    her breast!
"Now keep good watch!" and they kissed her. She heard the
    dead man say—
Look for me by moonlight;
    Watch for me by moonlight;

*I'll come to thee by moonlight, though hell should bar the
    way!*

She twisted her hands behind her; but all the knots held
    good!
She writhed her hands till her fingers were wet with sweat or
    blood!
They stretched and strained in the darkness, and the hours
    crawled by like years,
Till, now, on the stroke of midnight,
    Cold, on the stroke of midnight,
The tip of one finger touched it! The trigger at least was hers!

The tip of one finger touched it; she strove no more for the
    rest!
Up, she stood to attention, with the barrel beneath her
    breast,
She would not risk their hearing; she would not strive again;
For the road lay bare in the moonlight;
    Blank and bare in the moonlight;
And the blood of her veins in the moonlight throbbed to her
    love's refrain.

Tlot-tlot; tlot-tlot! Had they heard it? The horse-hoofs ring-
    ing clear;
Tlot-tlot, tlot-tlot, in the distance? Were they deaf that they
    did not hear?
Down the ribbon of moonlight, over the brow of the hill,

The highwayman came riding,
  Riding, riding!
The red-coats looked to their priming! She stood up, straight
  and still!

Tlot-tlot, in the frosty silence! *Tlot-tlot*, in the echoing night!
Nearer he came and nearer! Her face was like a light!
Her eyes grew wide for a moment; she drew one last deep
  breath,
Then her finger moved in the moonlight,
  Her musket shattered the moonlight,
Shattered her breast in the moonlight and warned him—
  with her death.

He turned; he spurred to the West; he did not know who
  stood
Bowed, with her head o'er the musket, drenched with her
  own red blood!
Not till the dawn he heard it, his face grew grey to hear
How Bess, the landlord's daughter,
  The landlord's black-eyed daughter,
Had watched for her love in the moonlight, and died in the
  darkness there.

Back, he spurred like a madman, shrieking a curse to the sky,
With the white road smoking behind him and his rapier
  brandished high!
Blood-red were his spurs i' the golden noon; wine-red was his
  velvet coat,

When they shot him down on the highway,
    Down like a dog on the highway,
And he lay in his blood on the highway, with the bunch of
    lace at his throat.

*   *   *

And still of a winter's night, they say, when the wind is in
    the trees,
When the moon is a ghostly galleon tossed upon cloudy seas,
When the road is a ribbon of moonlight over the purple
    moor,
A highwayman comes riding—
    Riding—riding—
A highwayman comes riding, up to the old inn-door.

Over the cobbles he clatters and clangs in the dark inn-yard;
He taps with his whip on the shutters, but all is locked and
    barred;
He whistles a tune to the window, and who should be wait-
    ing there
But the landlord's black-eyed daughter,
    Bess, the landlord's daughter,
Plaiting a dark red love-knot into her long black hair.

                                        ALFRED NOYES

[117]

LOCHINVAR

O young Lochinvar is come out of the west,
Through all the wide border his steed was the best,
And save his good broad-sword he weapons had none;
He rode all unarmed, and he rode all alone.
So faithful in love, and so dauntless in war,
There never was knight like the young Lochinvar.

He stay'd not for brake, and he stopp'd not for stone,
He swam the Esk river where ford there was none;
But, ere he alighted at Netherby gate,
The bride had consented, the gallant came late:
For a laggard in love, and a dastard in war,
Was to wed the fair Ellen of brave Lochinvar.

So boldly he entered the Netherby Hall,
Among bride's-men and kinsmen, and brothers and all:
Then spoke the bride's father, his hand on his sword
(For the poor craven bridegroom said never a word),
"O come ye in peace here, or come ye in war,
Or to dance at our bridal, young Lord Lochinvar?"

"I long wooed your daughter, my suit you denied:—
Love swells like the Solway, but ebbs like its tide—
And now I am come, with this lost love of mine

To lead but one measure, drink one cup of wine.
There are maidens in Scotland more lovely by far
That would gladly be bride to the young Lochinvar."

The bride kiss'd the goblet; the knight took it up,
He quaff'd off the wine, and he threw down the cup;
She look'd down to blush, and she look'd up to sigh,
With a smile on her lips and a tear in her eye.
He took her soft hand, ere her mother could bar,—
"Now tread we a measure!" said young Lochinvar.

So stately his form, and so lovely her face,
That never a hall such a galliard did grace;
While her mother did fret, and her father did fume,
And the bridegroom stood dangling his bonnet and plume;
And the bride-maidens whisper'd, " 'Twere better by far
To have match'd our fair cousin with young Lochinvar."

One touch to her hand and one word in her ear,
When they reach'd the hall door and the charger stood near;
So light to the croup the fair lady he swung,
So light to the saddle before her he sprung!
"She is won! we are gone, over bank, bush, and scaur;
They'll have fleet steeds that follow," quoth young Loch-
        invar.

There was mounting 'mong Graemes of the Netherby clan;
Forsters, Fenwicks, and Musgraves, they rode and they ran:

There was racing and chasing on Cannobie Lee,
But the lost bride of Netherby ne'er did they see.
So daring in love, and so dauntless in war,
Have ye e'er heard of gallant like young Lochinvar?

SIR WALTER SCOTT

EARL MAR'S DAUGHTER

It was intill a pleasant time,
   Upon a simmer's day
The noble Earl Mar's daughter
   Went forth to sport and play.

And while she play'd and sported
   Before a green aik tree,
There she saw a sprightly doo
   Set on a tower sae hie.

"O Coo-me-doo, my love sae true,
   If ye'll come doun to me,
Ye'se hae a cage o' gude red gowd
   Instead o' simple tree.

"I'll put gowd hingers roun' your cage,
   And siller roun' your wa';
I'll gar ye shine as fair a bird
   As ony o' them a'."

But she had nae these words well spoke,
   Nor yet these words well said,
Till Coo-me-doo flew frae the tower
   And lichted on her head.

Then she has brought this pretty bird
    Hame to her bowers and ha',
And made him shine as fair a bird
    As ony o' them a'.

When day was gone, and night was come,
    About the evening-tide,
This lady spied a gallant youth
    Stand straight up by her side.

"From whence cam' ye, young man?" she said;
    "That does surprise me sair;
My door was bolted right secure,
    What way hae ye come here?"—

"O haud your tongue, ye lady fair,
    Lat a' your folly be;
Mind ye not o' your turtle-doo
    Ye wiled from aff the tree?"—

"What country come ye frae?" she said,
    "An' what's your pedigree?"—
"O it was but this verra day
    That I cam' ower the sea.

"My mither lives on foreign isles,
    A queen o' high degree;
And by her spells I am a doo
    With you to live an' dee."—

[122]

"O Coo-me-doo, my love sae true,
    Nae mair frae me ye'se gae."—
"That's never my intent, my love;
    As ye said, it shall be sae."

Then he has stay'd in bower wi' her
    For six lang years and ane,
Till six young sons to him she bare,
    And the seventh she's brought hame.

But aye, as ever a child was born,
    He carried them away,
And brought them to his mither's care
    As fast as he could fly.

When he had stay'd in bower wi' her
    For seven lang years an' mair
There cam' a lord o' high reknown
    To court this lady fair.

But still his proffer she refused
    And a' his presents too;
Says, "I'm content to live alane
    Wi' my bird Coo-me-doo."

Her father swore a michty oath
    Amang the nobles all,
"The morn, or ere I eat or drink,
    This bird I will gar kill."

[123]

The bird was sitting in his cage
   And heard what they did say;
Says, "Wae is me, and you forlorn,
   If I do langer stay!"

Then Coo-me-doo took flight and flew
   And afar beyond the sea,
And lichted near his mither's castle
   On a tower o' gowd sae hie.

His mither she was walking out
   To see what she could see,
And there she saw her one young son
   Set on the tower sae hie.

"Get dancers here to dance," she said,
   "And minstrels for to play;
For here's my young son Florentine
   Come hame wi' me to stay."—

"Get nae dancers to dance, mither,
   Nor minstrels for to play;
For the mither o' my seven sons,
   The morn's her wedding-day."—

"O tell me, tell me, Florentine,
   Tell me, an tell me true;
Tell me this day without a flaw
   What I will do for you?"—

"Instead of dancers to dance, mither,
    Or minstrels for to play,
Turn four-and-twenty well-wight men
    Like storks in feathers gray:

"My seven sons in seven swans
    Aboon their heads to flee;
And I mysel' a gay goshawk,
    A bird o' high degree."

Then siching said the Queen hersel',
    "That thing's too high for me!"
But she applied to an auld woman
    Wha had mair skill than she.

Instead o' dancers to dance a dance,
    Or minstrels for to play,
Four-and-twenty well-wight men
    Turn'd birds o' feathers gray.

Her seven sons in seven swans,
    Aboon their heads to flee;
And he himsel' a gay goshawk,
    A bird o' high degree.

This flock o' birds took flight and flew
    Beyond the raging sea,
And landed near the Earl Mar's castle,
    Took shelter in every tree.

[125]

They were a flock o' pretty birds
   Right comely to be seen;
The people view'd them wi' surprise
   As they dancéd on the green.

These birds flew out frae every tree
   And lichted on the ha',
And frae the roof with force did flee
   Amang the nobles a'.

The storks there seized ilk wedding-guest
   —They could not fight nor flee;
The swans they bound the bridegroom fast
   Below a gree aik tree.

They lichted next on the bride-maidens,
   Then on the bride's own head;
And wi' the twinkling o' an e'e
   The bride an' them were fled.

There's ancient men at weddings been
   For sixty years or more,
But siccan a curious wedding-day
   They never saw before.

For naething could the companie do,
   Nor naething could they say;
But they saw a flock o' pretty birds
   That took their bride away.

               TRADITIONAL: SCOTS

BINNORIE

There were twa sisters sat in a bour;
    Binnorie, O Binnorie!
There cam a knight to be their wooer,
    By the bonnie mildams o' Binnorie.

He courted the eldest with glove and ring,
But he lo'ed the youngest abune a' thing.

The eldest she was vexed sair,
And sair envied her sister fair.

Upon a morning fair and clear,
She cried upon her sister dear:

"O sister, sister, tak my hand,
And we'll see our father's ships to land."

She's ta'en her by the lily hand,
And led her down to the river-strand.

The youngest stood upon a stane,
The eldest cam and push'd her in.

"O sister, sister, reach your hand!
And ye sall be heir o' half my land:

"O sister, reach me but your glove!
And sweet William sall be your love."—

"Foul fa' the hand that I should take;
It twin'd me o' my warldis make.

"Your cherry cheeks and your yellow hair
Gar'd me gang maiden evermair."

Sometimes she sank, sometimes she swam.
Until she cam to the miller's dam.

Out then cam the miller's son,
And saw the fair maid soummin' in.

"O father, father, draw your dam!
There's either a mermaid or a milk-white swan!"

The miller hasted and drew his dam,
And there he found a drown'd woman.

You couldna see her middle sma',
Her gowden girdle was sae braw.

You couldna see her lily feet,
Her gowden fringes were sae deep.

You couldna' see her yellow hair
For the strings o' pearls twisted there.

You couldna see her fingers sma',
Wi' diamond rings they were cover'd a'.

And by there cam a harper fine,
That harpit to the king at dine.

And when he look'd that lady on,
He sigh'd and made a heavy moan.

He's made a harp of her breast-bane,
Whose sound wad melt a heart of stane.

He's ta'en three locks o' her yellow hair,
And wi' them strung his harp sae rare.

He went into her father's hall,
And there was the court assembled all.

He laid his harp upon a stane,
And straight it began to play by lane.

"O yonder sits my father, the King,
And yonder sits my mother, the Queen;

"And yonder stands my brother Hugh,
And by him my William, sweet and true."

But the last tune that the harp play'd then—
    Binnorie, O Binnorie!
Was, "Woe to my sister, false Helen!"
    By the bonnie milldams o' Binnorie.

TRADITIONAL: SCOTS

[129]

LORD RANDAL

"O where hae ye been, Lord Randal, my son?
O where hae ye been, my handsome young man?"—
"I hae been to the wild wood; mother, make my bed soon,
For I'm weary wi' hunting, and fain wald lie down."

"Where gat ye your dinner, Lord Randal, my son?
Where gat ye your dinner, my handsome young man?"—
"I dined wi' my true-love; mother, make my bed soon,
For I'm weary wi' hunting, and fain wald lie down."

"What gat ye to your dinner, Lord Randal, my son?
What gat ye to your dinner, my handsome young man?"—
"I gat eels boil'd in broo'; mother, make my bed soon,
For I'm weary wi' hunting, and fain wald lie down."

"What became of your bloodhounds, Lord Randal, my son?
What became of your bloodhounds, my handsome young
       man?"—
"O they swell'd and they died; mother, make my bed soon,
For I'm weary wi' hunting, and fain wald lie down."

"O I fear ye are poison'd, Lord Randal, my son!
O I fear ye are poison'd, my handsome young man!"—
"O yes! I am poison'd; mother, make my bed soon,
For I'm sick at the heart, and I fain wald lie down."

TRADITIONAL: ENGLISH

THE DOUGLAS TRAGEDY

"Rise up, rise up, now Lord Douglas," she says,
    "And put on your armor so bright;
Let it never be said that a daughter of thine
    Was married to a lord under night.

"Rise up, rise up, my seven bold sons,
    And put on your armor so bright,
And take better care of your youngest sister,
    For your eldest's awa the last night."

He's mounted her on a milk-white steed,
    And himself on a dapple grey,
With a bugelet horn hung down his side;
    And lightly they rode away.

Lord William look'd o'er his left shoulder,
    To see what he could see,
And there he spy'd her seven brethren bold
    Come riding over the lea.

"Light down, light down, Lady Margret," he said,
    "And hold my steed in your hand,
Until that against your seven brethren bold,
    And your father, I mak' a stand."

O, there she stood, and bitter she stood,
   And never did shed one tear,
Until that she saw her seven brethren fa',
   And her father, who lov'd her so dear.

"O hold your hand, Lord William!" she said,
   "For your strokes they are wondrous sair;
True lovers I can get many an ane,
   But a father I can never get mair."

O she's ta'en out her handkerchief,
   It was o' the holland sae fine,
And aye she dighted her father's wounds,
   That were redder than the wine.

"O chuse, O chuse, Lady Margret," he said,
   "O whether will ye gang or bide?"
"I'll gang, I'll gang, Lord William," she said,
   "For ye've left me no other guide."

He's lifted her on a milk-white steed,
   And himself on a dapple grey,
With a bugelet horn hung down by his side;
   And slowly they baith rade away.

O they rade on, and on they rade,
   And a' by the light of the moon,
Until they came to yon wan water,
   And there they lighted doun.

They lighted doun to tak' a drink
   Of the spring that ran sae clear
And doun the stream ran his gude heart's blood
   And sair she gan to fear.

"Hold up, hold up, Lord William," she says,
   "For I fear that you are slain."—
" 'Tis naething but the shadow of my scarlet cloak,
   That shines in the water sae plain."

O they rade on, and on they rade,
   And a' by the light of the moon,
Until they cam' to his mother's ha' door,
   And there they lighted doun.

"Get up, get up, lady mother," he says,
   "Get up, and let me in!
Get up, get up, lady mother," he says,
   "For this night my fair lady I've win.

"O mak my bed, lady mother," he says,
   "O mak it braid and deep,
And lay Lady Margret close at my back,
   And the sounder I will sleep."

Lord William was dead lang ere midnight,
   Lady Margret lang ere day,
And all true lovers that go thegither,
   May they have mair luck than they!

Lord William was buried in St. Mary's kirk,
   Lady Margret in Mary's quire;
Out o' the lady's grave grew a bonny red rose,
   And out o' the knight's a brier.

And they twa met, and they twa plat,
   And fain they wad be near;
And a' the warld might ken right weel
   They were twa lovers dear.

But bye and rade the Black Douglas,
   And wow but he was rough!
For he pull'd up the bonny brier,
   And flang't in St. Mary's Lough.

TRADITIONAL: SCOTS

THE BAILIFF'S DAUGHTER
OF ISLINGTON

There was a youth, and a well-belovéd youth,
   And he was an esquire's son,
He loved the bailiff's daughter dear,
   That lived in Islington.

But she was coy, and she would not believe
   That he did love her so,
No, nor at any time she would
   Any countenance to him show.

But when his friends did understand
   His fond and foolish mind,
They sent him up to fair London,
   An apprentice for to bind.

And when he had been seven long years,
   And his love he had not seen;
"Many a tear have I shed for her sake
   When she little thought of me."

All the maids of Islington
   Went forth to sport and play;
All but the bailiff's daughter dear;
   She secretly stole away.

She put off her gown of gray,
  And put on her puggish attire;
She's up to fair London gone,
  Her true-love to require.

As she went along the road,
  The weather being hot and dry,
There was she aware of her true-love,
  At length came riding by.

She stept to him, as red as any rose,
  And took him by the bridle-ring:
"I pray you, kind sir, give me one penný,
  To ease my weary limb."—

"I prithee, sweetheart, canst thou tell me
  Where that thou wast born?"—
"At Islington, kind sir," said she,
  "Where I have had many a scorn."—

"I prithee, sweetheart, canst thou tell me
  Whether thou dost know
The bailiff's daughter of Islington?"—
  "She's dead, sir, long ago."—

"Then will I sell my goodly steed,
  My saddle and my bow;
I will into some far countrey,
  Where no man doth me know."—

"Oh stay, O stay, thou goodly youth!
  She's alive, she is not dead;
Here she standeth by thy side,
  And is ready to be thy bride."—

"O farewell grief, and welcome joy,
  Ten thousand times and o'er!
For now I have seen my own true-love,
  That I thought I should have seen no more."

TRADITIONAL: ENGLISH

BARBARA ALLEN'S CRUELTY

In Scarlet town, where I was born,
　　There was a fair maid dwellin'
Made every youth cry Well-a-way!
　　Her name was Barbara Allen.

All in the merry month of May,
　　When green buds they were swellin',
Young Jemmy Grove on his death-bed lay,
　　For love of Barbara Allen.

He sent his man in to her then,
　　To the town where she was dwellin';
"O haste and come to my master dear,
　　If your name be Barbara Allen."

So slowly, slowly rase she up,
　　And slowly she came nigh him,
And when she drew the curtain by—
　　"Young man, I think you're dyin',"

"O it's I am sick and very very sick,
　　And it's all for Barbara Allen."—
"O the better for me ye'se never be,
　　Tho' your heart's blood were a-spillin'!

[138]

"O dinna ye mind, young man," says she,
 "When the red wine ye were fillin',
That ye made the healths go round and round,
 And slighted Barbara Allen?"

He turn'd his face unto the wall,
 And death was with him dealin':
"Adieu, adieu, my dear friends all,
 And be kind to Barbara Allen!"

As she was walking o'er the fields,
 She heard the dead-bell knellin';
And every jow the dead-bell gave
 Cried "Woe to Barbara Allen."

"O mother, mother, make my bed,
 O make it saft and narrow:
My love has died for me today,
 I'll die for him tomorrow.

"Farewell," she said, "ye virgins all,
 And shun the fault I fell in:
Henceforth take warning by the fall
 Of cruel Barbara Allen."

TRADITIONAL: ENGLISH

THE WRAGGLE TAGGLE GIPSIES

There were three gipsies a-come to my door,
And downstairs ran this a-lady, O!
One sang high, and another sang low,
And the other sang, Bonny, bonny Biscay, O!

Then she pulled off her silk-finished gown
And put on hose of leather, O!
The ragged, ragged rags about our door—
She's gone with the wraggle taggle gipsies, O!

It was late last night, when my lord came home,
Enquiring for his a-lady, O!
The servants said, on every hand:
"She's gone with the wraggle taggle gipsies, O!"

"O saddle to me my milk-white steed,
Go and fetch me my pony, O!
That I may ride and seek my bride,
Who is gone with the wraggle taggle gipsies, O!"

O he rode high and he rode low,
He rode through woods and copses too,
Until he came to an open field,
And there he espied his a-lady, O!

"What makes you leave your house and land?
What makes you leave your money, O?
What makes you leave your new-wedded lord;
To go with the wraggle taggle gipsies, O!"

"What care I for my house and land?
What care I for my money, O?
What care I for my new-wedded lord?
I'm off with the wraggle taggle gipsies, O!"

"Last night you slept on a goose-feather bed,
With the sheet turned down so bravely, O!
And tonight you'll sleep in a cold open field,
Along with the wraggle taggle gipsies, O!"

"What care I for a goose-feather bed,
With the sheet turned down so bravely, O?
For tonight I shall sleep in a cold open field,
Along with the wraggle taggle gipsies, O!"

TRADITIONAL: ENGLISH

GREEN BROOM

There was an old man lived out in the wood,
    His trade was a-cutting of Broom, green Broom;
He had but one son without thrift, without good,
    Who lay in his bed till 'twas noon, bright noon.

The old man awoke one morning and spoke,
    He swore he would fire the room, that room,
If his John would not rise and open his eyes,
    And away to the wood to cut Broom, green Broom.

So Johnny arose, and he slipped on his clothes,
    And away to the wood to cut Broom, green Broom,
He sharpened his knives, for once he contrives
    To cut a great bundle of Broom, green Broom.

When Johnny passed under a lady's fine house,
    Passed under a lady's fine room, fine room,
She called to her maid, "Go fetch me," she said,
    "Go fetch me the boy that sells Broom, green Broom."

When Johnny came in to the lady's fine house,
    And stood in the lady's fine room, fine room;
"Young Johnny," she said, "Will you give up your trade,
    And marry a lady in bloom, full bloom?"

Johnny gave his consent, and to church they both went,
   And he wedded the lady in bloom, full bloom,
At market and fair, all folks do declare,
    There is none like the Boy that sold Broom, green Broom.

                TRADITIONAL: ENGLISH

LORD LOVEL

Lord Lovel he stood at his castle-gate,
    Combing his milk-white steed,
When up came Lady Nancy Belle,
    To wish her lover good speed.

"Where are you going, Lord Lovel?" she said,
    "Oh where are you going?" said she.
"I'm going, my Lady Nancy Belle,
    Strange countries for to see."

"When will you be back, Lord Lovel?" she said,
    "Oh when will you come back?" said she.
"In a year, or two, or three at the most,
    I'll return to my fair Nancy."

But he had not been gone a year and a day,
    Strange countries for to see,
When languishing thoughts came into his head,
    Lady Nancy Belle he would go see.

So he rode, and he rode, on his milk-white steed,
    Till he came to London town,
And there he heard St. Pancras' bells,
    And the people all mourning around.

"Oh what is the matter?" Lord Lovel he said,
  "Oh what is the matter?" said he;
"A lord's lady is dead," a woman replied,
  "And some call her Lady Nancý."

So he order'd the grave to be open'd wide,
  And the shroud he turnéd down,
And there he kiss'd her clay-cold lips,
  Till the tears came trickling down.

Lady Nancy she died, as it might be, today,
  Lord Lovel he died as tomorrow;
Lady Nancy she died out of pure, pure grief,
  Lord Lovel he died out of sorrow.

Lady Nancy was laid in St. Pancras' Church,
  Lord Lovel was laid in the choir;
And out of her bosom there grew a red rose,
  And out of her lover's a briar.

They grew, and they grew, to the church-steeple top,
  And then they could grow no higher;
So there they entwined in a true-lovers' knot,
  For all lovers true to admire.

                    TRADITIONAL: ENGLISH

LORD ULLIN'S DAUGHTER

A Chieftain to the Highlands bound
   Cries, "Boatman, do not tarry!
And I'll give thee a silver pound
   To row us o'er the ferry!"

"Now, who be ye would cross Lochgyle
   This dark and stormy water?"
"O I'm the chief of Ulva's isle,
   And this, Lord Ullin's daughter.

"And fast before her father's men
   Three days we've fled together,
For should he find us in the glen,
   My blood should stain the heather.

"His horsemen hard behind us ride—
   Should they our steps discover,
Then who will cheer my bonny bride
   When they have slain her lover?"

Out spoke the hardy Highland wight,
   "I'll go, my chief, I'm ready:
It is not for your silver bright,
   But for your winsome lady:—

"And by my word! the bonny bird
   In danger shall not tarry;
So though the waves are raging white,
   I'll row you o'er the ferry."

By this the storm grew loud apace,
   The water-wraith was shrieking;
And in the scowl of heaven each face
   Grew dark as they were speaking.

But still as wilder blew the wind,
   And as the night grew drearer,
Adown the glen rode arméd men,
   Their trampling sounded nearer.

"O haste thee, haste!" the lady cries,
   "Though tempest round us gather;
I'll meet the raging of the skies,
   But not an angry father!"

The boat has left a stormy land,
   A stormy sea before her—
When, O! too strong for human hand
   The tempest gather'd o'er her.

And still they row'd amidst the roar
   Of waters fast prevailing:
Lord Ullin reach'd that fatal shore,—
   His wrath was turned to wailing.

[147]

For, sore dismayed, through storm and shade
   His child he did discover:—
One lovely hand she stretch'd for aid,
   And one was round her lover.

"Come back! come back!" he cried in grief,
   Across this stormy water:
And I'll forgive your Highland chief:—
   My daughter!— O my daughter!"

'Twas vain: the loud waves lash'd the shore,
   Return or aid preventing;
The waters wild went o'er his child,
   And he was left lamenting.

THOMAS CAMPBELL

THE SINGING LEAVES

"What fairings will ye that I bring?"
  Said the King to his daughters three;
"For I to Vanity Fair am bound,
  Now say what shall they be?"

Then up and spake the eldest daughter,
  That lady tall and grand:
"Oh, bring me pearls and diamonds great,
  And gold rings for my hand."

Thereafter spake the second daughter,
  That was both white and red:
"For me bring silks that will stand alone,
  And a gold comb for my head."

Then came the turn of the least daughter,
  That was whiter than thistle-down,
And among the gold of her blithesome hair
  Dim shone the golden crown.

"There came a bird this morning,
  And sang 'neath my bower eaves,
Till I dreamed, as his music made me,
  'Ask thou for the Singing Leaves.'"

Then the brow of the King swelled crimson
　　With a flush of angry scorn:
"Well have ye spoken, my two eldest,
　　And chosen as ye were born;

"But she, like a thing of peasant race,
　　That is happy binding the sheaves;"
Then he saw her dear mother in her face,
　　And said, "Thou shalt have thy leaves."

II

He mounted and rode three days and nights,
　　Till he came to Vanity Fair,
And 'twas easy to buy the gems and the silk,
　　But no Singing Leaves were there.

Then deep in the greenwood rode he,
　　And asked of every tree,
"Oh, if you have ever a Singing Leaf,
　　I pray you give it to me!"

But the trees all kept their counsel,
　　And never a word said they,
Only there sighed from the pine-tops
　　A music of seas far away.

Only the pattering aspen
　　Made a sound of growing rain,
That fell ever faster and faster,
　　Then faltered to silence again.

"Oh, where shall I find a little foot-page
    That would win both hose and shoon,
And will bring to me the Singing Leaves
    If they grow under the moon?"

Then lightly turned him Walter the page,
    By the stirrup as he ran:
"Now pledge you me the truesome word
    Of a king and gentleman,

"That you will give me the first, first thing
    You meet at your castle-gate,
And the Princess will get the Singing Leaves,
    Or mine be a traitor's fate."

The King's head dropt upon his breast
    A moment, as it might be;
'Twill be my dog, he thought, and said,
    "My faith I plight to thee."

Then Walter took from next his heart
    A packet small and thin,
"Now give you this to the Princess Anne,
    The Singing Leaves are therein."

III

As the King rode in at his castle-gate,
    A maiden to meet him ran,
And "Welcome, father!" she laughed and cried
    Together, the Princess Anne.

"Lo, here the Singing Leaves," quoth he,
   "And woe, but they cost me dear!"
She took the packet, and the smile
   Deepened down beneath the tear.

It deepened down till it reached her heart,
   And then gushed up again,
And lighted her tears as the sudden sun
   Transfigures the summer rain.

And the first Leaf, when it was opened,
   Sang: "I am Walter the page,
And the songs I sing 'neath thy window
   Are my only heritage."

And the second Leaf sang: "But in the land
   That is neither on earth nor sea,
My lute and I are lords of more
   Than thrice this kingdom's fee."

And the third leaf sang, "Be mine! Be mine!"
   And ever it sang, "Be mine!"
Then sweeter it sang and ever sweeter,
   And said, "I am thine, thine, thine!"

At the first Leaf she grew pale enough,
   At the second she turned aside,
At the third, 'twas as if a lily flushed
   With a rose's red heart's tide.

"Good counsel gave the bird," said she
  "I have my hope thrice o'er,
For they sing to my very heart," she said,
  "And it sings to them evermore."

She brought to him her beauty and truth,
  But and broad earldoms three,
And he made her queen of the broader lands
  He held of his lute in fee.

JAMES RUSSELL LOWELL

THE FORSAKEN MERMAN

Come, dear children, let us away;
Down and away below.
Now my brothers call from the bay;
Now the great winds shoreward blow;
Now the salt tides seaward flow;
Now the wild white horses play,
Champ and chafe and toss in the spray.
Children dear, let us away.
This way, this way.

Call her once before you go.
Call once yet.
In a voice that she will know:
"Margaret! Margaret!"
Children's voices should be dear
(Call once more) to a mother's ear:
Children's voices, wild with pain.
Surely she will come again.
Call her once and come away.
"Mother dear, we cannot stay."
The wild white horses foam and fret.
Margaret! Margaret!

Come, dear children, come away down.
Call no more.

[154]

One last look at the white-wall'd town,
And the little grey church on the windy shore.
Then come down.
She will not come though you call all day.
Come away, come away.

Children dear, was it yesterday
We heard the sweet bells over the bay?
In the caverns where we lay,
Through the surf and through the swell,
The far-off sound of a silver bell?
Sand-strewn caverns, cool and deep,
Where the winds are all asleep;
Where the spent lights quiver and gleam;
Where the salt weed sways in the stream;
Where the sea-beasts rang'd all round
Feed in the ooze of their pasture ground;
Where the sea-snakes coil and twine,
Dry their mail and bask in the brine;
Where great whales come sailing by,
Sail and sail with unshut eye,
Round the world for ever and aye?
When did music come this way?
Children dear, was it yesterday?

Children dear, was it yesterday
(Call yet once) that she went away?
Once she sate with you and me,
On a red gold throne in the heart of the sea,

[155]

And the youngest sate on her knee.
She comb'd its bright hair, and she tended it well,
When down swung the sound of the far-off bell.
She sigh'd, she look'd up through the clear green sea.
She said; "I must go, for my kinsfolk pray
In the little grey church on the shore today.
'Twill be Easter-time in the world—ah me!
And I lose my poor soul, Merman, here with thee."
I said; "Go up, dear heart, through the waves;
Say thy prayer, and come back to the kind sea-caves."
She smil'd, she went up through the surf in the bay.
Children dear, was it yesterday?

Children dear, were we long alone?
"The sea grows stormy, the little ones moan,
Long prayers," I said, "in the world they say.
Come," I said, and we rose through the surf in the bay.
We went up the beach, by the sandy down
Where the sea-stocks bloom, to the white-wall'd town.
Through the narrow pav'd streets, where all was still,
To the little grey church on the windy hill.
From the church came a murmur of folk at their prayers,
But we stood without in the cold blowing airs.
We climb'd on the graves, on the stones, worn with rains,
And we gaz'd up the aisle through the small leaded panes.
She sate by the pillar; we saw her clear:
"Margaret, hist! come quick, we are here.
Dear heart," I said, "we are long alone.
The sea grows stormy, the little ones moan."

But, ah, she gave me never a look,
For her eyes were seal'd to the holy book.
"Loud prays the priest; shut stands the door."
Come away, children call no more.
Come away, come down, call no more.

Down, down, down.
Down to the depths of the sea.
She sits at her wheel in the humming town,
Singing most joyfully.
Hark, what she sings; "O joy, O joy,
For the humming street, and the child with its toy.
For the priest, and the bell, and the holy well.
For the wheel where I spun,
And the blessed light of the sun."
And so she sings her fill,
Singing most joyfully,
Till the shuttle falls from her hand,
And the whizzing wheel stands still.
She steals to the window, and looks at the sand;
And over the sand at the sea;
And her eyes are set in a stare;
And anon there breaks a sigh,
And anon there drops a tear,
From a sorrow-clouded eye,
And a heart sorrow-laden,
A long, long sigh,
For the cold strange eyes of a little Mermaiden,
And the gleam of her golden hair.

Come away, away children.
Come children, come down.
The hoarse wind blows colder;
Lights shine in the town.
She will start from her slumber
When gusts shake the door;
She will hear the winds howling,
Will hear the waves roar.
We shall see, while above us
The waves roar and whirl,
A ceiling of amber,
A pavement of pearl.
Singing, "Here came a mortal,
But faithless was she.
And alone dwell for ever
The kings of the sea."

But, children, at midnight,
When soft the winds blow;
When clear falls the moonlight;
When spring-tides are low:
When sweet airs come seaward
From heaths starr'd with broom;
And high rocks throw mildly
On the blanch'd sands a gloom:
Up the still, glistening beaches,
Up the creeks we will hie;
Over banks of bright seaweed
The ebb-tide leaves dry.

We will gaze, from the sand-hills,
At the white, sleeping town;
At the church on the hill-side—
And then come back down.
Singing, "There dwells a lov'd one,
But cruel is she.
She left lonely for ever
The kings of the sea."

MATTHEW ARNOLD

THE EVE OF ST. AGNES

St. Agnes' Eve— Ah, bitter chill it was!
The owl, for all his feathers, was a-cold;
The hare limp'd trembling through the frozen grass,
And silent was the flock in woolly fold:
Numb were the Beadsman's fingers, while he told
His rosary, and while his frosted breath,
Like pious incense from a censer old,
Seem'd taking flight for heaven, without a death,
Past the sweet Virgin's picture, while his prayer he saith.

His prayer he saith, this patient, holy man;
Then takes his lamp, and riseth from his knees,
And back returneth, meager, barefoot, wan,
Along the chapel aisle by slow degrees:
The sculptur'd dead, on each side, seem to freeze,
Emprison'd in black, purgatorial rails:
Knights, ladies, praying in dumb orat'ries,
He passeth by; and his weak spirit fails
To think how they may ache in icy hoods and mails.

Northward he turneth through a little door,
And scarce three steps, ere Music's golden tongue
Flatter'd to tears this aged man and poor;
But no—already had his deathbell rung:

The joys of all his life were said and sung:
His was harsh penance on St. Agnes' Eve:
Another way he went, and soon among
Rough ashes sat he for his soul's reprieve,
And all night kept awake, for sinners' sake to grieve.

That ancient Beadsman heard the prelude soft;
And so it chanc'd, for many a door was wide,
From hurry to and fro. Soon, up aloft,
The silver, snarling trumpets 'gan to chide:
The level chambers, ready with their pride,
Were glowing to receive a thousand guests:
The carved angels, ever eager-eyed,
Star'd, where upon their heads the cornice rests,
With hair blown back, and wings put cross-wise on their
        breasts.

At length burst in the argent revelry,
With plume, tiara, and all rich array,
Numerous as shadows haunting faerily
The brain, new stuff'd, in youth, with triumphs gay
Of old romance. These let us wish away,
And turn, sole-thoughted, to one Lady there,
Whose heart had brooded, all that wintry day,
On love, and wing'd St. Agnes' saintly care,
As she had heard old dames full many times declare.

They told her how, upon St. Agnes' Eve,
Young virgins might have visions of delight,

[161]

And soft adorings from their loves receive
Upon the honey'd middle of the night,
If ceremonies due they did aright;
As, supperless to bed they must retire,
And couch supine their beauties, lily white;
Nor look behind, nor sideways, but require
Of Heaven with upward eyes for all that they desire.

Full of this whim was thoughtful Madeline:
The music, yearning like a God in pain,
She scarcely heard: her maiden eyes divine,
Fix'd on the floor, saw many a sweeping train
Pass by—she heeded not at all: in vain
Came many a tiptoe, amorous cavalier,
And back retir'd; not cool'd by high disdain,
But she saw not: her heart was otherwhere:
She sigh'd for Agnes' dreams, the sweetest of the year.

She danc'd along with vague, regardless eyes,
Anxious her lips, her breathing quick and short:
The hallow'd hour was near at hand: she sighs
Amid the timbrels, and the throng'd resort
Of whisperers in anger, or in sport;
'Mid looks of love, defiance, hate, and scorn,
Hoodwink'd with faery fancy; all amort,
Save to St. Agnes and her lambs unshorn,
And all the bliss to be before tomorrow morn.

So, purposing each moment to retire,
She linger'd still. Meantime, across the moors,

Had come young Porphyro, with heart on fire
For Madeline. Beside the portal doors,
Buttress'd from moonlight, stands he, and implores
All saints to give him sight of Madeline,
But for one moment in the tedious hours,
That he might gaze and worship all unseen;
Perchance speak, kneel, touch, kiss—in sooth such things
        have been.

He ventures in: let no buzz'd whisper tell:
All eyes be muffled, or a hundred swords
Will storm his heart, Love's fev'rous citadel:
For him, those chambers held barbarian hordes,
Hyena foemen, and hot-blooded lords,
Whose very dogs would execrations howl
Against his lineage: not one breast affords
Him any mercy, in that mansion foul,
Save one old beldame, weak in body and in soul.

Ah, happy chance! the aged creature came,
Shuffling along with ivory-headed wand,
To where he stood, hid from the torch's flame,
Behind a broad hall-pillar, far beyond
The sound of merriment and chorus bland:
He startled her; but soon she knew his face,
And grasp'd his fingers in her palsied hand,
Saying, "Mercy, Porphyro! hie thee from this place:
"They are all here tonight, the whole blood-thirsty race!

"Get hence! get hence! there's dwarfish Hildebrand;
"He had a fever late, and in the fit
"He cursed thee and thine, both house and land:
"Then there's that old Lord Maurice, not a whit
"More tame for his gray hairs— Alas me! flit!
"Flit like a ghost away."—"Ah, Gossip dear,
"We're safe enough; here in this arm-chair sit,
"And tell me how"— "Good Saints! not here, not here;
"Follow me, child, or else these stones will be thy bier."

He follow'd through a lowly arched way,
Brushing the cobwebs with his lofty plume,
And as she mutter'd "Well-a—well-a-day!"
He found him in a little moonlight room,
Pale, lattic'd, chill, and silent as a tomb.
"Now tell me where is Madeline," said he,
"O tell me, Angela, by the holy loom
"Which none but secret sisterhood may see,
"When they St. Agnes' wool are weaving piously."

"St. Agnes! Ah! it is St. Agnes' Eve—
"Yet men will murder upon holy days:
"Thou must hold water in a witch's sieve,
"And be liege-lord of all the Elves and Fays,
"To venture so: it fills me with amaze
"To see thee, Porphyro!—St. Agnes' Eve!
"God's help! my lady fair the conjuror plays
"This very night: good angels her deceive!
"But let me laugh awhile, I've mickle time to grieve."

[164]

Feebly she laugheth in the languid moon,
While Porphyro upon her face doth look,
Like puzzled urchin on an aged crone
Who keepeth clos'd a wond'rous riddle-book,
As spectacled she sits in chimney nook.
But soon his eyes grew brilliant, when she told
His lady's purpose; and he scarce could brook
Tears, at the thought of those enchantments cold,
And Madeline asleep in lap of legends old.

Sudden a thought came like a full-blown rose,
Flushing his brow, and in his pained heart
Made purple riot: then doth he propose
A stratagem, that makes the beldame start:
"A cruel man and impious thou art:
"Sweet lady, let her pray, and sleep, and dream
"Alone with her good angels, far apart
"From wicked men like thee. Go, go!—I deem
"Thou canst not surely be the same that thou didst seem."

"I will not harm her, by all saints I swear,"
Quoth Porphyro: "O may I ne'er find grace
"When my weak voice shall whisper its last prayer,
"If one of her soft ringlets I displace,
"Or look with ruffian passion in her face:
"Good Angela, believe me by these tears;
"Or I will, even in a moment's space,
"Awake, with horrid shout, my foemen's ears,

"And beard them, though they be more fang'd than wolves
        and bears."

  "Ah! why wilt thou affright a feeble soul?
  "A poor, weak, palsy-stricken, churchyard thing,
  "Whose passing-bell may ere midnight toll;
  "Whose prayers for thee, each morn and evening,
  "Were never miss'd."—Thus plaining, doth she bring
A gentler speech from burning Porphyro;
So woeful, and of such deep sorrowing,
That Angela gives promise she will do
Whatever he shall wish, betide her weal or woe.

  Which was, to lead him, in close secrecy,
Even to Madeline's chamber, and there hide
Him in a closet, of such privacy
That he might see her beauty unespied,
And win perhaps that night a peerless bride,
While legion'd faeries pac'd the coverlet,
And pale enchantment held her sleepy-eyed.
Never on such a night have lovers met,
Since Merlin paid his Demon all the monstrous debt.

  "It shall be as thou wishest," said the Dame:
  "All cates and dainties shall be stored there
  "Quickly on this feast-night: by the tambour frame
  "Her own lute thou wilt see: no time to spare,
  "For I am slow and feeble, and scarce dare
  "On such a catering trust my dizzy head.

"Wait here, my child, with patience; kneel in prayer
"The while: Ah! thou must needs the lady wed,
"Or may I never leave my grave among the dead."

So saying, she hobbled off with busy fear.
The lover's endless minutes slowly pass'd;
The dame return'd, and whisper'd in his ear
To follow her; with aged eyes aghast
From fright of dim espial. Safe at last,
Through many a dusky gallery, they gain
The maiden's chamber, silken, hush'd, and chaste;
Where Porphyro took covert, pleas'd amain.
His poor guide hurried back with agues in her brain.

Her falt'ring hand upon the balustrade,
Old Angela was feeling for the stair,
When Madeline, St. Agnes' charmed maid,
Rose, like a mission'd spirit, unaware:
With silver taper's light, and pious care,
She turn'd, and down the aged gossip led
To a safe level matting. Now prepare,
Young Porphyro, for gazing on that bed;
She comes, she comes again, like ring-dove fray'd and fled.

Out went the taper as she hurried in;
Its little smoke, in pallid moonshine died:
She clos'd the door, she panted, all akin
To spirits of the air, and visions wide:
No uttered syllable, or, woe betide!

But to her heart, her heart was voluble,
Paining with eloquence her balmy side;
As though a tongueless nightingale should swell
Her throat in vain, and die, heart-stifled, in her dell.

A casement high and triple-arch'd there was,
All garlanded with carven imag'ries
Of fruits, and flowers, and bunches of knot-grass,
And diamonded with panes of quaint device,
Innumerable of stains and splendid dyes,
As are the tiger-moth's deep-damask'd wings;
And in the midst, 'mong thousand heraldries,
And twilight saints, and dim emblazonings,
A shielded scutcheon blush'd with blood of queens and
          kings.

Full on this casement shone the wintry moon,
And threw warm gules on Madeline's fair breast,
As down she knelt for heaven's grace and boon;
Rose-bloom fell on her hands, together prest,
And on her silver cross soft amethyst,
And on her hair a glory, like a saint:
She seem'd a splendid angel, newly drest,
Save wings, for heaven:—Porphyro grew faint:
She knelt, so pure a thing, so free from mortal taint.

Anon his heart revives: her vespers done,
Of all its wreathed pearls her hair she frees;
Unclasps her warmed jewels one by one;

Loosens her fragrant bodice; by degrees
Her rich attire creeps rustling to her knees:
Half-hidden, like a mermaid in sea-weed,
Pensive awhile she dreams awake, and sees,
In fancy, fair St. Agnes in her bed,
But dares not look behind, or all the charm is fled.

Soon, trembling in her soft and chilly nest,
In sort of wakeful swoon, perplex'd she lay,
Until the poppied warmth of sleep oppress'd
Her soothed limbs, and soul fatigued away;
Flown, like a thought, until the morrow-day;
Blissfully haven'd both from joy and pain;
Clasp'd like a missal where swart Paynims pray;
Blinded alike from sunshine and from rain,
As though a rose should shut, and be a bud again.

Stol'n to this paradise, and so entranced,
Porphyro gazed upon her empty dress,
And listen'd to her breathing, if it chanced
To wake into a slumberous tenderness;
Which when he heard, that minute did he bless,
And breath'd himself: then from the closet crept,
Noiseless as fear in a wide wilderness,
And over the hush'd carpet, silent, stept,
And 'tween the curtains peep'd, where, lo!—how fast she
        slept.

Then by the bed-side, where the faded moon
Made a dim, silver twilight, soft he set

[169]

A table, and, half anguish'd, threw thereon
A cloth of woven crimson, gold, and jet:—
O for some drowsy Morphean amulet!
The boisterous, midnight, festive clarion,
The kettle-drum, and far-heard clarinet,
Affray his ears, though but in dying tone:—
The hall door shuts again, and all the noise is gone.

And still she slept an azure-lidded sleep,
In blanched linen, smooth, and lavender'd,
While he from forth the closet brought a heap
Of candied apple, quince, and plum, and gourd;
With jellies soother than the creamy curd,
And lucent syrops, tinct with cinnamon;
Manna and dates, in argosy transferr'd
From Fez; and spiced dainties, every one,
From silken Samarcand to cedar'd Lebanon.

These delicates he heap'd with glowing hand
On golden dishes and in baskets bright
Of wreathed silver: sumptuous they stand
In the retired quiet of the night,
Filling the chilly room with perfume light.—
"And now, my love, my seraph fair, awake!
"Thou art my heaven, and I thine eremite:
"Open thine eyes, for meek St. Agnes' sake,
"Or I shall drowse beside thee, so my soul doth ache."

Thus whispering, his warm, unnerved arm
Sank in her pillow. Shaded was her dream

By the dusk curtains:—'twas a midnight charm
Impossible to melt as iced stream:
The lustrous salvers in the moonlight gleam;
Broad golden fringe upon the carpet lies:
It seem'd he never, never could redeem
From such a stedfast spell his lady's eyes;
So mus'd awhile, entoil'd in woofed phantasies.

Awakening up, he took her hollow lute,—
Tumultuous,—and, in chords that tenderest be,
He play'd an ancient ditty, long since mute,
In Provence call'd, "La belle dame sans mercy:"
Close to her ear touching the melody;—
Wherewith disturb'd, she utter'd a soft moan:
He ceased—she panted quick—and suddenly
Her blue affrayed eyes wide open shone:
Upon his knees he sank, pale as smooth-sculptured stone.

Her eyes were open, but she still beheld,
Now wide awake, the vision of her sleep:
There was a painful change, that nigh expell'd
The blisses of her dream so pure and deep
At which fair Madeline began to weep,
And moan forth witless words with many a sigh;
While still her gaze on Porphyro would keep;
Who knelt, with joined hands and piteous eye,
Fearing to move or speak, she look'd so dreamingly.

"Ah, Porphyro!" said she, "but even now
"Thy voice was at sweet tremble in mine ear,

[171]

"Made tuneable with every sweetest vow;
"And those sad eyes were spiritual and clear:
"How chang'd thou art! how pallid, chill, and drear!
"Give me that voice again, my Porphyro,
"Those looks immortal, those complainings dear!
"Oh leave me not in this eternal woe,
"For if thou diest, my Love, I know not where to go."

Beyond a mortal man impassion'd far
At these voluptuous accents, he arose,
Ethereal, flush'd, and like a throbbing star
Seen mid the sapphire heaven's deep repose;
Into her dream he melted, as the rose
Blendeth its odor with the violet,—
Solution sweet: meantime the frost-wind blows
Like Love's alarum pattering the sharp sleet
Against the window-panes; St. Agnes' moon hath set.

'Tis dark: quick pattereth the flaw-blown sleet:
"This is no dream, my bride, my Madeline!"
'Tis dark: the iced gusts still rave and beat:
"No dream, alas! alas! and woe is mine!
"Porphyro will leave me here to fade and pine.—
"Cruel! what traitor could thee hither bring?
"I curse not, for my heart is lost in thine,
"Though thou forsakest a deceived thing;—
"A dove forlorn and lost with sick unpruned wing."

"My Madeline! sweet dreamer! lovely bride!
"Say, may I be for aye thy vassal blest?

"Thy beauty's shield, heart-shap'd and vermeil dyed?
"Ah, silver shrine, here will I take my rest
"After so many hours of toil and quest,
"A famish'd pilgrim,—sav'd by miracle.
"Though I have found, I will not rob thy nest
"Saving of thy sweet self; if thou think'st well
"To trust, fair Madeline, to no rude infidel.

"Hark! 'tis an elfin-storm from faery land,
"Of haggard seeming, but a boon indeed:
"Arise—arise! the morning is at hand;—
"The bloated wassaillers will never heed:—
"Let us away, my love, with happy speed;
"There are no ears to hear, or eyes to see,—
"Drown'd all in Rhenish and the sleepy mead:
"Awake! arise! my love, and fearless be,
"For o'er the southern moors I have a home for thee."

She hurried at his words, beset with fears,
For there were sleeping dragons all around,
At glaring watch, perhaps, with ready spears—
Down the wide stairs a darkling way they found.—
In all the house was heard no human sound.
A chain-droop'd lamp was flickering by each door;
The arras, rich with horseman, hawk, and hound,
Flutter'd in the besieging wind's uproar;
And the long carpets rose along the gusty floor.

They glide, like phantoms, into the wide hall;
Like phantoms, to the iron porch, they glide;

Where lay the Porter, in uneasy sprawl,
With a huge empty flaggon by his side:
The wakeful bloodhound rose, and shook his hide,
But his sagacious eye an inmate owns:
By one, and one, the bolts full easy slide:—
The chains lie silent on the footworn stones;—
The key turns, and the door upon its hinges groans.

And they are gone: aye, ages long ago
These lovers fled away into the storm.
That night the Baron dreamt of many a woe,
And all his warrior-guests, with shade and form
Of witch, and demon, and large coffin-worm,
Were long be-nightmar'd. Angela the old
Died palsy-twitch'd, with meager face deform;
The Beadsman, after thousand aves told,
For aye unsought for slept among his ashes cold.

JOHN KEATS

[174]

POEMS ABOUT PEOPLE

ABOU BEN ADHEM

Abou Ben Adhem (may his tribe increase!)
Awoke one night from a deep dream of peace,
And saw, within the moonlight in his room,
Making it rich, and like a lily in bloom,
An angel writing in a book of gold:—
Exceeding peace had made Ben Adhem bold,
And to the presence in the room he said,
"What writest thou?"— The vision rais'd its head,
And with a look made all of sweet accord,
Answer'd, "The names of those that love the Lord."
"And is mine one?" said Abou. "Nay, not so,"
Replied the angel. Abou spoke more low,
But cheerly still; and said, "I pray thee, then,
Write me as one that loves his fellow men."
The angel wrote, and vanished. The next night
It came again with a great awakening light,
And show'd the names whom love of God had blest,
And lo! Ben Adhem's name led all the rest.

LEIGH HUNT

EDDI'S SERVICE

Eddi, priest of St. Wilfrid
   In his chapel at Manhood End,
Ordered a midnight service
   For such as cared to attend.

But the Saxons were keeping Christmas,
   And the night was stormy as well,
Nobody came to service,
   Though Eddi rang the bell.

"Wicked weather for walking,"
   Said Eddi of Manhood End.
"But I must go on with the service
   For such as care to attend."

The altar lamps were lighted,—
   An old marsh-donkey came,
Bold as a guest invited,
   And stared at the guttering flame.

The storm beat on at the windows,
   The water splashed on the floor,
And a wet, yoke-weary bullock
   Pushed in through the open door.

"How do I know what is greatest,
    How do I know what is least?
That is My Father's business,"
    Said Eddi, Wilfrid's priest.

"But—three are gathered together—
    Listen to me and attend.
I bring good news, my brethren!"
    Said Eddi of Manhood End.

And he told the Ox of a Manger
    And a stall in Bethlehem,
And he spoke to the Ass of a Rider
    That rode to Jerusalem.

They steamed and dripped in the chancel,
    They listened and never stirred,
While, just as though they were Bishops,
    Eddi preached them The Word,

Till the gale blew off on the marshes
    And the windows showed the day,
And the Ox and the Ass together
    Wheeled and clattered away.

And when the Saxons mocked him,
    Said Eddi of Manhood End,
"I dare not shut His chapel
    On such as care to attend."

                          RUDYARD KIPLING

THE LEAK IN THE DIKE

The good dame looked from her cottage
  At the close of the pleasant day,
And cheerily called to her little son
  Outside the door at play:
"Come, Peter! come! I want you to go,
  While there is light to see,
To the hut of the blind old man who lives
  Across the dike, for me;
And take these cakes I made for him—
  They are hot and smoking yet;
You have time enough to go and come
  Before the sun is set."

Then the good wife turned to her labor,
  Humming a simple song,
And thought of her husband working hard
  At the sluices all day long;
And set the turf a-blazing,
  And brought the coarse black bread:
That he might find a fire at night,
  And find the table spread.

And Peter left the brother,
  With whom all day he had played,

And the sister who had watched their sports
  In the willow's tender shade;
And told them they'd see him back before
  They saw a star in sight,
Though he wouldn't be afraid to go
  In the very darkest night!
For he was a brave, bright fellow,
  With eye and conscience clear;
He could do whatever a boy might do,
  And he had not learned to fear.
Why, he wouldn't have robbed a bird's nest
  Nor brought a stork to harm,
Though never a law in Holland
  Had stood to stay his arm!

And now with his face all glowing,
  And eyes as bright as the day
With the thoughts of his pleasant errand,
  He trudged along the way;
And soon his joyous prattle
  Made glad a lonesome place—
Alas! if only the blind old man
  Could have seen that happy face!
Yet he somehow caught the brightness
  Which his voice and presence lent
And he felt the sunshine come and go
  As Peter came and went.

And now, as the day was sinking,
  And the winds began to rise,

The mother looked from her door again,
  Shading her anxious eyes,
And saw the shadows deepen
  And birds to their home come back,
But never a sign of Peter
  Along the level track.
But she said: "He will come at morning,
  So I need not fret or grieve—
Though it isn't like my boy at all
  To stay without my leave."

But where was the child delaying?
  On the homeward way was he,
And across the dike while the sun was up
  An hour above the sea.
He was stopping now to gather flowers,
  Now listening to the sound,
As the angry waters dashed themselves
  Against their narrow bound.
"Ah! well for us," said Peter,
  "That the gates are good and strong,
And my father tends them carefully,
  Or they would not hold you long!
You're a wicked sea," said Peter;
  "I know why you fret and chafe;
You would like to spoil our lands and homes;
  But our sluices keep you safe."

But hark! through the noise of waters
  Comes a low, clear, trickling sound;

And the child's face pales with terror,
   And his blossoms drop to the ground.
He is up the bank in a moment,
   And, stealing through the sand,
He sees a stream not yet so large
   As his slender, childish hand.

'Tis a leak in the dike!— He is but a boy,
   Unused to fearful scenes;
But, young as he is, he has learned to know
   The dreadful thing that means.
A *leak in the dike!* The stoutest heart
   Grows faint that cry to hear,
And the bravest man in all the land
   Turns white with mortal fear.
For he knows the smallest leak may grow
   To a flood in a single night;
And he knows the strength of the cruel sea
   When loosed in its angry might.

And the Boy! he has seen the danger
   And, shouting a wild alarm,
He forces back the weight of the sea
   With the strength of his single arm!
He listens for the joyful sound
   Of a footstep passing nigh;
And lays his ear to the ground, to catch
   The answers to his cry.

And he hears the rough winds blowing,
   And the waters rise and fall,
But never an answer comes to him
   Save the echo of his call.
He sees no hope, no succor,
   His feeble voice is lost;
Yet what shall he do but watch and wait
   Though he perish at his post!

So, faintly calling and crying
   Till the sun is under the sea;
Crying and moaning till the stars
   Come out for company;
He thinks of his brother and sister,
   Asleep in their safe warm bed;
He thinks of his father and mother,
   Of himself as dying—and dead;
And of how, when the night is over,
   They must come and find him at last;
But he never thinks he can leave the place
   Where duty holds him fast.

The good dame in the cottage
   Is up and astir with the light,
For the thought of her little Peter
   Has been with her all the night.
And now she watches the pathway,
   As yester-eve she had done;

[183]

But what does she see so strange and black
   Against the rising sun?
Her neighbors are bearing between them
   Something straight to her door;
Her child is coming home, but not
   As he ever came before!

"He is dead!" she cries, "my darling!"
   And the startled father hears,
And comes and looks the way she looks,
   And fears the thing she fears;
Till a glad shout from the bearers
   Thrills the stricken man and wife—
"Give thanks, for your son has saved our land,
   And God has saved his life!"
So, there in the morning sunshine
   They knelt about the boy;
And every head was bared and bent
   In tearful, reverent joy.

'Tis many a year since then; but still,
   When the sea roars like a flood,
The boys are taught what a boy can do
   Who is brave and true and good;
For every man in that country
   Takes his son by the hand
And tells him of little Peter,
   Whose courage saved the land.

They have many a valiant hero,
  Remembered through the years;
But never one whose name so oft
  Is named with loving tears.
And his deed shall be sung by the cradle,
  And told to the child on the knee,
So long as the dikes of Holland
  Divide the land from the sea!

PHOEBE CARY

PLAIN LANGUAGE
FROM TRUTHFUL JAMES

Which I wish to remark,
And my language is plain,
That for ways that are dark
And for tricks that are vain,
The heathen Chinee is peculiar,
Which the same I would rise to explain.

Ah Sin was his name;
And I shall not deny,
In regard to the same,
What that name might imply;
But his smile it was pensive and childlike,
As I frequent remarked to Bill Nye.

It was August the third,
And quite soft was the skies;
Which it might be inferred
That Ah Sin was likewise;
Yet he played it that day upon William
And me in a way I despise.

Which we had a small game,
And Ah Sin took a hand:
It was Euchre. The same

He did not understand;
But he smiled as he sat by the table,
With the smile that was childlike and bland.

Yet the cards they were stocked
In a way that I grieve,
And my feelings were shocked
At the state of Nye's sleeve,
Which was stuffed full of aces and bowers,
And the same with intent to deceive.

But the hands that were played
By that heathen Chinee,
And the points that he made,
Were quite frightful to see—
Till at last he put down a right bower,
Which the same Nye had dealt unto me.

Then I looked up at Nye,
And he gazed upon me;
And he rose with a sigh,
And said, "Can this be?
We are ruined by Chinese cheap labor"—
And he went for that heathen Chinee.

In the scene that ensued
I did not take a hand,
But the floor it was strewed
Like the leaves on the strand

With the cards that Ah Sin had been hiding,
In the game "he did not understand."

In his sleeves, which were long,
He had twenty-four packs—
Which was coming it strong.
Yet I state but the facts;
And we found on his nails, which were taper,
What is frequent in tapers—that's wax.

Which is why I remark,
And my language is plain,
That for ways that are dark,
And for tricks that are vain,
The heathen Chinee is peculiar—
Which the same I am free to maintain.

BRET HARTE

EDWARD, EDWARD

"Why does your brand sae drop wi' blude,
  Edward, Edward?
Why does your brand sae drop wi' blude,
  And why sae sad gang ye, O?"—
"O I hae kill'd my hawk sae gude,
  Mither, mither;
O I hae kill'd my hawk sae gude,
  And I had nae mair but he, O."

"Your hawk's blude was never sae red,
  Edward, Edward;
Your hawk's blude was never sae red,
  My dear son, I tell thee, O."—
"O I hae kill'd my red-roan steed,
  Mither, mither;
O I hae kill'd my red-roan steed,
  That erst was sae fair and free, O."

"Your steed was auld, and ye hae got mair,
  Edward, Edward;
Your steed was auld, and ye hae got mair;
  Some other dule ye dree, O."—
"O I hae kill'd my father dear,
  Mither, mither;

O I hae kill'd my father dear,
 Alas, and wae is me, O!"

"And whatten penance will ye dree for that,
 Edward, Edward?
Whatten penance will ye dree for that?
 My dear son, now tell me, O."—
"I'll set my feet in yonder boat,
 Mither, mither;
I'll set my feet in yonder boat
 And I'll fare over the sea, O."—

"And what will ye do wi' your tow'rs and your ha',
 Edward, Edward?
And what will ye do wi' your tow'rs and your ha',
 That were sae fair to see, O?"—
"I'll let them stand till they doun fa',
 Mither, mither;
I'll let them stand till they doun fa',
 For here never mair maun I be, O."

"And what will ye leave to your ain mither dear,
 Edward, Edward?
And what will ye leave to your ain mither dear,
 My dear son, now tell me, O?"—
"The curse of hell frae me sall ye bear,
 Mither, mither;
The curse of hell frae me sall ye bear:
 Sic counsels ye gave to me, O!"

TRADITIONAL: SCOTS

[190]

THE CHILDREN IN THE WOOD

Now ponder well, you parents dear,
    These words which I shall write;
A doleful story you shall hear,
    In time brought forth to light.
A gentleman of good account
    In Norfolk dwelt of late,
Who did in honor far surmount
    Most men of his estate.

Sore sick he was and like to die,
    No help his life could save;
His wife by him as sick did lie,
    And both possest one grave,
No love between these two was lost,
    Each was to other kind;
In love they lived, in love they died,
    And left two babes behind:

The one a fine and pretty boy
    Not passing three years old,
The other a girl more young than he,
    And framed in beauty's mould.
The father left his little son,
    As plainly did appear,

When he to perfect age should come,
   Three hundred pounds a year;

And to his little daughter Jane,
   Five hundred pounds in gold,
To be paid down on marriage-day,
   Which might not be controll'd.
But if the children chanced to die
   Ere they to age should come,
Their uncle should possess their wealth;
   For so the will did run.

"Now, brother," said the dying man,
   "Look to my children dear;
Be good unto my boy and girl,
   No friends else have they here:
To God and you I recommend
   My children dear this day;
But little while be sure we have
   Within this world to stay.

"You must be father and mother both,
   And uncle, all in one;
God knows what will become of them
   When I am dead and gone."
With that bespake their mother dear:
   "O brother kind," quoth she,
"You are the man must bring our babes
   To wealth or misery!

"And if you keep them carefully,
   Then God will you reward;
But if you otherwise should deal,
   God will your deeds regard."
With lips as cold as any stone,
   They kiss'd their children small:
"God bless you both, my children dear!"
   With that the tears did fall.

These speeches then their brother spake
   To this sick couple there:
"The keeping of your little ones,
   Sweet sister, do not fear;
God never prosper me nor mine,
   Nor aught else that I have,
If I do wrong your children dear
   When you are laid in grave!"

The parents being dead and gone,
   The children home he takes,
And brings them straight unto his house,
   Where much of them he makes.
He had not kept these pretty babes
   A twelvemonth and a day,
But, for their wealth, he did devise
   To make them both away.

He bargain'd with two ruffians strong,
   Which were of furious mood,

That they should take these children young,
 And slay them in a wood.
He told his wife an artful tale:
 He would the children send
To be brought up in London town
 With one that was his friend.

Away then went those pretty babes,
 Rejoicing at that tide,
Rejoicing with a merry mind
 They should on cock-horse ride.
They prate and prattle pleasantly,
 As they ride on the way,
To those that should their butchers be
 And work their lives' decay:

So that the pretty speech they had
 Made Murder's heart relent;
And they that undertook the deed
 Full sore did now repent.
Yet one of them, more hard of heart,
 Did vow to do his charge,
Because the wretch that hired him
 Had paid him very large.

The other won't agree thereto,
 So here they fall to strife;
With one another they did fight
 About the children's life:

[194]

And he that was of mildest mood
   Did slay the other there,
Within an unfrequented wood.—
   The babes did quake for fear!

He took the children by the hand,
   Tears standing in their eye,
And bade them straightway follow him,
   And look they did not cry;
And two long miles he led them on,
   While they for food complain:
"Stay here," quoth he; "I'll bring you bread
   When I come back again."

These pretty babes, with hand in hand,
   Went wandering up and down;
But never more could see the man
   Approaching from the town.
Their pretty lips with blackberries
   Were all besmear'd and dyed;
And when they saw the darksome night,
   They sat them down and cried.

Thus wander'd these poor innocents,
   Till death did end their grief;
In one another's arms they died,
   As wanting due relief:
No burial this pretty pair
   From any man receives,

[195]

Till Robin Redbreast piously
  Did cover them with leaves.

And now the heavy wrath of God
  Upon their uncle fell;
Yea, fearful fiends did haunt his house,
  His conscience felt an hell:
His barns were fired, his goods consumed,
  His lands were barren made,
His cattle died within the field,
  And nothing with him stay'd.

And in a voyage to Portugal
  Two of his sons did die;
And, to conclude, himself was brought
  To want and misery:
He pawn'd and mortgaged all his land
  Ere seven years came about.
And now at last his wicked act
  Did by this means come out.

The fellow that did take in hand
  These children for to kill
Was for a robbery judged to die,
  Such was God's blessed will:
Who did confess the very truth,
  As here hath been display'd:
The uncle having died in jail,
  Where he for debt was laid.

[196]

You that executors be made,
     And overseers eke,
Of children that be fatherless,
     And infants mild and meek,
Take you example by this thing,
     And yield to each his right,
Lest God with suchlike misery
     Your wicked minds requite.

TRADITIONAL: ENGLISH

SKIPPER IRESON'S RIDE

Of all the rides since the birth of time,
Told in story or sung in rhyme,—
On Apuleius's Golden Ass,
Or one-eyed Calender's horse of brass,
Witch astride of a human back,
Islam's prophet on Al-Borak,—
The strangest ride that ever was sped
Was Ireson's, out from Marblehead!
  Old Floyd Ireson, for his hard heart,
  Tarred and feathered and carried in a cart
    By the women of Marblehead!

Body of turkey, head of owl,
Wings a-droop like a rained-on fowl,
Feathered and ruffled in every part,
Skipper Ireson stood in the cart.
Scores of women, old and young,
Strong of muscle and glib of tongue,
Pushed and pulled up the rocky lane,
Shouting and singing the shrill refrain:
  "Here's Flud Oirson, fur his horrd horrt,
  Torr'd an' futherr'd an' corr'd in a corrt
    By the women o' Morble'ead!"

Wrinkled scolds with hands on hips,
Girls in bloom of cheek and lips,
Wild-eyed, free-limbed, such as chase
Bacchus round some antique vase,
Brief of skirt, with ankles bare,
Loose of kerchief and loose of hair,
With conch-shells blowing and fish-horns' twang,
Over and over the Maenads sang:
 "Here's Flud Oirson, fur his horrd horrt,
 Torr'd an' futherr'd an' corr'd in a corrt
  By the women o' Morble'ead!"

Small pity for him!— He sailed away
From a leaking ship in Chaleur Bay,—
Sailed away from a sinking wreck,
With his own town's-people on her deck!
"Lay by! lay by!" they called to him.
Back he answered, "Sink or swim!
Brag of your catch of fish again!"
And off he sailed through the fog and rain!
 Old Floyd Ireson, for his hard heart,
 Tarred and feathered and carried in a cart
  By the women of Marblehead!

Fathoms deep in dark Chaleur
That wreck shall lie forevermore.
Mother and sister, wife and maid,
Looked from the rocks of Marblehead
Over the moaning and rainy sea,—

Looked for the coming that might not be!
What did the winds and the sea-birds say
Of the cruel captain who sailed away?—
  Old Floyd Ireson, for his hard heart,
  Tarred and feathered and carried in a cart
    By the women of Marblehead.

Through the street, on either side,
Up flew windows, doors swung wide;
Sharp-tongued spinsters, old wives gray,
Treble lent the fish-horn's bray.
Sea-worn grandsires, cripple-bound,
Hulks of old sailors run aground,
Shook head, and fist, and hat, and cane,
And cracked with curses the hoarse refrain:
  "Here's Flud Oirson, fur his horrd horrt,
  Torr'd an' futherr'd an' corr'd in a corrt
    By the women o' Morble'ead!"

Sweetly along the Salem road
Bloom of orchard and lilac showed.
Little the wicked skipper knew
Of the fields so green and the sky so blue.
Riding there in his sorry trim,
Like an Indian idol glum and grim,
Scarcely he seemed the sound to hear
Of voices shouting, far and near:
  "Here's Flud Oirson, fur his horrd horrt,

Torr'd an' futherr'd an' corr'd in a corrt
By the women o' Morble'ead!"

"Hear me, neighbors!" at last he cried,—
"What to me is this noisy ride?
What is the shame that clothes the skin
To the nameless horror that lives within?
Waking or sleeping, I see a wreck,
And hear a cry from a reeling deck!
Hate me and curse me,—I only dread
The hand of God and the face of the dead!"
  Said old Floyd Ireson, for his hard heart,
  Tarred and feathered and carried in a cart
    By the women of Marblehead!

Then the wife of the skipper lost at sea
Said, "God has touched him! why should we!"
Said an old wife mourning her only son,
"Cut the rogue's tether and let him run!"
So with soft relentings and rude excuse,
Half scorn, half pity, they cut him loose,
And gave him a cloak to hide him in,
And left him alone with his shame and sin.
  Poor Floyd Ireson, for his hard heart,
  Tarred and feathered and carried in a cart
    By the women of Marblehead!
                JOHN GREENLEAF WHITTIER

MAUD MULLER

Maud Muller on a summer's day
Raked the meadow sweet with hay.

Beneath her torn hat glowed the wealth
Of simple beauty and rustic health.

Singing, she wrought, and her merry glee
The mock-bird echoed from his tree.

But when she glanced to the far-off town,
White from its hill-slope looking down,

The sweet song died, and a vague unrest
And a nameless longing filled her breast,—

A wish that she hardly dared to own,
For something better than she had known.

The Judge rode slowly down the lane,
Smoothing his horse's chestnut mane.

He drew his bridle in the shade
Of the apple-trees, to greet the maid,

And asked a draught from the spring that flowed
Through the meadow across the road.

She stooped where the cool spring bubbled up,
And filled for him her small tin cup,

And blushed as she gave it, looking down
On her feet so bare, and her tattered gown.

"Thanks!" said the Judge; "a sweeter draught
From a fairer hand was never quaffed."

He spoke of the grass and flowers and trees,
Of the singing birds and the humming bees;

Then talked of the haying, and wondered whether
The cloud in the west would bring foul weather.

And Maud forgot her brier-torn gown,
And her graceful ankles bare and brown;

And listened, while a pleased surprise
Looked from her long-lashed hazel eyes.

At last, like one who for delay
Seeks a vain excuse, he rode away.

Maud Muller looked and sighed: "Ah me!
That I the Judge's bride might be!

"He would dress me up in silks so fine,
And praise and toast me at his wine.

"My father should wear a broadcloth coat;
My brother should sail a painted boat.

"I'd dress my mother so grand and gay,
And the baby should have a new toy each day.

"And I'd feed the hungry and clothe the poor,
And all should bless me who left our door."

The Judge looked back as he climbed the hill,
And saw Maud Muller standing still.

"A form more fair, a face more sweet,
Ne'er hath it been my lot to meet.

"And her modest answer and graceful air
Show her wise and good as she is fair.

"Would she were mine, and I today,
Like her, a harvester of hay;

"No doubtful balance of rights and wrongs,
Nor weary lawyers with endless tongues,

"But low of cattle and song of birds,
And health and quiet and loving words."

But he thought of his sisters, proud and cold,
And his mother, vain of her rank and gold.

So, closing his heart, the Judge rode on,
And Maud was left in the field alone.

But the lawyers smiled that afternoon,
When he hummed in court an old love-tune;

And the young girl mused beside the well
Till the rain on the unraked clover fell.

He wedded a wife of richest dower,
Who lived for fashion, as he for power.

Yet oft, in his marble hearth's bright glow,
He watched a picture come and go;

And sweet Maud Muller's hazel eyes
Looked out in their innocent surprise.

Oft, when the wine in his glass was red,
He longed for the wayside well instead;

And closed his eyes on his garnished rooms
To dream of meadows and clover-blooms.

And the proud man sighed, with a secret pain,
"Ah, that I were free again!

"Free as when I rode that day,
Where the barefoot maiden raked her hay."

She wedded a man unlearned and poor,
And many children played round her door.

But care and sorrow, and childbirth pain,
Left their traces on heart and brain.

And oft, when the summer sun shone hot
On the new-mown hay in the meadow lot,

And she heard the little spring brook fall
Over the roadside, through the wall,

In the shade of the apple-tree again
She saw a rider draw his rein;

And, gazing down with timid grace,
She felt his pleased eyes read her face.

Sometimes her narrow kitchen walls
Stretched away into stately halls;

The weary wheel to a spinnet turned,
The tallow candle an astral burned,

And for him who sat by the chimney lug,
Dozing and grumbling o'er pipe and mug,

A manly form at her side she saw,
And joy was duty and love was law.

Then she took up her burden of life again,
Saying only, "It might have been."

Alas for maiden, alas for Judge,
For rich repiner and household drudge!

God pity them both! and pity us all,
Who vainly the dreams of youth recall.

For of all sad words of tongue or pen,
The saddest are these: "It might have been!"

Ah, well! for us all some sweet hope lies
Deeply buried from human eyes;

And, in the hereafter, angels may
Roll the stone from its grave away!

JOHN GREENLEAF WHITTIER

THE PRISONER OF CHILLON

My hair is grey, but not with years,
  Nor grew it white
  In a single night,
As men's have grown from sudden fears:
My limbs are bow'd, though not with toil,
  But rusted with a vile repose,
For they have been a dungeon's spoil,
  And mine has been the fate of those
To whom the goodly earth and air
Are bann'd, and barr'd—forbidden fare:
But this was for my father's faith
I suffer'd chains and courted death;
That father perish'd at the stake
For tenets he would not forsake;
And for the same his lineal race
In darkness found a dwelling-place;
We were seven—who now are one,
  Six in youth, and one in age,
Finish'd as they had begun,
  Proud of Persecution's rage;
One in fire, and two in field,
Their belief with blood have seal'd,
Dying as their father died,
For the God their foes denied;

Three were in a dungeon cast,
Of whom this wreck is left the last.

There are seven pillars of Gothic mould,
In Chillon's dungeons deep and old,
There are seven columns, massy and grey,
Dim with a dull imprison'd ray,
A sunbeam which hath lost its way,
And through the crevice and the cleft
Of the thick wall is fallen and left;
Creeping o'er the floor so damp,
Like a marsh's meteor lamp:
   And in each pillar there is a chain;
That iron is a cankering thing,
   For in these limbs its teeth remain,
With marks that will not wear away,
Till I have done with this new day,
Which now is painful to these eyes,
Which have not seen the sun so rise
For years—I cannot count them o'er,
I lost their long and heavy score,
When my last brother droop'd and died,
And I lay living by his side.

They chain'd us each to a column stone,
And we were three—yet, each alone;
We could not move a single pace,
We could not see each other's face,
But with that pale and livid light

That made us strangers in our sight:
And thus together—yet apart,
Fetter'd in hand, but join'd in heart,
'Twas still some solace, in the dearth
Of the pure elements of earth,
To hearken to each other's speech,
And each turn comforter to each,
With some new hope, or legend old,
Or song heroically bold;
But even these at length grew cold.
Our voices took a dreary tone,
An echo of the dungeon stone,
 A grating sound, not full and free,
 As they of yore were wont to be:
 It might be fancy, but to me
They never sounded like our own.

I was the eldest of the three,
 And to uphold and cheer the rest
 I ought to do—and did my best —
And each did well in his degree.
 The youngest, whom my father loved,
Because our mother's brow was given
To him, with eyes as blue as heaven—
 For him my soul was sorely moved;
And truly might it be distress'd
To see such bird in such a nest;
For he was beautiful as day—
 (When day was beautiful to me

As to young eagles, being free)—
A polar day, which will not see
A sunset till its summer's gone,
　Its sleepless summer of long light,
The snow-clad offspring of the sun:
　And thus he was as pure and bright,
And in his natural spirit gay,
With tears for naught but others' ills,
And then they flow'd like mountain rills,
Unless he could assuage the woe
Which he abhorr'd to view below.

The other was as pure of mind,
But form'd to combat with his kind;
Strong in his frame, and of a mood
Which 'gainst the world in war had stood,
And perish'd in the foremost rank
　With joy:—but not in chains to pine:
His spirit wither'd with their clank,
　I saw it silently decline—
　And so perchance in sooth did mine:
But yet I forced it on to cheer
Those relics of a home so dear.
He was a hunter of the hills,
　Had follow'd there the deer and wolf;
　To him his dungeon was a gulf,
And fetter'd feet the worst of ills.

　Lake Leman lies by Chillon's walls:
A thousand feet in depth below

Its massy waters meet and flow;
Thus much the fathom-line was sent
From Chillon's snow-white battlement,
   Which round about the wave inthrals:
A double dungeon wall and wave
Have made—and like a living grave
Below the surface of the lake
The dark vault lies wherein we lay,
We heard it ripple night and day;
   Sounding o'er our heads it knock'd
And I have felt the winter's spray
Wash through the bars when winds were high
And wanton in the happy sky;
   And then the very rock hath rock'd,
   And I have felt it shake, unshock'd,
Because I could have smiled to see
The death that would have set me free.

I said my nearer brother pined,
I said his mighty heart declined,
He loathed and put away his food;
It was not that 'twas coarse and rude,
For we were used to hunter's fare,
And for the like had little care:
The milk drawn from the mountain goat
Was changed for water from the moat,
Our bread was such as captives' tears
Have moistened many a thousand years,

Since man first pent his fellow men
Like brutes within an iron den;
But what were these to us or him?
These wasted not his heart or limb;
My brother's soul was of that mould
Which in a palace had grown cold,
Had his free breathing been denied
The range of the steep mountain's side;
But why delay the truth?—he died.
I saw, and could not hold his head,
Nor reach his dying hand—nor dead.—
Though hard I strove, but strove in vain,
To rend and gnash my bonds in twain.
He died, and they unlocked his chain,
And scoop'd for him a shallow grave
Even from the cold earth of our cave.
I begg'd them as a boon to lay
His corse in dust whereon the day
Might shine—it was a foolish thought,
But then within my brain it wrought,
That even in death his freeborn breast
In such a dungeon could not rest.
I might have spared my idle prayer—
They coldly laugh'd, and laid him there:
The flat and turfless earth above
The being we so much did love;
His empty chain above it leant,
Such murder's fitting monument!

But he, the favorite and the flower,
Most cherish'd since his natal hour,
His mother's image in fair face,
The infant love of all his race.
His martyr'd father's dearest thought,
My latest care, for whom I sought
To hoard my life, that his might be
Less wretched now, and one day free;
He, too, who yet had held untired
A spirit natural or inspired—
He, too, was struck, and day by day
Was wither'd on the stalk away.
Oh, God! it is a fearful thing
To see the human soul take wing
In any shape, in any mood:
I've seen it rushing forth in blood,
I've seen it on the breaking ocean
Strive with a swoln convulsive motion,
I've seen the sick and ghastly bed
Of Sin delirious with its dread;
But these were horrors—this was woe
Unmix'd with such—but sure and slow:
He faded, and so calm and meek,
So softly worn, so sweetly weak,
So tearless, yet so tender, kind,
And grieved for those he left behind;
With all the while a cheek whose bloom
Was as a mockery of the tomb,
Whose tints as gently sunk away

As a departing rainbow's ray;
An eye of most transparent light,
That almost made the dungeon bright,
And not a word of murmur, not
A groan o'er his untimely lot,—
A little talk of better days,
A little hope my own to raise,
For I was sunk in silence—lost
In this last loss, of all the most;
And then the sighs he would suppress
Of fainting nature's feebleness,
More slowly drawn, grew less and less:
I listen'd, but I could not hear;
I call'd, for I was wild with fear;
I knew 'twas hopeless, but my dread
Would not be thus admonished;
I call'd, and thought I heard a sound—
I burst my chain with one strong bound,
And rush'd to him:—I found him not,
I only stirr'd in this black spot,
I only liv'd, I only drew
The accursed breath of dungeon-dew;
The last, the sole, the dearest link
Between me and the eternal brink,
Which bound me to my failing race,
Was broken in this fatal place.
One on the earth, and one beneath—
My brothers—both had ceased to breathe:
I took that hand which lay so still,

Alas! my own was full as chill;
I had not strength to stir, or strive,
But felt that I was still alive—
A frantic feeling, when we know
That what we love shall ne'er be so.
   I know not why
   I could not die,
I had no earthly hope but faith,
And that forbade a selfish death.

What next befell me then and there
   I know not well—I never knew—
First came the loss of light, and air,
   And then of darkness too:
I had no thought, no feeling—none—
Among the stones I stood a stone,
And was, scarce conscious what I wist,
As shrubless crags within the mist;
For all was blank, and bleak, and grey;
It was not night, it was not day;
It was not even the dungeon-light,
So hateful to my heavy sight,
But vacancy absorbing space,
And fixedness without a place;
There were no stars, no earth, no time,
No check, no change, no good, no crime,
But silence, and a stirless breath
Which neither was of life nor death;

A sea of stagnant idleness,
Blind, boundless, mute, and motionless!

A light broke in upon my brain,—
   It was the carol of a bird;
It ceased, and then it came again,
   The sweetest song ear ever heard,
And mine was thankful till my eyes
Ran over with the glad surprise,
And they that moment could not see
I was the mate of misery;
But then by dull degrees came back
My senses to their wonted track;
I saw the dungeon walls and floor
Close slowly round me as before,
I saw the glimmer of the sun
Creeping as it before had done,
But through the crevice where it came
That bird was perch'd, as fond and tame,
   And tamer than upon the tree;
A lovely bird, with azure wings,
And song that said a thousand things,
   And seemed to say them all for me!
I never saw its like before,
I ne'er shall see its likeness more:
It seem'd like me to want a mate,
But was not half so desolate,
And it was come to love me when
None lived to love me so again,

And cheering from my dungeon's brink,
Had brought me back to feel and think.
I know not if it late were free,

   Or broke its cage to perch on mine,
But knowing well captivity,

   Sweet bird! I could not wish for thine!
Or if it were, in winged guise,
A visitant from Paradise;
For—Heaven forgive that thought! the while
Which made me both to weep and smile—
I sometimes deem'd that it might be
My brother's soul come down to me;
But then at last away it flew,
And then 'twas mortal well I knew,
For he would never thus have flown,
And left me twice so doubly lone,
Lone as the corse within its shroud,
Lone as a solitary cloud,—

   A single cloud on a sunny day,
While all the rest of heaven is clear,
A frown upon the atmosphere,
That hath no business to appear

   When skies are blue, and earth is gay.

A kind of change came in my fate,
My keepers grew compassionate;
I know not what had made them so,
They were inured to sights of woe,
But so it was:—my broken chain

With links unfasten'd did remain,
And it was liberty to stride
Along my cell from side to side,
And up and down, and then athwart,
And tread it over every part;
And round the pillars one by one,
Returning where my walk begun,
Avoiding only, as I trod,
My brothers' graves without a sod;
For if I thought with heedless tread
My step profaned their lowly bed,
My breath came gaspingly and thick,
And my crush'd heart felt blind and sick.

I made a footing in the wall,
    It was not therefrom to escape,
For I had buried one and all
    Who loved me in a human shape;
And the whole earth would henceforth be
A wider prison unto me:
No child, no sire, no kin had I,
No partner in my misery;
I thought of this, and I was glad,
For thought of them had made me mad;
But I was curious to ascend
To my barr'd windows, and to bend
Once more, upon the mountains high,
The quiet of a loving eye.

I saw them and they were the same,
They were not changed like me in frame;
I saw their thousand years of snow
On high—their wide long lake below,
And the blue Rhone in the fullest flow;
I heard the torrents leap and gush
O'er channel'd rock and broken bush;
I saw the white-wall'd distant town,
And whiter sails go skimming down;
And then there was a little isle,
Which in my very face did smile,
 The only one in view;
A small green isle, it seem'd no more,
Scarce broader than my dungeon floor,
But in it there were three tall trees,
And o'er it blew the mountain breeze,
And by it there were waters flowing,
And on it there were young flowers growing,
 Of gentle breath and hue.
The fish swam by the castle wall,
And they seem'd joyous each and all;
The eagle rode the rising blast,
Methought he never flew so fast
As then to me he seem'd to fly;
And then new tears came in my eye,
And I felt troubled—and would fain
I had not left my recent chain;
And when I did descend again,
The darkness of my dim abode

Fell on me as a heavy load;
It was as is a new-dug grave,
Closing o'er one we sought to save,—
And yet my glance, too much opprest,
Had almost need of such a rest.

It might be months, or years, or days,
    I kept no count, I took no note,
I had no hope my eyes to raise,
    And clear them of their dreary mote;
At last men came to set me free;
    I ask'd not why, and reck'd not where;
It was at length the same to me,
Fetter'd or fetterless to be,
    I learn'd to love despair.
And thus when they appear'd at last,
And all my bonds aside were cast,
These heavy walls to me had grown
A hermitage—and all my own!
And half I felt as they were come
To tear me from a second home:
With spiders I had friendship made,
And watch'd them in their sullen trade,
Had seen the mice by moonlight play,
And why should I feel less than they?
We were all inmates of one place,
And I, the monarch of each race,
Had power to kill—yet, strange to tell!
In quiet we had learn'd to dwell;

My very chains and I grew friends,
So much a long communion tends
To make us what we are:—even I
Regain'd my freedom with a sigh.

LORD BYRON

LUCY GRAY

Oft had I heard of Lucy Gray:
And, when I crossed the wild,
I chanced to see at break of day
The solitary child.

No mate, no comrade Lucy knew;
She dwelt on a wide moor,
—The sweetest thing that ever grew
Beside a human door!

You may yet spy the fawn at play,
The hare upon the green;
But the sweet face of Lucy Gray
Will never more be seen.

"Tonight will be a stormy night—
You to the town must go;
And take a lantern, Child, to light
Your mother through the snow."

"That, Father! will I gladly do:
'Tis scarcely afternoon—
The minster-clock has just struck two,
And yonder is the moon!"

At this the Father raised his hook,
And snapped a faggot-band;
He plied his work;—and Lucy took
The lantern in her hand.

Not blither is the mountain roe:
With many a wanton stroke
Her feet disperse the powdery snow,
That rises up like smoke.

The storm came on before its time:
She wandered up and down;
And many a hill did Lucy climb:
She never reached the town.

The wretched parents all that night
Went shouting far and wide;
But there was neither sound nor sight
To serve them for a guide.

At day-break on a hill they stood
That overlooked the moor;
And thence they saw the bridge of wood,
 A furlong from their door.

They wept—and, turning homeward, cried,
"In heaven we all shall meet";
—When in the snow the mother spied
The print of Lucy's feet.

[224]

Then downwards from the steep hill's edge
They tracked the footmarks small;
And through the broken hawthorn hedge,
And by the long stone-wall;

And then an open field they crossed:
The marks were still the same;
They tracked them on, nor ever lost;
And to the bridge they came.

They followed from the snowy bank
Those footmarks, one by one,
Into the middle of the plank;
And further there were none!

—Yet some maintain that to this day
She is a living child;
That you may see sweet Lucy Gray
Upon the lonesome wild.

O'er rough and smooth she trips along,
And never looks behind;
And sings a solitary song
That whistles in the wind.

WILLIAM WORDSWORTH

THE DIVERTING HISTORY
OF JOHN GILPIN

John Gilpin was a citizen
   Of credit and renown,
A train-band captain eke was he,
   Of famous London town.

John Gilpin's spouse said to her dear,
   "Though wedded we have been
These twice ten tedious years, yet we
   No holiday have seen.

"Tomorrow is our wedding-day,
   And we will then repair
Unto the 'Bell' at Edmonton,
   All in a chaise and pair.

"My sister, and my sister's child,
   Myself, and children three,
Will fill the chaise; so you must ride
   On horseback after we."

He soon replied, "I do admire
   Of womankind but one,
And you are she, my dearest dear,
   Therefore it shall be done.

"I am a linen-draper bold,
  As all the world doth know,
And my good friend the calender
  Will lend his horse to go."

Quoth Mrs. Gilpin, "That's well said;
  And for that wine is dear,
We will be furnished with our own,
  Which is both bright and clear."

John Gilpin kissed his loving wife;
  O'erjoyed was he to find,
That though on pleasure she was bent,
  She had a frugal mind.

The morning came, the chaise was brought,
  But yet was not allowed
To drive up to the door, lest all
  Should say that she was proud.

So three doors off the chaise was stayed,
  Where they did all get in;
Six precious souls, and all agog
  To dash through thick and thin.

Smack went the whip, round went the wheels,
  Were never folks so glad!
The stones did rattle underneath,
  As if Cheapside were mad.

John Gilpin at his horse's side
  Seized fast the flowing mane,
And up he got, in haste to ride,
  But soon came down again.

For saddletree scarce reached had he,
  His journey to begin,
When, turning round his head, he saw
  Three customers come in.

So down he came; for loss of time,
  Although it grieved him sore,
Yet loss of pence, full well he knew,
  Would trouble him much more.

'Twas long before the customers
  Were suited to their mind,
When Betty screaming came downstairs,
  "The wine is left behind!"

"Good lack!" quoth he, "yet bring it me,
  My leathern belt likewise,
In which I bear my trusty sword
  When I do exercise."

Now Mistress Gilpin (careful soul!)
  Had two stone bottles found,
To hold the liquor that she loved,
  And keep it safe and sound.

Each bottle had a curling ear,
　　Through which the belt he drew,
And hung a bottle on each side,
　　To make his balance true.

Then over all, that he might be
　　Equipped from top to toe,
His long red cloak, well brushed and neat;
　　He manfully did throw.

Now see him mounted once again,
　　Upon his nimble steed,
Full slowly pacing o'er the stones,
　　With caution and good heed.

But finding soon a smoother road
　　Beneath his well-shod feet,
The snorting beast began to trot,
　　Which galled him in his seat.

"So, fair and softly!" John he cried,
　　But John he cried in vain;
That trot became a gallop soon,
　　In spite of curb and rein.

So stooping down, as needs he must
　　Who cannot sit upright,
He grasped the mane with both his hands,
　　And eke with all his might.

His horse, who never in that sort
  Had handled been before,
What thing upon his back had got,
  Did wonder more and more.

Away went Gilpin, neck or nought;
  Away went hat and wig;
He little dreamt, when he set out,
  Of running such a rig.

The wind did blow, the cloak did fly
  Like streamer long and gay,
Till, loop and button failing both,
  At last it flew away.

Then might all people well discern
  The bottles he had slung;
A bottle swinging at each side,
  As hath been said or sung.

The dogs did bark, the children screamed,
  Up flew the windows all;
And every soul cried out, "Well done!"
  As loud as he could bawl.

Away went Gilpin—who but he?
  His fame soon spread around;
"He carries weight! he rides a race!
  'Tis for a thousand pound!"

And still as fast as he drew near,
　'Twas wonderful to view
How in a trice the turnpike-men
　Their gates wide open threw.

And now, as he went bowing down
　His reeking head full low,
The bottles twain behind his back
　Were shattered at a blow.

Down ran the wine into the road,
　Most piteous to be seen,
Which made the horse's flanks to smoke,
　As they had basted been.

But still he seemed to carry weight,
　With leathern girdle braced;
For all might see the bottle-necks
　Still dangling at his waist.

Thus all through merry Islington
　These gambols he did play,
Until he came unto the Wash
　Of Edmonton so gay;

And there he threw the wash about
　On both sides of the way,
Just like unto a trundling mop,
　Or a wild goose at play.

[2 3 1]

At Edmonton his loving wife
    From the balcony spied
Her tender husband, wondering much
    To see how he did ride.

"Stop, stop, John Gilpin!— Here's the house!"
    They all at once did cry;
"The dinner waits, and we are tired;"
    Said Gilpin— "So am I!"

But yet his horse was not a whit
    Inclined to tarry there;
For why?—his owner had a house
    Full ten miles off, at Ware.

So like an arrow swift he flew,
    Shot by an archer strong;
So did he fly—which brings me to
    The middle of my song.

Away went Gilpin, out of breath,
    And sore against his will,
Till at his friend the calender's
    His horse at last stood still.

The calender, amazed to see
    His neighbor in such trim,
Laid down his pipe, flew to the gate,
    And thus accosted him:

"What news? what news? your tidings tell;
  Tell me you must and shall—
Say why bareheaded you are come,
  Or why you come at all."

Now Gilpin had a pleasant wit,
  And loved a timely joke;
And thus unto the calender
  In merry guise he spoke:—

"I came because your horse would come;
  And, if I well forbode,
My hat and wig will soon be here—
  They are upon the road."

The calender, right glad to find
  His friend in merry pin,
Returned him not a single word,
  But to the house went in;

Whence straight he came with hat and wig;
  A wig that flowed behind,
A hat not much the worse for wear,
  Each comely in its kind.

He held them up, and in his turn,
  Thus showed his ready wit—
"My head is twice as big as yours,
  They therefore needs must fit.

[233]

"But let me scrape the dirt away
    That hangs upon your face;
And stop and eat, for well you may
    Be in a hungry case."

Said John—"It is my wedding-day,
    And all the world would stare,
If wife should dine at Edmonton
    And I should dine at Ware!"

So, turning to his horse, he said—
    "I am in haste to dine;
'Twas for your pleasure you came here,
    You shall go back for mine."

Ah, luckless speech, and bootless boast!
    For which he paid full dear;
For, while he spake, a braying ass
    Did sing most loud and clear;

Whereat his horse did snort, as he
    Had heard a lion roar,
And galloped off with all his might,
    As he had done before.

Away went Gilpin, and away
    Went Gilpin's hat and wig!
He lost them sooner than at first—
    For why?—they were too big.

Now, Mistress Gilpin, when she saw
  Her husband posting down
Into the country far away,
  She pulled out half a crown;

And thus unto the youth she said
  That drove them to the Bell—
"This shall be yours when you bring back
  My husband safe and well."

The youth did ride, and soon did meet
  John coming back amain;
Whom in a trice he tried to stop,
  By catching at his rein;

But, not performing what he meant,
  And gladly would have done,
The frighted steed he frighted more,
  And made him faster run.

Away went Gilpin, and away
  Went post-boy at his heels!—
The post-boy's horse right glad to miss
  The lumb'ring of the wheels.

Six gentlemen upon the road,
  Thus seeing Gilpin fly,
With post-boy scamp'ring in the rear,
  They raised the hue and cry:

"Stop thief! stop thief!—a highwayman!"
  Not one of them was mute;
And all and each that passed that way
  Did join in the pursuit.

And now the turnpike gates again
  Flew open in short space;
The toll-men thinking, as before,
  That Gilpin rode a race.

And so he did—and won it too!—
  For he got first to town;
Nor stopped till where he had got up
  He did again get down.

Now let us sing— Long live the king,
  And Gilpin long live he;
And when he next doth ride abroad,
  May I be there to see!

WILLIAM COWPER

THE BALLAD OF
WILLIAM SYCAMORE

My father, he was a mountaineer,
His fist was a knotty hammer;
He was quick on his feet as a running deer,
And he spoke with a Yankee stammer.

My mother, she was merry and brave,
And so she came to her labor,
With a tall green fir for her doctor grave
And a stream for her comforting neighbor.

And some are wrapped in linen fine,
And some like a godling's scion;
But I was cradled on twigs of pine
In the skin of a mountain lion.

And some remember a white, starched lap
And a ewer with silver handles;
But I remember a coonskin cap
And the smell of bayberry candles.

The cabin logs, with the bark still rough,
And my mother who laughed at trifles,
And the tall, lank visitors, brown as snuff,
With their long, straight squirrel rifles.

[237]

I can hear them dance, like a foggy song,
Through the deepest one of my slumbers,
The fiddle squeaking the boots along
And my father calling the numbers.

The quick feet shaking the puncheon floor,
And the fiddle squeaking and squealing,
Till the dried herbs rattled above the door
And the dust went up to the ceiling.

There are children lucky from dawn till dusk,
But never a child so lucky!
For I cut my teeth on "Money Musk"
In the Bloody Ground of Kentucky!

When I grew as tall as the Indian corn,
My father had little to lend me,
But he gave me his great, old powderhorn
And his woodsman's skill to befriend me.

With a leather shirt to cover my back,
And a redskin nose to unravel
Each forest sign, I carried my pack
As far as a scout could travel.

Till I lost my boyhood and found my wife,
A girl like a Salem clipper!
A woman straight as a hunting-knife,
With eyes as bright as the Dipper!

[238]

We cleared our camp where the buffalo feed,
Unheard-of streams were our flagons;
And I sowed my sons like appleseed
On the trail of the Western wagons.

They were right, tight boys, never sulky or slow,
A fruitful, a goodly muster.
The eldest died at the Alamo.
The youngest fell with Custer.

The letter that told it burned my hand,
Yet we smiled and said, "So be it!"
But I could not live when they fenced the land,
For it broke my heart to see it.

I saddled a red, unbroken colt
And rode him into the day there;
And he threw me down like a thunderbolt
And rolled on me as I lay there.

The hunter's whistle hummed in my ear
As the city men tried to move me,
And I died in my boots like a pioneer
With the whole wide sky above me.

Now I lie in the heart of the fat, black soil,
Like the seed of a prairie thistle;
It has washed my bones with honey and oil
And picked them clean as a whistle.

And my youth returns, like the rains of Spring,
And my sons, like the wild geese flying;
And I lie and hear the meadow lark sing
And have much content in my dying.

Go play with the towns you have built of blocks
The towns where you would have bound me!
I sleep in my earth like a tired fox,
And my buffalo have found me.

STEPHEN VINCENT BENÉT

POEMS ABOUT MAGIC

GOBLIN MARKET

Morning and evening
Maids heard the goblins cry:
"Come buy our orchard fruits,
Come buy, come buy:
Apples and quinces,
Lemons and oranges,
Plump unpecked cherries,
Melons and raspberries,
Bloom-down-cheeked peaches,
Swart-headed mulberries,
Wild free-born cranberries,
Crab-apples, dewberries,
Pine-apples, blackberries,
Apricots, strawberries;—
All ripe together
In summer weather,—
Morns that pass by,
Fair eves that fly;
Come buy, come buy:
Our grapes fresh from the vine,
Pomegranates full and fine,
Dates and sharp bullaces,
Rare pears and greengages,
Damsons and bilberries,

Taste them and try:
Currants and gooseberries,
Bright-fire-like barberries,
Figs to fill your mouth,
Citrons from the South,
Sweet to tongue and sound to eye;
Come buy, come buy."

Evening by evening
Among the brookside rushes,
Laura bowed her head to hear,
Lizzie veiled her blushes:
Crouching close together
In the cooling weather,
With clasping arms and cautioning lips,
With tingling cheeks and finger tips.
"Lie close," Laura said,
Pricking up her golden head:
"We must not look at goblin men,
We must not buy their fruits:
Who knows upon what soil they fed
Their hungry thirsty roots?"
"Come buy," call the goblins
Hobbling down the glen.
"Oh," cried Lizzie, "Laura, Laura,
You should not peep at goblin men."
Lizzie covered up her eyes,
Covered close lest they should look;
Laura reared her glossy head,

And whispered like the restless brook:
"Look, Lizzie, look, Lizzie,
Down the glen tramp little men.
One hauls a basket,
One bears a plate,
One lugs a golden dish
Of many pounds' weight.
How fair the vine must grow
Whose grapes are so luscious;
How warm the wind must blow
Through those fruit bushes."
"No," said Lizzie: "No, no, no;
Their offers should not charm us,
Their evil gifts would harm us."
She thrust a dimpled finger
In each ear, shut eyes and ran:
Curious Laura chose to linger
Wondering at each merchant man.
One had a cat's face,
One whisked a tail,
One tramped at a rat's pace,
One crawled like a snail,
One like a wombat prowled obtuse and furry,
One like a ratel tumbled hurry skurry.
She heard a voice like voice of doves
Cooing all together:
They sounded kind and full of loves
In the pleasant weather.

Laura stretched her gleaming neck
Like a rush-imbedded swan,
Like a lily from the beck,
Like a moonlit poplar branch,
Like a vessel at the launch
When its last restraint is gone.

Backwards up the mossy glen
Turned and trooped the goblin men,
With their shrill repeated cry,
"Come buy, come buy."
When they reached where Laura was
They stood stock still upon the moss,
Leering at each other,
Brother with queer brother;
Signaling each other,
Brother with sly brother.
One set his basket down,
One reared his plate;
One began to weave a crown
Of tendrils, leaves, and rough nuts brown
(Men sell not such in any town);
One heaved the golden weight
Of dish and fruit to offer her:
"Come buy, come buy," was still their cry.
Laura stared but did not stir,
Longed but had no money:
The whisk-tailed merchant bade her taste
In tones as smooth as honey,

The cat-faced purr'd,
The rat-paced spoke a word
Of welcome, and the snail-paced even was heard;
One parrot-voiced and jolly
Cried "Pretty Goblin" still for "Pretty Polly";—
One whistled like a bird.

But sweet-tooth Laura spoke in haste:
"Good folk, I have no coin;
To take were to purloin:
I have no copper in my purse,
I have no silver either,
And all my gold is on the furze
That shakes in windy weather
Above the rusty heather."
"You have much gold upon your head,"
They answered all together:
"Buy from us with a golden curl."
She clipped a precious golden lock,
She dropped a tear more rare than pearl,
Then sucked their fruit globes fair or red:
Sweeter than honey from the rock,
Stronger than man-rejoicing wine,
Clearer than water flowed that juice;
She never tasted such before,
How should it cloy with length of use?
She sucked and sucked and sucked the more
Fruits which that unknown orchard bore;
She sucked until her lips were sore;

Then flung the emptied rinds away
But gathered up one kernel-stone,
And knew not was it night or day
As she turned home alone.

Lizzie met her at the gate
Full of wise upbraidings:
"Dear, you should not stay so late,
Twilight is not good for maidens;
Should not loiter in the glen
In the haunts of goblin men.
Do you not remember Jeanie,
How she met them in the moonlight,
Took their gifts both choice and many,
Ate their fruits and wore their flowers
Plucked from bowers
Where summer ripens at all hours?
But ever in the moonlight
She pined and pined away;
Sought them by night and day,
Found them no more, but dwindled and grew grey,
Then fell with the first snow,
While to this day no grass will grow
Where she lies low:
I planted daisies there a year ago
That never blow.
You should not loiter so."
"Nay, hush," said Laura:
"Nay, hush, my sister:

I ate and ate my fill,
Yet my mouth waters still;
Tomorrow night I will
Buy more": and kissed her:
"Have done with sorrow;
I'll bring you plums tomorrow
Fresh on their mother twigs,
Cherries worth getting;
You cannot think what figs
My teeth have met in,
What melons icy-cold
Piled on a dish of gold
Too huge for me to hold,
What peaches with a velvet nap,
Pellucid grapes without one seed:
Odorous indeed must be the mead
Whereon they grow, and pure the wave they drink
With lilies at the brink,
And sugar-sweet their sap."

Golden head by golden head,
Like two pigeons in one nest,
Folded in each other's wings,
They lay down in their curtained bed:
Like two blossoms on one stem,
Like two flakes of new-fall'n snow,
Like two wands of ivory
Tipped with gold for awful kings.
Moon and stars gazed in at them,

Wind sang to them lullaby,
Lumbering owls forbore to fly,
Not a bat flapped to and fro
Round their nest:
Cheek to cheek and breast to breast
Locked together in one nest.

   Early in the morning
When the first cock crowed his warning,
Neat like bees, as sweet and busy,
Laura rose with Lizzie:
Fetched in honey, milked the cows,
Aired and set right the house,
Kneaded cakes of whitest wheat,
Cakes for dainty mouths to eat,
Next churned butter, whipped up cream,
Fed their poultry, sat and sewed;
Talked as modest maidens should:
Lizzie with an open heart,
Laura in an absent dream,
One content, one sick in part;
One warbling for the mere bright day's delight,
One longing for the night.

   At length slow evening came:
They went with pitchers to the reedy brook;
Lizzie most placid in her look,
Laura most like a leaping flame.
They drew the gurgling water from its deep;

Lizzie plucked purple and rich golden flags,
Then turning homewards said: "The sunset flushes
Those furthest loftiest crags;
Come, Laura, not another maiden lags,
No wilful squirrel wags,
The beasts and birds are fast asleep."
But Laura loitered still among the rushes
And said the bank was steep.

And said the hour was early still,
The dew not fall'n, the wind not chill:
Listening ever, but not catching
The customary cry,
"Come buy, come buy,"
With its iterated jingle
Of sugar-baited words:
Not for all her watching
Once discerning even one goblin
Racing, whisking, tumbling, hobbling;
Let alone the herds
That used to tramp along the glen,
In groups or single,
Of brisk fruit-merchant men.

Till Lizzie urged, "O Laura, come;
I hear the fruit-call, but I dare not look:
You should not loiter longer at this brook:
Come with me home.
The stars rise, the moon bends her arc,

Each glowworm winks her spark,
Let us get home before the night grows dark:
For clouds may gather
Though this is summer weather,
Put out the lights and drench us through;
Then if we lost our way what should we do?"

    Laura turned cold as stone
To find her sister heard that cry alone,
That goblin cry,
"Come buy our fruits, come buy."
Must she then buy no more such dainty fruit?
Must she no more such succous pasture find,
Gone deaf and blind?
Her tree of life drooped from the root:
She said not one word in her heart's sore ache;
But peering thro' the dimness, naught discerning,
Trudged home, her pitcher dripping all the way;
So crept to bed, and lay
Silent till Lizzie slept;
Then sat up in a passionate yearning,
And gnashed her teeth for baulked desire, and wept
As if her heart would break.

    Day after day, night after night,
Laura kept watch in vain
In sullen silence of exceeding pain.
She never caught again the goblin cry:
"Come buy, come buy";—

She never spied the goblin men
Hawking their fruits along the glen:
But when the moon waxed bright
Her hair grew thin and grey;
She dwindled, as the fair full moon doth turn
To swift decay and burn
Her fire away.

One day remembering her kernel-stone
She set it by a wall that faced the south;
Dewed it with tears, hoped for a root,
Watched for a waxing shoot,
But there came none;
It never saw the sun,
It never felt the trickling moisture run:
While with sunk eyes and faded mouth
She dreamed of melons, as a traveler sees
False waves in desert drouth
With shade of leaf-crowned trees,
And burns the thirstier in the sandful breeze.

She no more swept the house,
Tended the fowls or cows,
Fetched honey, kneaded cakes of wheat,
Brought water from the brook:
But sat down listless in the chimney-nook
And would not eat.

Tender Lizzie could not bear
To watch her sister's cankerous care

Yet not to share.
She night and morning
Caught the goblins' cry:
"Come buy our orchard fruits,
Come buy, come buy":—
Beside the brook, along the glen,
She heard the tramp of goblin men,
The voice and stir
Poor Laura could not hear;
Longed to buy fruit to comfort her,
But feared to pay too dear.
She thought of Jeanie in her grave,
Who should have been a bride;
But who for joys brides hope to have
Fell sick and died
In her gay prime,
In earliest Winter time,
With the first glazing rime,
With the first snow-fall of crisp Winter time.

Till Laura dwindling
Seemed knocking at Death's door:
Then Lizzie weighed no more
Better and worse;
But put a silver penny in her purse,
Kissed Laura, crossed the heath with clumps of furze
At twilight, halted by the brook:
And for the first time in her life
Began to listen and look.

Laughed every goblin
When they spied her peeping:
Came toward her hobbling,
Flying, running, leaping,
Puffing and blowing,
Chuckling, clapping, crowing,
Clucking and gobbling,
Mopping and mowing,
Full of airs and graces,
Pulling wry faces,
Demure grimaces,
Cat-like and rat-like,
Ratel- and wombat-like,
Snail-paced in a hurry,
Parrot-voiced and whistler,
Helter skelter, hurry skurry,
Chattering like magpies,
Fluttering like pigeons,
Gliding like fishes,—
Hugged her and kissed her,
Squeezed and caressed her:
Stretched up their dishes,
Panniers, and plates:
"Look at our apples
Russet and dun,
Bob at our cherries,
Bite at our peaches,
Citrons and dates,
Grapes for the asking,

Pears red with basking
Out in the sun,
Plums on their twigs;
Pluck them and suck them,
Pomegranates, figs."—

"Good folk," said Lizzie,
Mindful of Jeanie:
"Give me much and many":—
Held out her apron,
Tossed them her penny.
"Nay, take a seat with us,
Honor and eat with us,"
They answered grinning:
"Our feast is but beginning.
Night is yet early,
Warm and dew-pearly,
Wakeful and starry:
Such fruits as these
No man can carry;
Half their bloom would fly,
Half their dew would dry,
Half their flavor would pass by.
Sit down and feast with us,
Be welcome guest with us,
Cheer you and rest with us."—
"Thank you," said Lizzie: "But one waits
At home alone for me:
So without further parleying,

If you will not sell me any
Of your fruits though much and many,
Give me back my silver penny
I tossed you for a fee."—
They began to scratch their pates,
No longer wagging, purring,
But visibly demurring,
Grunting and snarling.
One called her proud,
Cross-grained, uncivil;
Their tones waxed loud,
Their looks were evil.
Lashing their tails
They trod and hustled her,
Elbowed and jostled her,
Clawed with their nails,
Barking, mewing, hissing, mocking,
Tore her gown and soiled her stocking,
Twitched her hair out by the roots,
Stamped upon her tender feet,
Held her hands and squeezed their fruits
Against her mouth to make her eat.

White and golden Lizzie stood,
Like a lily in a flood,—
Like a rock of blue-veined stone
Lashed by tides obstreperously,—
Like a beacon left alone
In a hoary roaring sea,

Sending up a golden fire,—
Like a fruit-crowned orange-tree,
White with blossoms honey-sweet,
Sore beset by wasp and bee,—
Like a royal virgin town
Topped with gilded dome and spire
Close beleaguered by a fleet
Mad to tug her standard down.

One may lead a horse to water,
Twenty cannot make him drink.
Though the goblins cuffed and caught her,
Coaxed and fought her,
Bullied and besought her,
Scratched her, pinched her black as ink,
Kicked and knocked her,
Mauled and mocked her,
Lizzie uttered not a word;
Would not open lip from lip
Lest they should cram a mouthful in:
But laughed in heart to feel the drip
Of juice that syruped all her face,
And lodged in dimples of her chin,
And streaked her neck which quaked like curd.
At last the evil people
Worn out by her resistance
Flung back her penny, kicked their fruit
Along whichever road they took,
Not leaving root or stone or shoot;

Some writhed into the ground,
Some dived into the brook
With ring and ripple,
Some scudded on the gale without a sound,
Some vanished in the distance.

    In a smart, ache, tingle,
Lizzie went her way;
Knew not was it night or day;
Sprang up the bank, tore thro' the furze,
Threaded copse and dingle;
And heard her penny jingle
Bouncing in her purse,—
Its bounce was music to her ear.
She ran and ran
As if she feared some goblin man
Dogged her with jibe or curse
Or something worse:
But not one goblin skurried after,
Nor was she pricked by fear;
The kind heart that made her windy-paced
That urged her home quite out of breath with haste
And inward laughter.

    She cried, "Laura," up the garden,
"Did you miss me?
Come and kiss me.
Never mind my bruises,
Hug me, kiss me, suck my juices

Squeezed from goblin fruits for you,
Goblin pulp and goblin dew.
Eat me, drink me, love me;
Laura, make much of me:
For your sake I have braved the glen
And had to do with goblin merchant men."

Laura started from her chair,
Flung her arms up in the air,
Clutched her hair:
"Lizzie, Lizzie, have you tasted
For my sake the fruit forbidden?
Must your light like mine be hidden,
Your young life like mine be wasted,
Undone in my undoing
And ruined in my ruin,
Thirsty, cankered, goblin-ridden?"—
She clung about her sister,
Kissed and kissed and kissed her:
Tears once again
Refreshed her shrunken eyes,
Dropping like rain
After long sultry drouth;
Shaking with aguish fear, and pain,
She kissed and kissed her with a hungry mouth.

Her lips began to scorch,
That juice was wormwood to her tongue,
She loathed the feast:

Writhing as one possessed she leaped and sung,
Rent all her robe, and wrung
Her hands in lamentable haste,
And beat her breast.
Her locks streamed like the torch
Borne by a racer at full speed,
Or like the mane of horses in their flight,
Or like an eagle when she stems the light
Straight toward the sun,
Or like a caged thing freed,
Or like a flying flag when armies run.

Swift fire spread through her veins, knocked at her heart,
Met the fire smouldering there
And overbore its lesser flame;
She gorged on bitterness without a name:
Ah! fool, to choose such part
Of soul-consuming care!
Sense failed in the mortal strife:
Like the watch-tower of a town
Which an earthquake shatters down,
Like a lightning-stricken mast,
Like a wind-uprooted tree
Spun about,
Like a foam-topped waterspout
Cast headlong in the sea,
She fell at last;
Pleasure past and anguish past,
Is it death or is it life?

Life out of death.
That night long Lizzie watched by her,
Counted her pulses flagging stir,
Felt for her breath,
Held water to her lips, and cooled her face
With tears and fanning leaves:
But when the first birds chirped about their eaves,
And early reapers plodded to the place
Of golden sheaves,
And dew-wet grass
Bowed in the morning winds so brisk to pass,
And new buds with new day
Opened of cup-like lilies on the stream,
Laura awoke as from a dream,
Laughed in the old innocent way,
Hugged Lizzie but not twice or thrice;
Her gleaming locks showed not one thread of grey,
Her breath was sweet as May
And light danced in her eyes.

Days, weeks, months, years,
Afterwards, when both were wives
With children of their own;
Their mother-hearts beset with fears,
Their lives bound up in tender lives;
Laura would call the little ones
And tell them of her early prime,
Those pleasant days long gone
Of not-returning time:

Would talk about the haunted glen,
The wicked quaint fruit-merchant men,
Their fruits like honey to the throat
But poison in the blood;
(Men sell not such in any town):
Would tell them how her sister stood
In deadly peril to do her good,
And win the fiery antidote:
Then joining hands to little hands
Would bid them cling together,
"For there is no friend like a sister
In calm or stormy weather;
To cheer one on the tedious way,
To fetch one if one goes astray,
To lift one if one totters down,
To strengthen whilst one stands."

CHRISTINA ROSSETTI

BERRIES

There was an old woman
  Went blackberry picking
Along the hedges
  From Weep to Wicking.
Half a pottle—
  No more had she got,
When out steps a Fairy
  From her green grot;
And says, "Well, Jill,
  Would 'ee pick 'ee mo?"
And Jill, she curtseys,
  And looks just so.
"Be off," says the Fairy,
  "As quick as you can,
Over the meadows
  To the little green lane,
That dips to the hayfields
  Of Farmer Grimes:
I've berried those hedges
  A score of times;
Bushel on bushel
  I'll promise 'ee, Jill,
This side of supper
  If 'ee pick with a will."

She glints very bright
  And speaks her fair;
Then lo, and behold!
  She had faded in air.

Be sure Old Goodie
  She trots betimes
Over the meadows
  To Farmer Grimes.
And never was queen
  With jewelry rich
As those same hedges
  From twig to ditch;
Like Dutchmen's coffers,
  Fruit, thorn, and flower—
They shone like William
  And Mary's bower.
And be sure Old Goodie
  Went back to Weep
So tired with her basket
  She scarce could creep.

When she comes in the dusk
  To her cottage door,
There's Towser wagging
  As never before,
To see his Missus
  So glad to be
Come from her fruit-picking

Back to he.
As soon as next morning
  Dawn was grey,
The pot on the hob
  Was simmering away;
And all in a stew
  And a hugger-mugger
Towser and Jill
  A-boiling of sugar,
And the dark clear fruit
  That from Faerie came,
For syrup and jelly
  And blackberry jam
Twelve jolly gallipots
  Jill put by;
And one little teeny one,
  One inch high;
And that she's hidden
  A good thumb deep,
Halfway over
  From Wicking to Weep.

WALTER DE LA MARE

THE SONG OF
WANDERING AENGUS

I went out to the hazel wood,
Because a fire was in my head,
And cut and peeled a hazel wand,
And hooked a berry to a thread;
And when white moths were on the wing,
And moth-like stars were flickering out,
I dropped the berry in a stream
And caught a little silver trout.

When I had laid it on the floor
I went to blow the fire a-flame,
But something rustled on the floor,
And someone called me by my name:
It had become a glimmering girl
With apple blossom in her hair
Who called me by my name and ran
And faded through the brightening air.

Though I am old with wandering
Through hollow lands and hilly lands,
I will find out where she has gone,
And kiss her lips and take her hands;

And walk among long dappled grass,
And pluck till time and times are done
The silver apples of the moon,
The golden apples of the sun.

WILLIAM BUTLER YEATS

LA BELLE DAME SANS MERCI

"O what can ail thee, knight-at-arms,
  Alone and palely loitering?
The sedge is wither'd from the lake,
  And no birds sing.

"O what can ail thee, knight-at-arms,
  So haggard and so woe-begone?
The squirrel's granary is full,
  And the harvest's done.

"I see a lily on thy brow
  With anguish moist and fever dew;
And on thy cheek a fading rose
  Fast withereth too."

"I met a lady in the meads,
  Full beautiful—a faery's child,
Her hair was long, her foot was light,
  And her eyes were wild.

"I made a garland for her head,
  And bracelets too, and fragrant zone;
She look'd at me as she did love,
  And made sweet moan.

"I set her on my pacing steed
  And nothing else saw all day long,
For sideways would she lean, and sing
  A faery's song.

"She found me roots of relish sweet,
  And honey wild and manna dew,
And sure in language strange she said,
  'I love thee true!'

"She took me to her elfin grot,
  And there she wept and sigh'd full sore;
And there I shut her wild, wild eyes
  With kisses four.

"And there she lulléd me asleep,
  And there I dreamed— Ah! woe betide!
The latest dream I ever dream'd
  On the cold hill's side.

"I saw pale kings and princes too,
  Pale warriors, death-pale were they all;
Who cried—'La belle Dame sans Merci
  Hath thee in thrall!'

"I saw their starved lips in the gloam
  With horrid warning gapéd wide,
And I awoke and found me here
  On the cold hill's side.

"And this is why I sojourn here
   Alone and palely loitering,
Though the sedge is wither'd from the lake,
   And no birds sing."

JOHN KEATS

THE CHINESE NIGHTINGALE

"How, how," he said. "Friend Chang," I said,
"San Francisco sleeps as the dead—
Ended license, lust and play:
Why do you iron the night away?
Your big clock speaks with a deadly sound,
With a tick and a wail till dawn comes round.
While the monster shadows glower and creep,
What can be better for man than sleep?"

"I will tell you a secret," Chang replied;
"My breast with vision is satisfied,
And I see green trees and fluttering wings,
And my deathless bird from Shanghai sings."
Then he lit five firecrackers in a pan.
"Pop, pop," said the firecrackers, "cra-cra-crack."
He lit a joss stick long and black.
Then the proud gray joss in the corner stirred;
On his wrist appeared a gray small bird,
And this was the song of the gray small bird:
"Where is the princess, loved forever,
Who made Chang first of the kings of men?"

And the joss in the corner stirred again;
And the carved dog, curled in his arms, awoke,

Barked forth a smoke-cloud that whirled and broke.
It piled in a maze round the ironing-place,
And there on the snowy table wide
Stood a Chinese lady of high degree,
With a scornful, witching, tea-rose face . . .
Yet she put away all form and pride,
And laid her glimmering veil aside
With a childlike smile for Chang and me.

The walls fell back, night was aflower,
The table gleamed in a moonlit bower,
While Chang, with a countenance carved of stone,
Ironed and ironed, all alone.
And thus she sang to the busy man Chang:
"Have you forgotten . . .
Deep in the ages, long, long ago,
I was your sweetheart, there on the sand—
Storm-worn beach of the Chinese land?
We sold our grain in the peacock town—
Built on the edge of the sea-sands brown—
Built on the edge of the sea-sands brown . . .

When all the world was drinking blood
From the skulls of men and bulls
And all the world had swords and clubs of stone,
We drank our tea in China beneath the sacred spice-trees,
And heard the curled waves of the harbor moan.
And this gray bird, in Love's first spring,
With a bright-bronze breast and a bronze-brown wing,

Captured the world with his caroling.
Do you remember, ages after,
At last the world we were born to own?
You were the heir of the yellow throne—
The world was the field of the Chinese man
And we were the pride of the Sons of Han?
We copied deep books and we carved in jade,
And wove blue silks in the mulberry shade . . ."
"I remember, I remember
That Spring came on forever,
That Spring came on forever,"
Said the Chinese nightingale.

My heart was filled with marvel and dream,
Though I saw the western street-lamps gleam,
Though dawn was bringing the western day,
Though Chang was a laundryman ironing away . . .
Mingled there with the streets and alleys,
The railroad-yard and the clock-tower bright,
Demon clouds crossed ancient valleys;
Across wide lotus-ponds of light
I marked a giant firefly's flight.

And the lady, rosy-red,
Flourished her fan, her shimmering fan,
Stretched her hand toward Chang, and said:
"Do you remember,
Ages after,
Our palace of heart-red stone?

Do you remember
The little doll-faced children
With their lanterns full of moon-fire,
That came from all the empire
Honoring the throne?—
The loveliest fête and carnival
Our world had ever known?
The sages sat about us
With their heads bowed in their beards,
With proper meditation on the sight.
Confucius was not born;
We lived in those great days
Confucius later said were lived aright . . .
And this gray bird, on that day of spring,
With a bright-bronze breast and a bronze-brown wing,
Captured the world with his caroling.
Late at night his tune was spent.
Peasants,
Sages,
Children,
Homeward went,
And then the bronze bird sang for you and me.
We walked alone. Our hearts were high and free.
I had a silvery name, I had a silvery name,
I had a silvery name—do you remember
The name you cried beside the tumbling sea?"

Chang turned not to the lady slim—
He bent to his work, ironing away;

But she was arch, and knowing and glowing,
For the bird on his shoulder spoke for him.
"Darling . . . darling . . . darling . . . darling . . ."
Said the Chinese nightingale.

The great gray joss on the rustic shelf,
Rakish and shrewd, with his collar awry,
Sang impolitely, as though by himself,
Drowning with his bellowing the nightingale's cry:
"Back through a hundred, hundred years
Hear the waves as they climb the piers,
Hear the howl of the silver seas,
Hear the thunder.
Hear the gongs of holy China
How the waves and tunes combine
In a rhythmic clashing wonder,
Incantation old and fine:
     'Dragons, dragons, Chinese dragons,
      Red firecrackers, and green firecrackers
      And dragons, dragons, Chinese dragons,' "

Then the lady, rosy-red,
Turned to her lover Chang and said:
"Dare you forget that turquoise dawn
When we stood in our mist-hung velvet lawn,
And worked a spell this great joss taught
Till a God of the Dragons was charmed and caught?
From the flag high over our palace home
He flew to our feet in rainbow-foam—

[275]

A king of beauty and tempest and thunder
Panting to tear our sorrows asunder,
A dragon of fair adventure and wonder.
We mounted the back of that royal slave
With thoughts of desire that were noble and grave.
We swam down the shore to the dragon-mountains,
We whirled to the peaks and the fiery fountains.
To our secret ivory house we were borne.
We looked down the wonderful wing-filled regions
Where the dragons darted in shimmering legions.
Right by my breast the nightingale sang;
The old rhymes rang in the sunlit mist
That we this hour regain—
Song-fire for the brain.
When my hands and my hair and my feet you kissed,
When you cried for your heart's new pain,
What was my name in the dragon-mist,
In the rings of rainbowed rain?"

"Sorrow and love, glory and love,"
Said the Chinese nightingale.
"Sorrow and love, glory and love,"
Said the Chinese nightingale.

And now the joss broke in with his song:
"Dying ember, bird of Chang,
Soul of Chang, do you remember?—
Ere you returned to the shining harbor
There were pirates by ten thousand

Descended on the town
In vessels mountain-high and red and brown,
Moon-ships that climbed the storms and cut the skies.
On their prows were painted terrible bright eyes.
But I was then a wizard and a scholar and a priest;
I stood upon the sand;
With lifted hand I looked upon them
And sunk their vessels with my wizard eyes,
And the stately lacquer-gate made safe again.
Deep, deep below the bay, the seaweed and the spray,
Embalmed in amber every pirate lies,
Embalmed in amber every pirate lies."

Then this did the noble lady say:
"Bird, do you dream of our home-coming day
When you flew like a courier on before
From the dragon-peak to our palace-door,
And we drove the steed in your singing path—
The ramping dragon of laughter and wrath:
And found our city all aglow,
And knighted this joss that decked it so?
There were golden fishes in the purple river,
And silver fishes and rainbow fishes.
There were golden junks in the laughing river,
And silver junks and rainbow junks:
There were golden lilies by the bay and river,
And silver lilies and tiger-lilies,
And tinkling wind-bells in the gardens of the town
By the black-lacquer gate

[277]

Where walked in state
The kind king Chang
And his sweetheart mate . . .
With his flag-born dragon
And his crown of pearl . . . and . . . jade,
And his nightingale reigning in the mulberry shade,
And sailors and soldiers on the sea-sands brown,
And priests who bowed them down to your song—
By the city called Han, the peacock town,
By the city called Han, the nightingale town,
The nightingale town."

Then sang the bird, so strangely gay,
Fluttering, fluttering, ghostly and gray,
A vague, unraveling, final tune,
Like a long unwinding silk cocoon;
Sang as though for the soul of him
Who ironed away in that bower dim:—

    "I have forgotten
    Your dragons great,
    Merry and mad and friendly and bold.
Dim is your proud lost palace-gate.
I vaguely know
There were heroes of old,
Troubles more than the heart could hold,
There were wolves in the woods
Yet lambs in the fold,
Nests in the top of the almond tree . . .
The evergreen tree . . . and the mulberry tree . . .

[278]

Life and hurry and joy forgotten,
Years on years I but half-remember . . .
Man is a torch, then ashes soon,
May and June, then dead December,
Dead December, then again June.
Who shall end my dream's confusion?
Life is a loom, weaving illusion . . .
I remember, I remember
There were ghostly veils and laces . . .
In the shadowy bowery places . . .
With lovers' ardent faces
Bending to one another,
Speaking each his part.
They infinitely echo
In the red cave of my heart.
'Sweetheart, sweetheart, sweetheart,'
They said to one another.
They spoke, I think, of perils past.
They spoke, I think, of peace at last.
One thing I remember:
Spring came on forever,
Spring came on forever,"
Said the Chinese nightingale.

VACHEL LINDSAY

THE RIME OF
THE ANCIENT MARINER

It is an ancient Mariner,
And he stoppeth one of three.
"By thy long grey beard and glittering eye,
Now wherefore stopp'st thou me?

The Bridegroom's doors are opened wide,
And I am next of kin;
The guests are met, the feast is set:
May'st hear the merry din."

He holds him with his skinny hand,
"There was a ship," quoth he.
"Hold off! unhand me, grey-beard loon!"
Eftsoons his hand dropt he.

He holds him with his glittering eye—
The Wedding-Guest stood still,
And listens like a three years' child:
The Mariner hath his will.

The Wedding-Guest sat on a stone:
He cannot choose but hear;
And thus spake on that ancient man,
The bright-eyed Mariner.

"The ship was cheered, the harbor cleared,
Merrily we did drop
Below the kirk, below the hill,
Below the lighthouse top.

The Sun came up upon the left,
Out of the sea came he!
And he shone bright, and on the right
Went down into the sea.

Higher and higher every day,
Till over the mast at noon—"
The Wedding-Guest here beat his breast,
For he heard the loud bassoon.

The bride hath paced into the hall,
Red as a rose is she;
Nodding their heads before her goes
The merry minstrelsy.

The Wedding-Guest he beat his breast,
Yet he cannot choose but hear;
And thus spake on that ancient man,
The bright-eyed Mariner.

"And now the STORM-BLAST came, and he
Was tyrannous and strong:
He struck with his o'ertaking wings,
And chased us south along.

With sloping masts and dipping prow,
As who pursued with yell and blow
Still treads the shadow of his foe,
And forward bends his head,
The ship drove fast, loud roared the blast,
And southward aye we fled.

And now there came both mist and snow,
And it grew wondrous cold:
And ice, mast-high, came floating by,
As green as emerald.

And through the drifts the snowy clifts
Did send a dismal sheen:
Nor shapes of men nor breasts we ken—
The ice was all between.

The ice was here, the ice was there,
The ice was all around:
It cracked and growled, and roared and howled,
Like noises in a swound!

At length did cross an Albatross,
Through the fog it came;
As if it had been a Christian soul,
We hailed it in God's name.

It ate the food it ne'er had eat,
And round and round it flew.

The ice did split with a thunder-fit;
The helmsman steered us through!

And a good south wind sprung up behind;
The Albatross did follow,
And every day, for food or play,
Came to the mariner's hollo!

In mist or cloud, on mast or shroud,
It perched for vespers nine;
Whiles all the night, through fog-smoke white,
Glimmered the white Moon-shine."

"God save thee, ancient Mariner!
From the fiends that plague thee thus!—
Why look'st thou so?"—With my cross-bow
I shot the Albatross.

PART II

The Sun now rose upon the right:
Out of the sea came he,
Still hid in mist, and on the left
Went down into the sea.

And the good south wind still blew behind,
But no sweet bird did follow,
Nor any day for food or play
Came to the mariners' hollo!

[283]

And I had done a hellish thing,
And it would work 'em woe:
For all averred, I had killed the bird
That made the breeze to blow.
Ah wretch! said they, the bird to slay,
That made the breeze to blow!

Nor dim nor red, like God's own head,
The glorious Sun uprist:
Then all averred, I had killed the bird
That brought the fog and mist.
'Twas right, said they, such birds to slay,
That bring the fog and mist.

The fair breeze blew, the white foam flew,
The furrow followed free;
We were the first that ever burst
Into that silent sea.

Down dropt the breeze, the sails dropt down,
'Twas sad as sad could be;
And we did speak only to break
The silence of the sea!

All in a hot and copper sky,
The bloody Sun, at noon,
Right up above the mast did stand,
No bigger than the Moon.

Day after day, day after day,
We stuck, nor breath nor motion;

[284]

As idle as a painted ship
Upon a painted ocean.

Water, water, everywhere,
And all the boards did shrink;
Water, water, everywhere,
Nor any drop to drink.

The very deep did rot: O Christ!
That ever this should be!
Yea, slimy things did crawl with legs
Upon the slimy sea.

About, about, in reel and rout
The death-fires danced at night;
The water, like a witch's oils,
Burnt green, and blue and white.

And some in dreams assuréd were
Of the Spirit that plagued us so;
Nine fathom deep he had followed us
From the land of mist and snow.

And every tongue, through utter drought,
Was withered at the root;
We could not speak, no more than if
We had been choked with soot.

Ah! well a-day! what evil looks
Had I from old and young!

Instead of the cross, the Albatross
About my neck was hung.

PART III

There passed a weary time. Each throat
Was parched, and glazed each eye.
A weary time! a weary time!
How glazed each weary eye,
When, looking westward, I beheld
A something in the sky.

At first it seemed a little speck,
And then it seemed a mist;
It moved and moved, and took at last
A certain shape, I wist.

A speck, a mist, a shape, I wist!
And still it neared and neared:
As if it dodged a water-sprite,
It plunged and tacked and veered.

With throats unslaked, with black lips baked,
We could not laugh nor wail;
Through utter drought all dumb we stood!
I bit my arm, I sucked the blood,
And cried, A sail! a sail!

With throats unslaked, with black lips baked,
Agaped they heard me call:

Gramercy! they for joy did grin,
And all at once their breath drew in,
As they were drinking all.

See! see! (I cried) as she tacks no more!
Hither to work us weal;
Without a breeze, without a tide,
She steadies with upright keel!

The western wave was all aflame.
The day was well nigh done!
Almost upon the western wave
Rested the broad bright Sun;
When that strange shape drove suddenly
Betwixt us and the Sun.

And straight the Sun was flecked with bars,
(Heaven's Mother send us grace!)
As if through a dungeon-grate he peered
With broad and burning face.

Alas! (thought I, and my heart beat loud)
How fast she nears and nears!
Are those *her* sails that glance in the Sun
Like restless gossameres?

Are those *her* ribs through which the Sun
Did peer, as through a grate?
And is that Woman all her crew?

[287]

Is that a DEATH? and are there two?
Is DEATH that woman's mate?

Her lips were red, *her* looks were free,
Her locks were yellow as gold:
Her skin was as white as leprosy,
The Night-mare LIFE-IN-DEATH was she,
Who thicks man's blood with cold.

The naked hulk alongside came,
And the twain were casting dice;
"The game is done! I've won! I've won!"
Quoth she, and whistles thrice.

The Sun's rim dips; the stars rush out:
At one stride comes the dark;
With far-heard whisper o'er the sea,
Off shot the specter-bark.

We listened and looked sideways up!
Fear at my heart, as at a cup,
My life-blood seemed to sip!
The stars were dim, and thick the night,
The steersman's face by his lamp gleamed white;
From the sails the dew did drip—
Till clomb above the eastern bar
The hornéd Moon, with one bright star
Within the nether tip.

[288]

One after one, by the star-dogged Moon,
Too quick for groan or sigh,
Each turned his face with a ghastly pang,
And cursed me with his eye.

Four times fifty living men,
(And I heard nor sigh nor groan)
With heavy thump, a lifeless lump,
They dropped down one by one.

The souls did from their bodies fly,—
They fled to bliss or woe!
And every soul, it passed me by,
Like the whizz of my cross-bow!

PART IV

"I fear thee, ancient Mariner!
I fear thy skinny hand!
And thou art long, and lank, and brown,
As is the ribbed sea-sand.

I fear thee and thy glittering eye,
And thy skinny hand, so brown."—
Fear not, fear not, thou Wedding-Guest!
This body dropt not down.

Alone, alone, all, all alone,
Alone on a wide wide sea!
And never a saint took pity on
My soul in agony.

[289]

The many men, so beautiful!
And they all dead did lie:
And a thousand thousand slimy things
Lived on; and so did I.

I looked upon the rotting sea,
And drew my eyes away;
I looked upon the rotting deck,
And there the dead men lay.

I looked to heaven, and tried to pray;
But or ever a prayer had gusht,
A wicked whisper came, and made
My heart as dry as dust.

I closed my lids, and kept them close,
And the balls like pulses beat;
For the sky and the sea, and the sea and the sky
Lay like a load on my weary eye,
And the dead were at my feet.

The cold sweat melted from their limbs,
Nor rot nor reek did they:
The look with which they looked on me
Had never passed away.

An orphan's curse would drag to hell
A spirit from on high;
But oh! more horrible than that

Is the curse in a dead man's eye!
Seven days, seven nights, I saw that curse,
And yet I could not die.

The moving Moon went up the sky,
And no where did abide:
Softly she was going up,
And a star or two beside—

Her beams bemocked the sultry main,
Like April hoar-frost spread;
But where the ship's huge shadow lay,
The charmèd water burnt alway
A still and awful red.

Beyond the shadow of the ship,
I watched the water-snakes:
They moved in tracks of shining white,
And when they reared, the elfish light
Fell off in hoary flakes.

Within the shadow of the ship
I watched their rich attire:
Blue, glossy green, and velvet black,
They coiled and swam; and every track
Was a flash of golden fire.

O happy living things! no tongue
Their beauty might declare:

A spring of love gushed from my heart,
And I blessed them unaware:
Sure my kind saint took pity on me,
And I blessed them unaware.

The self-same moment I could pray;
And from my neck so free
The Albatross fell off, and sank
Like lead into the sea.

PART V

Oh sleep! it is a gentle thing,
Beloved from pole to pole!
To Mary Queen the praise be given!
She sent the gentle sleep from Heaven,
That slid into my soul.

The silly buckets on the deck,
That had so long remained,
I dreamt that they were filled with dew;
And when I awoke, it rained.

My lips were wet, my throat was cold,
My garments all were dank;
Sure I had drunken in my dreams,
And still my body drank.

I moved, and could not feel my limbs:
I was so light—almost

I thought that I had died in sleep,
And was a blesséd ghost.

And soon I heard a roaring wind:
It did not come anear;
But with its sound it shook the sails,
That were so thin and sere.

The upper air burst into life!
And a hundred fire-flags sheen,
To and fro they were hurried about!
And to and fro, and in and out,
The wan stars danced between.

And the coming wind did roar more loud,
And the sails did sigh like sedge;
And the rain poured down from one black cloud;
The Moon was at its edge.

The thick black cloud was cleft, and still
The Moon was at its side:
Like waters shot from some high crag,
The lightning fell with never a jag,
A river steep and wide.

The loud wind never reached the ship,
Yet now the ship moved on!
Beneath the lightning and the Moon
The dead men gave a groan.

They groaned, they stirred, they all uprose,
Nor spake, nor moved their eyes;
It had been strange, even in a dream,
To have seen those dead men rise.

The helmsman steered, the ship moved on;
Yet never a breeze up-blew;
The mariners all 'gan to work the ropes,
Where they were wont to do;
They raised their limbs like lifeless tools—
We were a ghastly crew.

The body of my brother's son
Stood by me, knee to knee:
The body and I pulled at one rope,
But he said nought to me.

"I fear thee, ancient Mariner!"
Be calm, thou Wedding-Guest!
'Twas not those souls that fled in pain,
Which to their corses came again,
But a troop of spirits blest:

For when it dawned—they dropped their arms,
And clustered round the mast;
Sweet sounds rose slowly through their mouths,
And from their bodies passed.

Around, around, flew each sweet sound,
Then darted to the Sun;

Slowly the sounds came back again,
Now mixed, now one by one.

Sometimes a-dropping from the sky
I heard the sky-lark sing;
Sometimes all little birds that are,
How they seemed to fill the sea and air
With their sweet jargoning!

And now 'twas like all instruments,
Now like a lonely flute;
And now it is an angel's song,
That makes the heavens be mute.

It ceased; yet still the sails made on
A pleasant noise till noon,
A noise like of a hidden brook
In the leafy month of June,
That to the sleeping woods all night
Singeth a quiet tune.

Till noon we quietly sailed on,
Yet never a breeze did breathe:
Slowly and smoothly went the ship,
Moved onward from beneath.

Under the keel nine fathom deep,
From the land of mist and snow,
The spirit slid: and it was he

That made the ship to go.
The sails at noon left off their tune,
And the ship stood still also.

The Sun, right up above the mast,
Had fixed her to the ocean:
But in a minute she 'gan stir,
With a short uneasy motion—
Backwards and forwards half her length
With a short uneasy motion.

Then like a pawing horse let go,
She made a sudden bound:
It flung the blood into my head,
And I fell down in a swound.

How long in that same fit I lay,
I have not to declare;
But ere my living life returned,
I heard and in my soul discerned
Two voices in the air.

"Is it he?" quoth one, "Is this the man?
By him who died on cross,
With his cruel bow he laid full low
The harmless Albatross.

The spirit who bideth by himself
In the land of mist and snow,

[296]

He loved the bird that loved the man
Who shot him with his bow."

The other was a softer voice,
As soft as honey-dew:
Quoth he, "The man hath penance done,
And penance more will do."

PART VI

First Voice
"But tell me, tell me! speak again,
Thy soft response renewing—
What makes that ship drive on so fast?
What is the ocean doing?"

Second Voice
"Still as a slave before his lord,
The ocean hath no blast;
His great bright eye most silently
Up to the Moon is cast—

If he may know which way to go;
For she guides him smooth or grim.
See, brother, see! how graciously
She looketh down on him."

First Voice
"But why drives on that ship so fast,
Without or wave or wind?"

[297]

Second Voice

"The air is cut away before,
And closes from behind.

Fly, brother, fly! more high, more high!
Or we shall be belated:
For slow and slow that ship will go,
When the Mariner's trance is abated."

I woke, and we were sailing on
As in a gentle weather:
'Twas night, calm night, the moon was high;
The dead men stood together.

All stood together on the deck,
For a charnel-dungeon fitter:
All fixed on me their stony eyes,
That in the Moon did glitter.

The pang, the curse, with which they died,
Had never passed away:
I could not draw my eyes from theirs,
Nor turn them up to pray.

And now this spell was snapt: once more
I viewed the ocean green,
And looked far forth, yet little saw
Of what had else been seen—

[298]

Like one, that on a lonesome road
Doth walk in fear and dread,
And having once turned round walks on,
And turns no more his head;
Because he knows, a frightful fiend
Doth close behind him tread.

But soon there breathed a wind on me,
Nor sound nor motion made:
Its path was not upon the sea,
In ripple or in shade.

It raised my hair, it fanned my cheek
Like a meadow-gale of spring—
It mingled strangely with my fears,
Yet it felt like a welcoming.

Swiftly, swiftly flew the ship,
Yet she sailed softly too:
Sweetly, sweetly blew the breeze—
On me alone it blew.

Oh! dream of joy! is this indeed
The light-house top I see?
Is this the hill? is this the kirk?
Is this mine own countree?

We drifted o'er the harbor-bar,
And I with sobs did pray—

O let me be awake, my God!
Or let me sleep alway.

The harbor-bar was clear as glass,
So smoothly it was strewn!
And on the bay the moonlight lay,
And the shadow of the Moon.

The rock shone bright, the kirk no less,
That stands above the rock:
The moonlight steeped in silentness
The steady weathercock.

And the bay was white with silent light,
Till rising from the same,
Full many shapes, that shadows were,
In crimson colors came.

A little distance from the prow
Those crimson shadows were:
I turned my eyes upon the deck—
Oh, Christ! what saw I there!

Each corse lay flat, lifeless and flat,
And, by the holy rood!
A man all light, a seraph-man,
On every corse there stood.

This seraph-band, each waved his hand:
It was a heavenly sight!

They stood as signals to the land,
Each one a lovely light;

This seraph-band, each waved his hand,
No voice did they impart—
No voice; but oh! the silence sank
Like music on my heart.

But soon I heard the dash of oars,
I heard the Pilot's cheer;
My head was turned perforce away
And I saw a boat appear.

The Pilot and the Pilot's boy,
I heard them coming fast:
Dear Lord in Heaven! it was a joy
The dead men could not blast.

I saw a third—I heard his voice:
It is the Hermit good!
He singeth loud his godly hymns
That he makes in the wood.
He'll shrieve my soul, he'll wash away
The Albatross's blood.

PART VII

This Hermit good lives in that wood
Which slopes down to the sea.
How loudly his sweet voice he rears!

He loves to talk with marineres
That come from a far countree.

He kneels at morn, and noon, and eve—
He hath a cushion plump:
It is the moss that wholly hides
The rotted old oak-stump.

The skiff-boat neared: I heard them talk,
"Why, this is strange, I trow.
Where are those lights so many and fair,
That signal made but now?"

"Strange, by my faith!" the Hermit said—
"And they answered not our cheer!
The planks looked warped! and see those **sails**,
How thin they are and sere!
I never saw aught like to them,
Unless perchance it were

Brown skeletons of leaves that lag
My forest-brook along;
When the ivy-tod is heavy with snow,
And the owlet whoops to the wolf below,
That eats the she-wolf's young."

"Dear Lord! it hath a fiendish look—
(The Pilot made reply)

I am a-feared"—"Push on, push on!"
Said the Hermit cheerily.

The boat came closer to the ship,
But I nor spake nor stirred;
The boat came close beneath the ship,
And straight a sound was heard.

Under the water it rumbled on,
Still louder and more dread:
It reached the ship, it split the bay;
The ship went down like lead.

Stunned by that loud and dreadful sound,
Which sky and ocean smote,
Like one that hath been seven days drowned
My body lay afloat;
But swift as dreams, myself I found
Within the Pilot's boat.

Upon the whirl, where sank the ship,
The boat spun round and round;
And all was still, save that the hill
Was telling of the sound.

I moved my lips—the Pilot shrieked
And fell down in a fit;
The holy Hermit raised his eyes,
And prayed where he did sit.

I took the oars: the Pilot's boy,
Who now doth crazy go,
Laughed loud and long, and all the while
His eyes went to and fro.
"Ha! ha!" quoth he, "full plain I see,
The Devil knows how to row."

And now, all in my own countree,
I stood on the firm land!
The Hermit stepped forth from the boat,
And scarcely he could stand.

"O shrieve me, shrieve me, holy man!"
The Hermit crossed his brow.
"Say quick," quoth he, "I bid thee say—
What manner of man art thou?"

Forthwith this frame of mind was wrenched
With a woeful agony,
Which forced me to begin my tale;
And then it left me free.

Since then, at an uncertain hour,
That agony returns:
And till my ghastly tale is told,
This heart within me burns.

I pass, like night, from land to land;
I have strange power of speech;

That moment that his face I see,
I know the man that must hear me:
To him my tale I teach.

What loud uproar bursts from that door!
The wedding-guests are there:
But in the garden-bower the bride
And bride-maids singing are:
And hark the little vesper bell,
Which biddeth me to prayer!

O Wedding-Guest! this soul hath been
Alone on a wide wide sea:
So lonely 'twas, that God himself
Scarce seeméd there to be.

O sweeter than the marriage-feast,
'Tis sweeter far to me,
To walk together to the kirk
With a goodly company!—

To walk together to the kirk,
And all together pray,
While each to his great Father bends,
Old men, and babes, and loving friends
And youths and maidens gay!

Farewell, farewell! but this I tell
To thee, thou Wedding-Guest!

[305]

He prayeth well, who loveth well
Both man and bird and beast.

He prayeth best, who loveth best
All things both great and small;
For the dear God who loveth us,
He made and loveth all.

The Mariner, whose eye is bright,
Whose beard with age is hoar,
Is gone: and now the Wedding-Guest
Turned from the bridegroom's door.

He went like one that hath been stunned,
And is of sense forlorn:
A sadder and a wiser man,
He rose the morrow morn.

SAMUEL TAYLOR COLERIDGE

THE RAVEN

Once upon a midnight dreary, while I pondered, weak and
       weary,
Over many a quaint and curious volume of forgotten lore,—
While I nodded, nearly napping, suddenly there came a
       tapping,
As if someone gently rapping, rapping at my chamber door.
" 'Tis some visitor," I muttered, "tapping at my chamber
       door;
    Only this and nothing more."

Ah, distinctly I remember it was in the bleak December,
And each separate dying ember wrought its ghost upon the
       floor.
Eagerly I wished the morrow;—vainly had I sought to bor-
       row
From my books surcease of sorrow—sorrow for the lost Le-
       nore,
For the rare and radiant maiden whom the angels name
     Lenore:
    Nameless here for evermore.

And the silken sad uncertain rustling of each purple curtain
Thrilled me—filled me with fantastic terrors never felt be-
       fore;

So that now, to still the beating of my heart, I stood re-
      peating,
" 'Tis some visitor entreating entrance at my chamber door—
Some late visitor entreating entrance at my chamber door;
      This it is and nothing more."

Presently my soul grew stronger; hesitating then no longer,
"Sir," said I, "or Madam, truly your forgiveness I implore;
But the fact is I was napping, and so gently you came rapping,
And so faintly you came tapping, tapping at my chamber
      door,
That I scarce was sure I heard you"—here I opened wide the
      door:—
      Darkness there and nothing more.

Deep into that darkness peering, long I stood there wonder-
      ing, fearing,
Doubting, dreaming, dreams no mortals ever dared to dream
      before;
But the silence was unbroken, and the stillness gave no token,
And the only word there spoken was the whispered word,
      "Lenore?"
This I whispered, and an echo murmured back the word,
      "Lenore":
      Merely this and nothing more.

Back into the chamber turning, all my soul within me burn-
      ing,
Soon again I heard a tapping somewhat louder than before.

"Surely," said I, "surely that is something at my window
    lattice;
Let me see, then, what thereat is, and this mystery explore:
    'Tis the wind and nothing more."

Open here I flung the shutter, when, with many a flirt and
    flutter,
In there stepped a stately Raven of the saintly days of yore.
Not the least obeisance made he; not a minute stopped or
    stayed he;
But, with mien of lord or lady, perched above my chamber
    door,
Perched upon a bust of Pallas just above my chamber door:
    Perched, and sat, and nothing more.

Then this ebony bird beguiling my sad fancy into smiling
By the grave and stern decorum of the countenance it
    wore,—
"Though thy crest be shorn and shaven, thou," I said, "art
    sure no craven,
Ghastly grim and ancient Raven wandering from the Nightly
    shore:
Tell me what thy lordly name is on the Night's Plutonian
    shore!"
    Quoth the Raven, "Nevermore."

Much I marveled this ungainly fowl to hear discourse so
    plainly,
Though its answer little meaning—little relevancy bore;
For we cannot help agreeing that no living human being

Ever yet was blessed with seeing bird above his chamber
      door—
Bird or beast upon the sculptured bust above his chamber
      door,
    With such name as "Nevermore."

But the Raven, sitting lonely on the placid bust, spoke only
That one word, as if his soul in that one word he did out-
      pour.
Nothing further then he uttered, not a feather then he flut-
      tered,
Till I scarcely more than muttered,—"Other friends have
      flown before;
On the morrow *he* will leave me, as my Hopes have flown
      before."
    Then the bird said, "Nevermore."

Startled at the stillness broken by reply so aptly spoken,
"Doubtless," said I, "what it utters is its only stock and store,
Caught from some unhappy master whom unmerciful Dis-
      aster
Followed fast and followed faster till his songs one burden
      bore:
Till the dirges of his Hope that melancholy burden bore
    Of 'Never-nevermore.' "

But the Raven still beguiling all my sad soul into smiling,
Straight I wheeled a cushioned seat in front of bird and bust
      and door;
Then upon the velvet sinking, I betook myself to linking

Fancy unto fancy, thinking what this ominous bird of yore,
What this grim, ungainly, ghastly, gaunt, and ominous bird
     of yore
    Meant in croaking "Nevermore."

This I sat engaged in guessing, but no syllable expressing
To the fowl whose fiery eyes now burned into my bosom's
     core;
This and more I sat divining, with my head at ease reclining
On the cushion's velvet lining that the lamplight gloated
     o'er,
But whose velvet violet lining with the lamplight gloating
     o'er
    She shall press, ah, nevermore!

Then, methought, the air grew denser, perfumed from an
     unseen censer
Swung by seraphim whose foot-falls tinkled on the tufted
     floor.
"Wretch," I cried, "thy God hath lent thee—by these an-
     gels he hath sent thee
Respite—respite and nepenthe from thy memories of Le-
     nore!
Quaff, oh quaff this kind nepenthe, and forget this lost Le-
     nore!"
    Quoth the Raven, "Nevermore."

"Prophet!" said I, "thing of evil! prophet still, if bird or devil!
Whether Tempter sent or whether tempest tossed thee here
     ashore,

Desolate, yet all undaunted, on this desert land enchanted,
On this home by Horror haunted—tell me truly, I implore:
Is there—*is* there balm in Gilead?—tell me—tell me, I im-
    plore!"
      Quoth the Raven, "Nevermore."

"Prophet!" said I, "thing of evil—prophet still, if bird or
    devil!
By that Heaven that bends above us, by that God we both
    adore,
Tell this soul with sorrow laden if, within the distant Aidenn,
It shall clasp a sainted maiden whom the angels name Le-
    nore:
Clasp a rare and radiant maiden whom the angels name Le-
    nore!"
      Quoth the Raven, "Nevermore."

"Be that word our sign of parting, bird or fiend!" I shrieked,
    upstarting—
"Get thee back into the tempest and the Night's Plutonian
    shore!
Leave no black plume as a token of that lie thy soul hath
    spoken!
Leave my loneliness unbroken! quit the bust above my
    door!
Take thy beak from out my heart, and take thy form from
    off my door!"
      Quoth the Raven, "Nevermore."

And the Raven, never flitting, still is sitting, still is sitting
On the pallid bust of Pallas just above my chamber door;
And his eyes have all the seeming of a demon's that is
       dreaming,
And the lamp-light o'er him streaming throws his shadow on
       the floor;
And my soul from out that shadow that lies floating on the
       floor
    Shall be lifted—nevermore!

EDGAR ALLAN POE

KILMENY

Bonny Kilmeny gaed up the glen;
But it wasna to meet Duneira's men,
Nor the rosy monk of the isle to see,
For Kilmeny was pure as pure could be.
It was only to hear the yorlin sing,
And pull the blue cress-flower round the spring;
To pull the hip and the hindberrye,
And the nut that hung frae the hazel-tree;
For Kilmeny was pure as pure could be.
But lang may her minnie look o'er the wa',
And lang may she seek in the greenwood shaw;
Lang the Laird o' Duneira blame,
And lang, lang greet e'er Kilmeny come hame!

When many a day had come and fled,
When grief grew calm, and hope was dead,
When mass for Kilmeny's soul had been sung,
When the bedesman had prayed and the dead-bell rung;
Late, late in a gloaming, when all was still,
When the fringe was red on the westlin hill,
The wood was sere, the moon i' the wane,
The reek of the cot hung o'er the plain,
Like a little wee cloud in the world its lane;

[314]

When the ingle lowed with an eery gleam,
Late, late in the gloamin', Kilmeny came hame!

"Kilmeny, Kilmeny, where have you been?
Lang hae we sought baith holt and dene;
By linn, by ford, and greenwood tree,
Yet you are halesome and fair to see.
Where gat you that joup of the lily sheen?
That bonny snood of the birk sae green?
And these roses, the fairest that ever were seen?
Kilmeny, Kilmeny, where have you been?"
Kilmeny look'd up with a lovely grace,
But nae smile was seen on Kilmeny's face;
As still was her look, and as still was her e'e,
As the stillness that lay on the emerald lea,
Or the mist that sleeps on a waveless sea.
For Kilmeny had been she knew not where,
And Kilmeny had seen what she could not declare.
Kilmeny had been where the cock never crew,
Where the rain never fell, and the wind never blew.
But it seem'd as the harp of the sky had rung,
And the airs of heaven play'd round her tongue,
When she spake of the lovely forms she had seen,
And a land where sin had never been;
A land of love and a land of light,
Withouten sun, or moon, or night;
The land of vision it would seem,
And still an everlasting dream.

.   .   .   .   .

They lifted Kilmeny, they led her away,
And she walk'd in the light of a sunless day;
The sky was a dome of crystal bright,
The fountain of vision, and fountain of light:
The emerald fields were of dazzling glow,
And the flowers of everlasting blow.
Then deep in the stream her body they laid,
That her youth and beauty might never fade;
And they smil'd on heaven, when they saw her lie
In the stream of life that wander'd by.
And she heard a song, she heard it sung,
She kenn'd not where; but so sweetly it rung,
It fell on the ear like a dream of the morn:
"O blest be the day Kilmeny was born!"

.   .   .   .   .

To sing of the sights Kilmeny saw,
So far surpassing nature's law,
The singer's voice would sink away,
And the string of his harp would cease to play.
But she saw till the sorrows of man were by,
And all was love and harmony;
Till the stars of heaven fell calmly away,
Like the flakes of snow on a winter day.

.   .   .   .   .

When seven lang years had come and fled,
When grief was calm and hope was dead;
When scarce was remembered Kilmeny's name,

Late, late in a gloaming Kilmeny came hame!
And O, her beauty was fair to see,
But still and steadfast was her e'e!
Her seymar was the lily flower,
And her cheek the moss-rose in the shower;
And her voice like the distant melody
That floats along the twilight sea.
But she loved to raike the lanely glen,
And keepit away frae the haunts of men;
Her holy hymns unheard to sing,
To suck the flowers and drink the spring.
But wherever her peaceful form appear'd,
The wild beasts of the hill were cheer'd;
The wolf played blythly round the field,
The lordly bison low'd and kneel'd;
The dun deer woo'd with manner bland,
And cower'd aneath her lily hand.
And all in a peaceful ring were hurl'd;
It was like an eve in a sinless world!

When a month and a day had come and gane,
Kilmeny sought the green-wood wene;
There laid her down on the leaves sae gree,
And Kilmeny on earth was never mair seen.

                    JAMES HOGG (*abridged*)

THE PIED PIPER OF HAMELIN

Hamelin Town's in Brunswick,
   By famous Hanover city;
The river Weser, deep and wide,
Washes its wall on the southern side;
A pleasanter spot you never spied;
   But, when begins my ditty,
Almost five hundred years ago,
To see the townsfolk suffer so
   From vermin, was a pity.

   Rats!
They fought the dogs and killed the cats,
   And bit the babies in the cradles,
And ate the cheese out of the vats,
   And licked the soup from the cooks' own ladles,
Split open the kegs of salted sprats,
Made nests inside men's Sunday hats,
And even spoiled the women's chats
      By drowning their speaking
      With shrieking and squeaking
In fifty different sharps and flats.

At last the people in a body
   To the Town Hall came flocking:

" 'Tis clear," cried they, "our Mayor's a noddy;
    And as for our Corporation—shocking
To think we buy gowns lined with ermine
For dolts that can't or won't determine
What's best to rid us of our vermine!
You hope, because you're old and obese,
To find in the furry civic robe ease?
Rouse up, sirs! Give your brains a racking
To find the remedy we're lacking,
Or, sure as fate, we'll send you packing!"
At this the Mayor and Corporation
Quaked with a mighty consternation.

An hour they sat in council,
    At length the Mayor broke silence:
"For a guilder I'd my ermine gown sell,
    I wish I were a mile hence!
It's easy to bid one rack one's brain—
I'm sure my poor head aches again,
I've scratched it so, and all in vain.
Oh for a trap, a trap, a trap!"
Just as he said this, what should hap
At the chamber door but a gentle tap?
"Bless us," cried the Mayor, "what's that?"
(With the Corporation as he sat,
Looking little though wondrous fat;
Nor brighter was his eye, nor moister
Than a too-long-opened oyster,
Save when at noon his paunch grew mutinous

[319]

For a plate of turtle green and glutinous)
"Only a scraping of shoes on the mat?
Anything like the sound of a rat
Makes my heart go pit-a-pat!"

"Come in!"—the Mayor cried, looking bigger:
And in did come the strangest figure!
His queer long coat from heel to head
Was half of yellow and half of red,
And he himself was tall and thin,
With sharp blue eyes, each like a pin,
And light loose hair, yet swarthy skin,
No tuft on cheek nor beard on chin,
But lips where smiles went out and in;
There was no guessing his kith and kin:
And nobody could enough admire
The tall man and his quaint attire.
Quoth one: "It's as my great-grandsire,
Starting up at the Trump of Doom's tone,
Had walked this way from his painted tombstone!"

He advanced to the council-table:
And, "Please your honors," said he, "I'm able,
By means of a secret charm, to draw
    All creatures living beneath the sun,
    That creep or swim or fly or run,
After me so as you never saw!
And I chiefly use my charm
On creatures that do people harm,

The mole and toad and newt and viper;
And people call me the Pied Piper."
(And here they noticed round his neck
   A scarf of red and yellow stripe,
To match with his coat of the self-same cheque;
   And at the scarf's end hung a pipe;
And his fingers, they noticed, were ever astraying
As if impatient to be playing
Upon this pipe, as low it dangled
Over his vesture so old-fangled.)
"Yet," said he, "poor piper as I am,
In Tartary I freed the Cham,
   Last June, from his huge swarms of gnats;
I eased in Asia the Nizam
   Of a monstrous brood of vampyre-bats:
And as for what your brain bewilders,
   If I can rid your town of rats
Will you give me a thousand guilders?"
"One? fifty thousand!"—was the exclamation
Of the astonished Mayor and Corporation.

Into the street the Piper stept,
   Smiling first a little smile,
As if he knew what magic slept
   In his quiet pipe the while;
Then, like a musical adept,
To blow the pipe his lips he wrinkled,
And green and blue his sharp eyes twinkled,
Like a candle-flame where salt is sprinkled;

[321]

And ere three shrill notes the pipe uttered,
You heard as if an army muttered;
And the muttering grew to a grumbling;
And the grumbling grew to a mighty rumbling;
And out of the houses the rats came tumbling.
Great rats, small rats, lean rats, brawny rats,
Brown rats, black rats, grey rats, tawny rats,
Grave old plodders, gay young friskers,
    Fathers, mothers, uncles, cousins,
Cocking tails and pricking whiskers,
    Families by tens and dozens,
Brothers, sisters, husbands, wives—
Followed the Piper for their lives.
From street to street he piped advancing,
And step for step they followed dancing,
Until they came to the river Weser,
    Wherein all plunged and perished!
Save one who, stout as Julius Caesar,
Swam across and lived to carry
    (As he, the manuscript he cherished)
To Rat-land home his commentary:
Which was, "At the first shrill notes of the pipe,
I heard a sound as of scraping tripe,
And putting apples, wondrous ripe,
Into a cider-press's gripe:
And a moving away of pickle-tub-boards,
And a leaving ajar of conserve-cupboards,
And a drawing the corks of train-oil-flasks,
And a breaking the hoops of butter-casks:

[322]

And it seemed as if a voice
  (Sweeter far than by harp or by psaltery
Is breathed) called out, 'Oh rats, rejoice!
  The world is grown to one vast dry-saltery!
So munch on, crunch on, take your nuncheon,
Breakfast, supper, dinner, luncheon!'
And just as a bulky sugar-puncheon,
All ready staved, like a great sun shone
Glorious scarce an inch before me,
Just as methought it said, 'Come, bore me!'
—I found the Weser rolling o'er me."

You should have heard the Hamelin people
Ringing the bells till they rocked the steeple.
"Go," cried the Mayor, "and get long poles,
Poke out the nests and block up the holes!
Consult with carpenters and builders,
And leave in our town not even a trace
Of the rats!"—when suddenly, up the face
Of the Piper perked in the market-place,
With a, "First, if you please, my thousand guilders!"

A thousand guilders! The Mayor looked blue;
So did the Corporation too.
For council dinners made rare havoc
With Claret, Moselle, Vin-de-Grave, Hock;
And half the money would replenish
Their cellar's biggest butt with Rhenish.

[323]

To pay this sum to a wandering fellow
With a gipsy coat of red and yellow!
"Beside," quoth the Mayor with a knowing wink,
"Our business was done at the river's brink;
We saw with our eyes the vermin sink,
And what's dead can't come to life, I think.
So, friend, we're not the folks to shrink
From the duty of giving you something for drink,
And a matter of money to put in your poke;
But as for the guilders, what we spoke
Of them, as you very well know, was in joke.
Beside, our losses have made us thrifty.
A thousand guilders! Come, take fifty!"

The Piper's face fell, and he cried
"No trifling! I can't wait, beside!
I've promised to visit by dinnertime
Bagdat, and accept the prime
Of the Head-Cook's pottage, all he's rich in,
For having left, in the Caliph's kitchen,
Of a nest of scorpions no survivor:
With him I proved no bargain-driver,
With you, don't think I'll bate a stiver!
And folks who put me in a passion
May find me pipe after another fashion."

"How?" cried the Mayor, "d'ye think I'd brook
Being worse treated than a Cook?

Insulted by a lazy ribald
With idle pipe and vesture piebald?
You threaten us, fellow? Do your worst,
Blow your pipe there until you burst!"
Once more he stept into the street
 And to his lips again
 Laid his long pipe of smooth straight cane;
And ere he blew three notes (such sweet
Soft notes as yet musician's cunning
 Never gave the enraptured air)
There was a rustling that seemed like a bustling
Of merry crowds justling at pitching and hustling,
Small feet were pattering, wooden shoes clattering,
Little hands clapping and little tongues chattering,
And, like fowls in a farm-yard when barley is scattering,
Out came the children running.
All the little boys and girls,
With rosy cheeks and flaxen curls,
And sparkling eyes and teeth like pearls,
Tripping and skipping, ran merrily after
The wonderful music with shouting and laughter.

The Mayor was dumb, and the Council stood
As if they were changed into blocks of wood,
Unable to move a step, or cry
To the children merrily skipping by,
—Could only follow with the eye
That joyous crowd at the Piper's back.
But how the Mayor was on the rack,

[325]

And the wretched Council's bosoms beat,
As the Piper turned from the High Street
To where the Weser rolled its waters
Right in the way of their sons and daughters!
However he turned from South to West,
And to Koppelberg Hill his steps addressed,
And after him the children pressed;
Great was the joy in every breast.
"He never can cross that mighty top!
He's forced to let the piping drop,
And we shall see our children stop."
When, lo, as they reached the mountain-side
A wondrous portal opened wide,
As if a cavern was suddenly hollowed;
And the Piper advanced and the children followed,
And when all were in to the very last,
The door in the mountain-side shut fast.
Did I say, all? No! One was lame,
   And could not dance the whole of the way:
And in after years, if you would blame
   His sadness, he was used to say,—
"It's dull in our town since my playmates left!
I can't forget that I'm bereft
Of all the pleasant sights they see,
Which the Piper also promised me.
For he led us, he said, to a joyous land,
Joining the town and just at hand,
Where waters gushed and fruit-trees grew
And flowers put forth a fairer hue,

And everything was strange and new;
The sparrows were brighter than peacocks here,
And their dogs outran our fallow deer,
And honey-bees had lost their stings,
And horses were born with eagles' wings:
And just as I became assured
My lame foot would be speedily cured,
The music stopped and I stood still,
And found myself outside the hill,
Left alone against my will,
To go now limping as before,
And never hear of that country more!"

Alas, alas for Hamelin!
        There came into many a burgher's pate
        A text which says that heaven's gate
        Opes to the rich at as easy rate
As the needle's eye takes a camel in!
The Mayor sent East, West, North and South,
To offer the Piper, by word of mouth,
        Wherever it was men's lot to find him,
Silver and gold to his heart's content,
If he'd only return the way he went,
        And bring the children behind him.
But when they saw 'twas a lost endeavor,
And Piper and dancers were gone for ever,
They made a decree that lawyers never
        Should think their records dated duly

If, after the day of the month and year,
These words did not as well appear,
'And so long after what happened here
    On the Twenty-second of July,
Thirteen hundred and seventy-six:'
And the better in memory to fix
The place of the children's last retreat,
They called it, the Pied Piper's Street—
Where anyone playing on pipe or tabor
Was sure for the future to lose his labor.
Nor suffered they hostelry or tavern

    To shock with mirth a street so solemn;
But opposite the place of the cavern
    They wrote the story on a column,
And on the great church-window painted
The same, to make the world acquainted
How their children were stolen away,
And there it stands to this very day.
And I must not omit to say
That in Transylvania there's a tribe
Of alien people who ascribe
The outlandish ways and dress
On which their neighbors lay such stress,
To their fathers and mothers having risen
Out of some subterraneous prison
Into which they were trepanned
Long time ago in a mighty band
Out of Hamelin town in Brunswick land,
But how or why, they don't understand.

So, Willy, let me and you be wipers
Of scores out with all men—especially pipers!
And, whether they pipe us free from rats or from mice,
If we've promised them aught, let us keep our promise!

ROBERT BROWNING

TAM O'SHANTER

When chapman billies leave the street,
And drouthy neibors, neibors meet,
As market-days are wearing late,
An' folk begin to tak the gate;
While we sit bousing at the nappy,
An' getting fou and unco happy,
We thinkna on the lang Scots miles,
The mosses, waters, slaps, and stiles,
That lie between us and our hame,
Where sits our sulky, sullen dame,
Gathering her brows like gathering storm,
Nursing her wrath to keep it warm.

This truth fand honest Tam O'Shanter,
As he frae Ayr ae night did canter:
(Auld Ayr, whom ne'er a town surpasses
For honest men and bonie lasses).

O Tam! hadst thou but been sae wise,
As ta'en thy ain wife Kate's advice!
She tauld thee weel thou wast a skellum,
A blethering, blustering, drunken blellum;
That frae November to October,
Ae market-day thou was nae sober;
That ilka melder, wi' the miller,
Thou sat as lang as thou had siller;

That ev'ry naig was ca'd a shoe on,
The smith and thee gat roaring fou on;
That at the Lord's house, ev'n on Sunday,
Thou drank wi' Kirkton Jean till Monday.
She prophesied that, late or soon,
Thou wad be found deep drowned in Doon;
Or catch'd wi' warlocks in the mirk,
By Alloway's auld haunted kirk.

　　Ah, gentle dames! it gars me greet,
To think how mony counsels sweet,
How mony lengthen'd, sage advices,
The husband frae the wife despises!

　　But to our tale: Ae market night,
Tam had got planted unco right,
Fast by an ingle, bleezing finely,
Wi' reaming swats, that drank divinely;
And at his elbow, Souter Johnie,
His ancient, trusty, drouthy crony:
Tam lo'ed him like a very brither;
They had been fou for weeks thegither.
The night drave on wi' sangs and clatter;
And ay the ale was growing better:
The landlady and Tam grew gracious,
Wi' favors, secret, sweet, and precious:
The souter tauld his queerest stories;
The landlord's laugh was ready chorus:
The storm without might rair and rustle,
Tam didna mind the storm a whistle.

　　Care, mad to see a man sae happy,

E'en drowned himself amang the nappy!
As bees flee hame wi' lades o' treasure,
The minutes winged their way wi' pleasure:
Kings may be blest, but Tam was glorious,
O'er a' the ills of life victorious!

But pleasures are like poppies spread,
You seize the flow'r, its bloom is shed;
Or like the snow falls in the river,
A moment white—then melts forever;
Or like the borealis race,
That flit ere you can point their place;
Or like the rainbow's lovely form
Evanishing amid the storm.
Nae man can tether time or tide;—
The hour approaches Tam maun ride;
That hour, o' night's black arch the key-stane,
That dreary hour he mounts his beast in;
And sic a night he taks the road in,
As ne'er poor sinner was abroad in.

The wind blew as 'twad blawn its last;
The rattling show'rs rose on the blast;
The speedy gleams the darkness swallow'd;
Loud, deep, and lang, the thunder bellow'd:
That night, a child might understand,
The Deil had business on his hand.

Weel mounted on his grey mare, Meg,
A better never lifted leg,
Tam skelpit on thro' dub and mire,
Despising wind, and rain, and fire;

Whiles holding fast his gude blue bonnet;
Whiles crooning o'er some auld Scots sonnet;
Whiles glow'ring round wi' prudent cares,
Lest bogles catch him unawares;
Kirk Alloway was drawing nigh,
Where ghaists and houlets nightly cry.

By this time he was cross the ford,
Where in the snaw the chapman smoored;
And past the birks and meikle stane,
Where drunken Charlie brak's neck-bane:
And thro' the whins, and by the cairn,
Where hunters fand the murdered bairn;
And near the thorn, aboon the well,
Whare Mungo's mither hanged hersel.
Before him Doon pours all his floods;
The doubling storm roars thro' the woods;
The lightnings flash from pole to pole;
Near and more near the thunders roll:
When, glimmering thro' the groaning trees,
Kirk Alloway seemed in a bleeze;
Thro' ilka bore the beams were glancing;
And loud resounded mirth and dancing.

Inspiring bold John Barleycorn!
What dangers thou canst make us scorn!
Wi' tippenny, we fear nae evil;
Wi' usquebae, we'll face the Devil!
The swats sae ream'd in Tammie's noddle,
Fair play, he car'd na deils a boddle.
But Maggie stood right sair astonished,

Till, by the heel and hand admonished,
She ventured forward on the light;
And, wow! Tam saw an unco sight!
Warlocks and witches in a dance;
Nae cotillion brent new frae France,
But hornpipes, jigs, strathspeys, and reels,
Put life and mettle in their heels.
At winnock-bunker in the east,
There sat old Nick, in shape o' beast;
A towzie tyke, black, grim, and large,
To gie them music was his charge:
He screw'd the pipes and gart them skirl,
Till roof and rafters a' did dirl.—
Coffins stood round, like open presses,
That shaw'd the dead in their last dresses;
And by some devilish cantrip slight
Each in its cauld hand held a light,—
By which heroic Tam was able
To note upon the haly table,
A murderer's banes in gibbet airns;
Twa span-lang, wee, unchristen'd bairns;
A thief, new-cutted frae a rape,
Wi' his last gasp his gab did gape;
Five tomahawks, wi' blude red rusted;
Five scymitars, wi' murder crusted;
A garter, which a babe had strangled;
A knife, a father's throat had mangled,
Whom his ain son o' life bereft,
The grey hairs yet stack to the heft;

Wi' mair of horrible and awfu',
Which ev'n to name wad be unlawfu'.

　　As Tammie glowr'd, amazed and curious,
The mirth and fun grew fast and furious:
The piper loud and louder blew;
The dancers quick and quicker flew;
They reeled, they set, they crossed, they cleekit,
Till ilka carlin swat and reekit,
And coost her duddies to the wark,
And linket at it in her sark!

　　Now Tam, O Tam, had thae been queans
A' plump and strapping in their teens;
Their sarks, instead o' creeshie flannen,
Been snaw-white seventeen-hunder linnen!
Thir breek o' mine, my only pair,
That ance were plush, o' gude blue hair,
I wad hae gi'en them off my hurdies,
For ae blink o' the bonnie burdies!

　　But wither'd beldams, auld and droll,
Rigwoodie hags, wad spean a foal,
Lowping and flinging on a crummock,
I wonder didna turn thy stomach.

　　But Tam kend what was fu' brawlie.
There was ae winsome wench and walie,
That night enlisted in the core,
(Lang after kend on Carrick shore;
For mony a beast to dead she shot,
And perished mony a bonie boat,
And shook baith meikle corn and bear,

[335]

And kept the country-side in fear,)
Her cutty sark, o' Paisley harn,
That, while a lassie, she had worn,
In longitude tho' sorely scanty,
It was her best, and she was vauntie.—
Ah! little kend thy reverend grannie,
That sark she coft for her wee Nannie,
Wi' twa pund Scots, ('twas a' her riches,)
Wad ever graced a dance of witches!

But here my muse her wing maun cour;
Sic flights are far beyond her power;
To sing how Nannie lap and flang
(A souple jade she was, and strang),
And how Tam stood, like ane bewitched,
And thought his very een enriched;
Even Satan glowr'd, and fidg' fu' fain,
And hotch'd and blew wi' might and main:
Till first ae caper, syne anither,
Tam tint his reason a' thegither,
And roars out, 'Weel done, Cutty-sark!'
And in an instant all was dark;
And scarcely had he Maggie rallied,
When out the hellish legion sallied.

As bees bizz out wi' angry fyke,
When plundering herds assail their byke;
As open pussie's mortal foes,
When, pop! she starts before their nose;
As eager runs the market-crowd,
When 'Catch the thief!' resounds aloud;

So Maggie runs, the witches follow,
Wi' monie an eldritch skreech and hollow.
    Ah, Tam! ah, Tam! thou'll get thy fairin!
In hell they'll roast thee like a herrin!
In vain thy Kate awaits thy comin!
Kate soon will be a woefu' woman!
Now, do thy speedy utmost, Meg,
And win the key-stane of the brig;
There at them thou thy tail may toss,
A running stream they darena cross.
But ere the key-stane she could make,
The fient a tail she had to shake!
For Nannie, far before the rest,
Hard upon noble Maggie prest,
And flew at Tam wi' furious ettle;
But little wist she Maggie's mettle—
Ae spring brought off her master hale,
But left behind her ain grey tail:
The carlin claught her by the rump,
And left poor Maggie scarce a stump.
    Now, wha this tale o' truth shall read,
Ilk man and mother's son, tak heed;
Whene'er to drink you are inclined,
Or cutty-sarks run in your mind,
Think, ye may buy the joys o'er dear,
Remember Tam o' Shanter's mare.

ROBERT BURNS

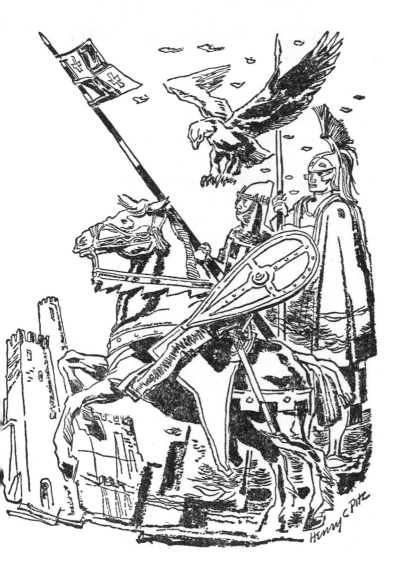

KINGS, KNIGHTS, AND
HEROES

KING ROBERT OF SICILY

Robert of Sicily, brother of Pope Urbane
And Valmond, Emperor of Allemaine,
Appareled in magnificent attire,
With retinue of many a knight and squire,
On St. John's eve, at vespers, proudly sat
And heard the priests chant the Magnificat.
And as he listened, o'er and o'er again
Repeated, like a burden or refrain,
He caught the words, *"Deposuit potentes*
De sede, et exaltavit humiles";
And slowly lifting up his kingly head
He to a learned clerk beside him said,
"What mean these words?" The clerk made answer meet,
"He has put down the mighty from their seat,
And has exalted them of low degree."
Thereat King Robert muttered scornfully,
" 'Tis well that such seditious words are sung
Only by priests and in the Latin tongue;
For unto priests and people be it known,
There is no power can push me from my throne!"
And leaning back, he yawned and fell asleep,
Lulled by the chant monotonous and deep.

When he awoke, it was already night;
The church was empty, and there was no light,

Save where the lamps, that glimmered few and faint,
Lighted a little space before some saint.
He started from his seat and gazed around,
But saw no living thing and heard no sound.
He groped towards the door, but it was locked;
He cried aloud, and listened, and then knocked,
And uttered awful threatenings and complaints,
And imprecations upon men and saints,
The sounds re-echoed from the roof and walls
As if dead priests were laughing in their stalls!

At length the sexton, hearing from without
The tumult of the knocking and the shout,
And thinking thieves were in the house of prayer,
Came with his lantern, asking, "Who is there?"
Half choked with rage, King Robert fiercely said,
"Open: 'Tis I, the King! art thou afraid?"
The frightened sexton, muttering, with a curse,
"This is some drunken vagabond, or worse!"
Turned the great key and flung the portal wide;
A man rushed by him at a single stride,
Haggard, half naked, without hat or cloak,
Who neither turned, nor looked at him, nor spoke,
But leaped into the blackness of the night,
And vanished like a specter from his sight.

Robert of Sicily, brother of Pope Urbane
And Valmond, Emperor of Allemaine,
Despoiled of his magnificent attire,

Bare-headed, breathless, and besprent with mire,
With sense of wrong and outrage desperate,
Strode on and thundered at the palace gate;
Rushed through the courtyard, thrusting in his rage
To right and left each seneschal and page,
And hurried up the broad and sounding stair,
His white face ghastly in the torches' glare.
From hall to hall he passed with breathless speed;
Voices and cries he heard, but did not heed,
Until at last he reached the banquet-room,
Blazing with light, and breathing with perfume.

There on the dais sat another king,
Wearing his robes, his crown, his signet-ring,
King Robert's self in features, form and height,
But all transfigured with angelic light!
It was an Angel; and his presence there
With a divine effulgence filled the air,
An exaltation, piercing the disguise,
Though none the hidden Angel recognize.

A moment speechless, motionless, amazed,
The throneless monarch on the Angel gazed,
Who met his looks of anger and surprise
With the divine compassion of his eyes;
Then said, "Who art thou? and why com'st thou here?"
To which King Robert answered, with a sneer,
"I am the King, and come to claim my own
From an impostor, who usurps my throne!"

And suddenly, at these audacious words,
Up sprang the angry guests, and drew their swords;
The Angel answered, with unruffled brow,
"Nay, not the King, but the King's Jester, thou
Henceforth shalt wear the bells and scalloped cape,
And for thy counsellor shalt lead an ape;
Thou shalt obey my servants when they call,
And wait upon my henchmen in the hall!"

Deaf to King Robert's threats and cries and prayers,
They thrust him from the hall and down the stairs;
A group of tittering pages ran before,
And as they opened wide the folding-door,
His heart failed, for he heard, with strange alarms,
The boisterous laughter of the men-at-arms,
And all the vaulted chamber roar and ring
With the mock plaudits of "Long live the King!"

Next morning, waking with the day's first beam,
He said within himself, "It was a dream!"
But the straw rustled as he turned his head,
There were the cap and bells beside his bed,
Around him rose the bare, discolored walls,
Close by, the steeds were champing in their stalls,
And in the corner, a revolting shape,
Shivering and chattering sat the wretched ape.
It was no dream; the world he loved so much
Had turned to dust and ashes at his touch!

Days came and went; and now returned again
To Sicily the old Saturnian reign;
Under the Angel's governance benign
The happy island danced with corn and wine,
And deep within the mountain's burning breast
Enceladus, the giant, was at rest.
Meanwhile King Robert yielded to his fate,
Sullen and silent and disconsolate.
Dressed in the motley garb that Jesters wear,
With looks bewildered and a vacant stare,
Close shaven above the ears, as monks are shorn,
By courtiers mocked, by pages laughed to scorn,
His only friend the ape, his only food
What others left,—he still was unsubdued.
And when the Angel met him on his way,
And half in earnest, half in jest, would say,
Sternly, though tenderly, that he might feel
The velvet scabbard held a sword of steel,
"Art thou the King?" the passion of his woe
Burst from him in resistless overflow,
And, lifting high his forehead, he would fling
The haughty answer back, "I am, I am the King!"

Almost three years were ended; when there came
Ambassadors of great repute and name
From Valmond, Emperor of Allemaine,
Unto King Robert, saying that Pope Urbane
By letter summoned them forthwith to come
On Holy Thursday to his city of Rome.

The Angel with great joy received his guests,
And gave them presents of embroidered vests,
And velvet mantles with rich ermine lined,
And rings and jewels of the rarest kind.
Then he departed with them o'er the sea
Into the lovely land of Italy,
Whose loveliness was more resplendent made
By the mere passing of that cavalcade,
With plumes, and cloaks, and housings, and the stir
Of jeweled bridle and of golden spur.

And lo! among the menials, in mock state,
Upon a piebald steed, with shambling gait,
His cloak of fox-tails flapping in the wind,
The solemn ape demurely perched behind,
King Robert rode, making huge merriment
In all the country towns through which they went.

The Pope received them with great pomp, and blare
Of bannered trumpets, on Saint Peter's square,
Giving his benediction and embrace,
Fervent, and full of apostolic grace.
While with congratulations and with prayers
He entertained the Angel unawares,
Robert, the Jester, bursting through the crowd,
Into their presence rushed, and cried aloud,
"I am the King! Look, and behold in me
Robert, your brother, King of Sicily!
This man, who wears my semblance to your eyes,

Is an imposter in a king's disguise.
Do you not know me? does no voice within
Answer my cry, and say we are akin?"
The Pope in silence, but with troubled mien,
Gazed at the Angel's countenance serene;
The Emperor, laughing, said, "It is strange sport
To keep a madman for thy Fool at court!"
And the poor, baffled Jester in disgrace
Was hustled back among the populace.

In solemn state the Holy Week went by,
And Easter Sunday gleamed upon the sky;
The presence of the Angel, with its light,
Before the sun rose, made the city bright,
And with new fervor filled the hearts of men,
Who felt that Christ indeed had risen again.
Even the Jester, on his bed of straw,
With haggard eyes the unwonted splendor saw,
He felt within a power unfelt before,
And, kneeling humbly on his chamber floor,
He heard the rushing garments of the Lord
Sweep through the silent air, ascending heavenward.

And now the visit ending, and once more
Valmond returning to the Danube's shore,
Homeward the Angel journeyed, and again
The land was made resplendent with his train,
Flashing along the towns of Italy
Unto Salerno, and from there by sea.
And when once more within Palermo's wall,
And, seated on the throne in his great hall,

He heard the Angelus from convent towers,
As if the better world conversed with ours,
He beckoned to King Robert to draw nigher,
And with a gesture bade the rest retire;
And when they were alone, the Angel said,
"Art thou the King?" Then bowing down his head,
King Robert crossed both hands upon his breast,
And meekly answered him: "Thou knowest best!
My sins as scarlet are; let me go hence,
And in some cloister's school of penitence,
Across those stones, that pave the way to heaven,
Walk barefoot, till my guilty soul is shriven!"
The Angel smiled, and from his radiant face
A holy light illumined all the place,
And through the open window, loud and clear,
They heard the monks chant in the chapel near,
Above the stir and tumult of the street:
"He has put down the mighty from their seat,
And has exalted them of low degree!"
And through the chant a second melody
Rose like the throbbing of a single string:
"I am an Angel, and thou art the King!"

King Robert, who was standing near the throne,
Lifted his eyes, and lo! he was alone!
But all appareled as in days of old,
With ermine mantle and with cloth of gold;
And when his courtiers came, they found him there
Kneeling upon the floor, absorbed in silent prayer.

HENRY WADSWORTH LONGFELLOW

[347]

SIR EGLAMORE

Sir Eglamore, that valiant knight,
   Fa, la, lanky down dilly,
He took up his sword and he went for to fight,
   Fa, la, lanky down dilly,
And as he rode o'er hill and dale,
All arméd with a coat of mail,
   Fa, lanky down, la, lanky down,
   Fa la lanky down dilly.

There starts a huge dragon out of his den,
Which had killed I know not how many men,
But when he see Sir Eglamore,
If you'd but heard how that dragon did roar.

This dragon had a plaguey hard hide,
Which could the strongest steel abide;
But as the dragon yawning did fall,
He thrust his sword down hilt and all.

The dragon laid him down and roared,
The knight was sorry for his sword;
The sword it was a right good blade,
As ever Turk or Spaniard made.

[348]

When all was done to the ale-house he went,
And presently his tuppence was spent;
He was so hot with fighting the dragon,
And nought could quench his thirst but a flagon.

Well now let us pray for the King and the Queen,
And eke in London that may be seen,
As many knights and as many more,
And all as good as Sir Eglamore.

Fa, lanky down, la, lanky down,
Fa la lanky down dilly.

TRADITIONAL: ENGLISH

THE ENCHANTED SHIRT

The King was sick. His cheek was red
   And his eye was clear and bright;
He ate and drank with a kingly zest,
   And peacefully snored at night.

But he said he was sick, and a king should know,
   And doctors came by the score.
They did not cure him. He cut off their heads
   And sent to the schools for more.

At last two famous doctors came,
   And one was poor as a rat,—
He had passed his life in studious toil,
   And never found time to grow fat.

The other had never looked in a book;
   His patients gave him no trouble.
If they recovered they paid him well,
   If they died their heirs paid double.

Together they looked at the royal tongue,
   As the King on his couch reclined;
In succession they thumped his august chest,
   But no trace of disease could find.

The old sage said, "You're as sound as a nut."
   "Hang him up!" roared the King in a gale,
In a ten-knot gale of royal rage.
   The other leech grew a shade pale;

But he pensively rubbed his sagacious nose,
   And thus his prescription ran—
The King will be well, if he sleeps one night
   In the Shirt of a Happy Man.

Wide o'er the realm the couriers rode,
   And fast their horses ran,
And many they saw, and to many they spoke,
   But they found no Happy Man.

They found poor men who would fain be rich
   And rich who thought they were poor;
And men who twisted their waists in stays,
   And women that short hose wore.

They saw two men by the roadside sit,
   And both bemoaned their lot;
For one had buried his wife, he said,
   And the other one had not.

At last they came to a village gate,
   A beggar lay whistling there;
He whistled and sang and laughed and rolled
   On the grass in the soft June air.

The weary couriers paused and looked
   At the scamp so blithe and gay;
And one of them said, "Heaven save you, friend!
   You seem to be happy today."

"O yes, fair sirs," the rascal laughed,
   And his voice rang free and glad,
"An idle man has so much to do
   That he never has time to be sad."

"This is our man," the courier said;
   "Our luck has led us aright.
I will give you a hundred ducats, friend,
   For the loan of your shirt tonight."

The merry blackguard lay back on the grass,
   And laughed till his face was black;
"I would do it, God wot," and he roared with the fun,
   "But I haven't a shirt to my back."

Each day to the King the reports came in
   Of his unsuccessful spies,
And the sad panorama of human woes
   Passed daily under his eyes.

And he grew ashamed of his useless life,
   And his maladies hatched in gloom;
He opened his windows and let the air
   Of the free heaven into his room.

And out he went in the world and toiled
   In his own appointed way;
And the people blessed him, the land was glad,
   And the King was well and gay.

JOHN HAY

MORTE D'ARTHUR

So all day long the noise of battle roll'd
Among the mountains by the winter sea;
Until King Arthur's table, man by man,
Had fall'n in Lyonnesse about their Lord,
King Arthur: then, because his wound was deep,
The bold Sir Bedivere uplifted him,
Sir Bedivere, the last of all his knights,
And bore him to a chapel nigh the field,
A broken chancel with a broken cross,
That stood on a dark strait of barren land.
On one side lay the Ocean, and on one
Lay a great water, and the moon was full.

    Then spake King Arthur to Sir Bedivere:
"The sequel of today unsolders all
The goodliest fellowship of famous knights
Whereof this world holds record. Such a sleep
They sleep—the men I loved. I think that we
Shall never more, at any future time,
Delight our souls with talk of knightly deeds,
Walking about the gardens and the halls
Of Camelot, as in the days that were.
I perish by this people which I made,—
Though Merlin sware that I should come again
To rule once more—but let what will be, be,

I am so deeply smitten through the helm
That without help I cannot last till morn.
Thou therefore take my brand Excalibur,
Which was my pride: for thou rememberest how
In those old days, one summer noon, an arm
Rose up from out the bosom of the lake,
Clothed in white samite, mystic, wonderful,
Holding the sword—and how I row'd across
And took it, and have worn it, like a king:
And, wheresoever I am sung or told
In aftertime, this also shall be known:
But now delay not: take Excalibur,
And fling him far into the middle mere:
Watch what thou seest, and lightly bring me word."

    To him replied the bold Sir Bedivere:
"It is not meet, Sir King, to leave thee thus,
Aidless, alone, and smitten through the helm.
A little thing may harm a wounded man.
Yet I thy hest will all perform at full,
Watch what I see, and lightly bring thee word."

    So saying, from the ruin'd shrine he stept
And in the moon athwart the place of tombs,
Where lay the mighty bones of ancient men,
Old knights, and over them the sea-wind sang
Shrill, chill, with flakes of foam. He, stepping down
By zig-zag paths, and juts of pointed rock,
Came on the shining levels of the lake.

    There drew he forth the brand Excalibur,
And o'er him, drawing it, the winter moon,

Brightening the skirts of a long cloud, ran forth
And sparkled keen with frost against the hilt:
For all the haft twinkled with diamond sparks,
Myriads of topaz-lights, and jacinth-work
Of subtlest jewelry. He gazed so long
That both his eyes were dazzled, as he stood,
This way and that dividing the swift mind,
In act to throw: but at the last it seem'd
Better to leave Excalibur conceal'd
There in the many-knotted waterflags,
That whistled stiff and dry about the marge.
So strode he back slow to the wounded king.

　　Then spake King Arthur to Sir Bedivere:
"Hast thou perform'd my mission which I gave?
What is it thou hast seen? or what hast heard?"

　　And answer made the bold Sir Bedivere:
"I heard the ripple washing in the reeds,
And the wild water lapping on the crag."

　　To whom replied King Arthur, faint and pale:
"Thou hast betray'd thy nature and thy name,
Not rendering true answer, as beseem'd
Thy fealty, nor like a noble knight:
For surer sign had follow'd, either hand,
Or voice, or else a motion of the mere.
This is a shameful thing for men to lie.
Yet now, I charge thee, quickly go again
As thou art lief and dear, and do the thing
I bade thee, watch, and lightly bring me word."

　　Then went Sir Bedivere the second time

Across the ridge, and pac'd beside the mere,
Counting the dewy pebbles, fix'd in thought;
But when he saw the wonder of the hilt,
How curiously and strangely chased, he smote
His palms together, and he cried aloud.

"And if indeed I cast the brand away,
Surely a precious thing, one worthy note,
Should thus be lost for ever from the earth,
Which might have pleas'd the eyes of many men.
What good should follow this, if this were done?
What harm, undone? deep harm to disobey,
Seeing obedience is the bond of rule.
Were it well to obey then, if a king demand
An act unprofitable, against himself?
The king is sick, and knows not what he does.
What record, or what relic of my lord
Should be to aftertime, but empty breath
And rumors of a doubt? but were this kept,
Stored in some treasure-house of mighty kings,
Someone might show it at a joust of arms,
Saying, 'King Arthur's sword, Excalibur,
Wrought by the lonely maiden of the Lake.
Nine years she wrought it, sitting in the deeps
Upon the hidden bases of the hills.'
So might some old man speak in the aftertime
To all the people, winning reverence.
But now much honor and much fame were lost,"

So spake he, clouded with his own conceit,
And hid Excalibur the second time.

And so strode back slow to the wounded King.
   Then spoke King Arthur, breathing heavily:
"What is it thou hast seen? or what hast heard?
   And answer made the bold Sir Bedivere:
"I heard the water lapping on the crag,
And the long ripple washing in the reeds."
   To whom replied King Arthur, much in wrath:
"Ah, miserable and unkind, untrue,
Unknightly, traitor-hearted! Woe is me!
Authority forgets a dying king,
Laid widow'd of the power in his eye
That bow'd the will. I see thee what thou art,
For thou, the latest-left of all my knights,
In whom should meet the offices of all,
Thou wouldst betray me for the precious hilt;
Either from lust of gold, or like a girl
Valuing the giddy pleasure of the eyes.
Yet, for a man may fail in duty twice,
And the third time may prosper, get thee hence:
But, if thou spare to fling Excalibur,
I will arise and slay thee with my hands."
   Then quickly rose Sir Bedivere, and ran,
And, leaping down the ridges lightly, plunged
Among the bulrush-beds, and clutch'd the sword,
And strongly wheel'd and threw it. The great brand
Made lightnings in the splendor of the moon,
And flashing round and round, and whirl'd in an arch,
Shot like a streamer of the northern morn,
Seen where the moving isles of winter shock

By night, with noises of the northern sea.
So flash'd and fell the brand Excalibur:
But ere he dipt the surface, rose an arm
Clothed in white samite, mystic, wonderful,
And caught him by the hilt, and brandish'd him
Three times, and drew him under in the mere.
And lightly went the other to the King.

Then spoke King Arthur, drawing thicker breath:
"Now see I by thine eyes that this is done.
Speak out: what is it thou hast heard, or seen?"

And answer made the bold Sir Bedivere:
"Sir King, I closed mine eyelids, lest the gems
Should blind my purpose, for I never saw,
Nor shall see, here or elsewhere, till I die,
Not though I live three lives of mortal men,
So great a miracle as yonder hilt.
Then with both hands I flung him, wheeling him;
But when I look'd again, behold an arm,
Clothed in white samite, mystic, wonderful,
That caught him by the hilt, and brandish'd him
Three times, and drew him under in the mere."

And answer made King Arthur, breathing hard:
"My end draws nigh; 'tis time that I were gone.
Make broad thy shoulders to receive my weight,
And bear me to the margin; yet I fear
My wound hath taken cold, and I shall die."

So saying, from the pavement he half rose,
Slowly, with pain, reclining on his arm,
And looking wistfully with wide blue eyes

[359]

As in a picture. Him Sir Bedivere
Remorsefully regarded through his tears,
And would have spoken, but he found not words,
Then took with care, and kneeling on one knee,
O'er both his shoulders drew the languid hands,
And rising, bore him through the place of tombs.

But, as he walk'd, King Arthur panted hard,
Like one that feels a nightmare on his bed
When all the house is mute. So sigh'd the King,
Muttering and murmuring at his ear, "Quick, quick!
I fear it is too late, and I shall die."
But the other swiftly strode from ridge to ridge,
Clothed with his breath, and looking as he walk'd
Larger than human on the frozen hills.
He heard the deep behind him, and a cry
Before. His own thought drove him like a goad.
Dry clash'd his harness in the icy caves
And barren chasms, and all to left and right
The bare black cliff clang'd round him, as he based
His feet on juts of slippery crag that rang
Sharp-smitten with the dint of armed heels—
And on a sudden, lo! the level lake,
And the long glories of the winter moon.

Then saw they how there hove a dusky barge,
Dark as a funeral scarf from stem to stern,
Beneath them; and descending they were ware
That all the decks were dense with stately forms
Black-stoled, black-hooded, like a dream—by these
Three Queens with crowns of gold—and from them rose

[360]

A cry that shiver'd to the tingling stars,
And, as it were one voice, an agony
Of lamentation, like a wind, that shrills
All night in a waste land, where no one comes,
Or hath come, since the making of the world.

    Then murmur'd Arthur, "Place me in the barge,"
And to the barge they came. There those three Queens
Put forth their hands, and took the King, and wept.
But she, that rose the tallest of them all
And fairest, laid his head upon her lap,
And loosed the shatter'd casque, and chafed his hands,
And call'd him by his name, complaining loud,
And dropping bitter tears against his brow
Striped with dark blood: for all his face was white
And colorless, and like the wither'd moon
Smote by the fresh beam of the springing east;
And all his greaves and cuisses dash'd with drops
Of onset; and the light and lustrous curls—
That made his forehead like a rising sun
High from the dais-throne—were parch'd with dust;
Or, clotted into points and hanging loose,
Mix'd with the knightly growth that fringed his lips.
So like a shatter'd column lay the King;
Not like that Arthur who, with lance in rest,
From spur to plume a star of tournament,
Shot through the lists at Camelot, and charged
Before the eyes of ladies and of kings.

    Then loudly cried the bold Sir Bedivere:
"Ah! my Lord Arthur, whither shall I go?

Where shall I hide my forehead and my eyes?
For now I see the true old times are dead,
When every morning brought a noble chance,
And every chance brought out a noble knight.
Such times have been not since the light that led
The holy Elders with the gift of myrrh.
But now the whole ROUND TABLE is dissolved
Which was an image of the mighty world;
And I, the last, go forth companionless,
And the days darken round me, and the years,
Among new men, strange faces, other minds."

    And slowly answer'd Arthur from the barge:
"The old order changeth, yielding place to new,
And God fulfils Himself in many ways,
Lest one good custom should corrupt the world.
Comfort thyself: what comfort is in me?
I have lived my life, and that which I have done
May He within Himself make pure! but thou,
If thou shouldst never see my face again,
Pray for my soul. More things are wrought by prayer
Than this world dreams of. Wherefore, let thy voice
Rise like a fountain for me night and day.
For what are men better than sheep or goats
That nourish a blind life within the brain,
If, knowing God, they lift not hands of prayer
Both for themselves and those who call them friend?
For so the whole round earth is every way
Bound by gold chains about the feet of God.
But now farewell. I am going a long way

With these thou seest—if indeed I go—
(For all my mind is clouded with a doubt)
To the island-valley of Avilion;
Where falls not hail, or rain, or any snow,
Nor ever wind blows loudly; but it lies
Deep-meadow'd, happy, fair with orchard-lawns
And bowery hollows crown'd with summer sea,
Where I will heal me of my grievous wound."
   So said he, and the barge with oar and sail
Moved from the brink, like some full-breasted swan
That, fluting a wild carol ere her death,
Ruffles her pure cold plume, and takes the flood
With swarthy webs. Long stood Sir Bedivere
Revolving many memories, till the hull
Looked one black dot against the verge of dawn,
And on the mere the wailing died away.

ALFRED TENNYSON

ROBIN HOOD AND ALAN A DALE

Come listen to me, you gallants so free,
   All you that love mirth for to hear,
And I will you tell of a bold outlaw,
   That lived in Nottinghamshire.

As Robin Hood in the forest stood,
   All under the green-wood tree,
There was he ware of a brave young man,
   As fine as fine might be.

The youngster was clothed in scarlet red,
   In scarlet fine and gay,
And he did frisk it over the plain,
   And chanted a roundelay.

As Robin Hood next morning stood,
   Amongst the leaves so gay,
There did he espy the same young man
   Come drooping along the way.

The scarlet he wore the day before,
   It was clean cast away;
And every step he fetcht a sigh,
   "Alack and a well a day!"

Then steppéd forth brave Little John,
  And Much, the miller's son,
Which made the young man bend his bow,
  When as he saw them come.

"Stand off, stand off!" the young man said,
  "What is your will with me?"—
"You must come before our master straight,
  Under yon green-wood tree."

And when he came bold Robin before,
  Robin askt him courteously,
"O hast thou any money to spare,
  For my merry men and me?"

"I have no money," the young man said,
  "But five shillings and a ring;
And that I have kept this seven long years,
  To have it at my wedding.

"Yesterday I should have married a maid,
  But she is now from me tane,
And chosen to be an old knight's delight,
  Whereby my poor heart is slain."

"What is thy name?" then said Robin Hood,
  "Come tell me, without any fail."—
"By the faith of my body," then said the young man,
  "My name it is Alan a Dale."

[365]

"What wilt thou give me," said Robin Hood,
  "In ready gold or fee,
To help thee to thy true-love again,
  And deliver her unto thee?"

"I have no money," then quoth the young man,
  "No ready gold nor fee,
But I will swear upon a book
  Thy true servant for to be."—

"But how many miles to thy true-love?
  Come tell me without any guile."—
"By the faith of my body," then said the young man,
  "It is but five little mile."

Then Robin he hasted over the plain,
  He did neither stint nor lin,
Until he came unto the church
  Where Alan should keep his wedding.

"What dost thou do here?" the Bishop he said,
  "I prithee now tell to me:"
"I am a bold harper," quoth Robin Hood,
  "And the best in the north countrey."

"O welcome, O welcome!" the Bishop he said,
  "That musick best pleaseth me."—
"You shall have no musick," quoth Robin Hood,
  "Till the bride and the bridegroom I see."

With that came in a wealthy knight,
  Which was both grave and old,
And after him a finikin lass,
  Did shine like glistering gold.

"This is no fit match," quoth bold Robin **Hood,**
  "That you do seem to make here;
For since we are come unto the church,
  The bride she shall chuse her own dear."

Then Robin Hood put his horn to his **mouth,**
  And blew blasts two or three;
When four and twenty bowmen bold
  Come leaping over the lee.

And when they came into the churchyard,
  Marching all on a row,
The first man was Alan a Dale,
  To give bold Robin his bow.

"This is thy true-love," Robin he said,
  "Young Alan, as I hear say;
And you shall be married at this same **time,**
  Before we depart away."

"That shall not be!" the Bishop he said,
  "For thy word it shall not stand;
They shall be three times askt in the **church,**
  As the law is of our land."

[367]

Robin Hood pull'd off the Bishop's coat,
   And put it upon Little John;
"By the faith of my body," then Robin said,
   "This cloath doth make thee a man."

When Little John went into the quire,
   The people began for to laugh;
He askt them seven times in the church,
   Least three should not be enough.

"Who gives me this maid?" then said Little John;
   Quoth Robin, "That do I!
And he that doth take her from Alan a Dale
   Full dearly he shall her buy."

And thus having ended this merry wedding,
   The bride lookt as fresh as a queen,
And so they return'd to the merry green-wood,
   Amongst the leaves so green.

TRADITIONAL: ENGLISH

THE DEATH OF ROBIN HOOD

When Robin Hood and Little John
  Down a-down, a-down, a-down
  Went o'er yon bank of broom,
Said Robin Hood bold to Little John,
  "We have shot for many a pound
  Hey, down a-down, a down!

"But I am not able to shoot one shot more,
  My broad arrows will not flee;
But I have a cousin lives down below,
  Please God, she will bleed me.

"I will never eat nor drink," he said,
  "Nor meat will do me good,
Till I have been to merry Kirkleys
  My veins for to let blood.

"The dame prior is my aunt's daughter,
  And nigh unto my kin;
I know she wo'ld me no harm this day,
  For all the world to win."

"That I rede not," said Little John,
  "Master, by th'assent of me,

Without half a hundred of your best bowmen
    You take to go with yee."—

"An' thou be afear'd, thou Little John,
    At home I rede thee be."—
"An' you be wroth, my deare master,
    You shall never hear more of me."

Now Robin is gone to merry Kirkleys
    And knockéd upon the pin:
Up then rose Dame Prioress
    And let good Robin in.

Then Robin gave to Dame Prioress
    Twenty pound in gold,
And bade her spend while that did last,
    She sho'ld have more when she wo'ld.

"Will you please to sit down, cousin Robin,
    And drink some beer with me?"—
"No, I will neither eat nor drink
    Till I am blooded· by thee."

Down then came Dame Prioress
    Down she came in that ilk,
With a pair of blood-irons in her hands,
    Were wrappéd all in silk.

"Set a chafing-dish to the fire," she said,
    "And strip thou up thy sleeve."

[370]

—I hold him but an unwise man
  That will no warning 'leeve!

She laid the blood-irons to Robin's vein,
  Alack, the more pitye!
And pierc'd the vein, and let out the blood
  That full red was to see.

And first it bled the thick, thick blood,
  And afterwards the thin,
And well then wist good Robin Hood
  Treason there was within.

And there she blooded bold Robin Hood
  While one drop of blood would run;
There did he bleed the live-long day,
  Until the next at noon.

He bethought him then of a casement there,
  Being locked up in the room;
But was so weak he could not leap,
  He could not get him down.

He bethought him then of his bugle-horn,
  That hung low down to his knee;
He set his horn unto his mouth,
  And blew out weak blasts three.

Then Little John he heard the horn
  Where he sat under a tree:

"I fear my master is now near dead,
    He blows so wearilye."

Little John is gone to merry Kirkleys,
    As fast as he can dree;
And when he came to merry Kirkleys,
    He broke locks two or three:

Until he came bold Robin to see,
    Then he fell on his knee;
"A boon, a boon!" cries Little John,
    "Master, I beg of thee!"

"What is that boon," said Robin Hood,
    "Little John, thou begs of me?"—
"It is to burn fair Kirkleys-hall,
    And all their nunnerye."

"Now nay, now nay," quoth Robin Hood,
    "That boon I'll not grant thee;
I never hurt woman in all my life,
    Nor men in their company.

"I never hurt maid in all my time,
    Nor at mine end shall it be;
But give me my bent bow in my hand,
    And a broad arrow I'll let flee;
And where this arrow is taken up
    There shall my grave digg'd be.

"But lay me a green sod under my head,
    And another at my feet;
And lay my bent bow at my side,
    Which was my music sweet;
And make my grave of gravel and green,
    Which is most right and meet.

"Let me have length and breadth enough,
    And under my head a sod;
That they may say when I am dead,
    —Here lies bold Robin Hood!"

TRADITIONAL: ENGLISH

KING JOHN AND THE ABBOT
OF CANTERBURY

An ancient story I'll tell you anon
Of a notable prince, that was calléd King John;
And he ruléd England with maine and with might,
For he did great wrong, and maintein'd little right.

And I'll tell you a story, a story so merrye,
Concerning the Abbot of Canterburye;
How, for his house-keeping and high renowne,
They rode poste for him to fair London towne.

An hundred men, the King did heare say,
The Abbot kept in his house every day;
And fifty golde chaynes, without any doubt,
In velvet coates waited the Abbot about.

"How now, Father Abbot, I heare it of thee
Thou keepest a farre better house than mee,
And for thy house-keeping and high renowne,
I feare thou work'st treason against my crown."

"My liege," quo' the Abbot, "I would it were knowne,
I never spend nothing, but what is my owne;
And I trust your Grace will doe me no deere
For spending of my owne true-gotten geere."

"Yes, yes, Father Abbot, thy fault it is highe,
And now for the same thou needest must dye;
For except thou canst answer me questions three,
Thy head shall be smitten from thy bodie.

"And first," quo' the King, "when I'm in this stead,
With my crowne of golde so faire on my head,
Among all my liege-men so noble of birthe,
Thou must tell me to one penny what I am worthe.

"Secondlye, tell me, without any doubt,
How soone I may ride the whole worlde about.
And at the third question thou must not shrinke,
But tell me here truly what I do thinke."—

"O these are hard questions for my shallow witt,
Nor I cannot answer your Grace as yet:
But if you will give me but three weekes space,
I'll do my endeavor to answer your Grace.

"Now three weekes space to thee will I give,
And that is the longest time thou hast to live;
For if thou dost not answer my questions three,
Thy lands and thy livings are forfeit to mee."

Away rode the Abbot all sad at that word,
And he rode to Cambridge, and Oxenford;
But never a doctor there was so wise,
That could with his learning an answer devise.

Then home rode the Abbot of comfort so cold,
And he mett with his shepheard a-going to fold:
"How now, my lord Abbot, you are welcome home;
What newes do you bring us from good King John?"—

"Sad newes, sad newes, shepheard, I must give;
That I have but three days more to live:
For if I do not answer him questions three,
My head will be smitten from my bodie.

"The first is to tell him there in that stead,
With his crowne of golde so fair on his head,
Among all his liege-men so noble of birthe,
To within one penny of what he is worthe.

"The seconde, to tell him, without any doubt,
How soone he may ride this whole worlde about:
And at the third question I must not shrinke,
But tell him there truly what he does thinke."—

"Now cheare up, sire Abbot, did you never hear yet,
That a fool he may learn a wise man witt?
Lend me horse, and serving-men, and your apparel,
And I'll ride to London to answere your quarrel.

"Nay frowne not, if it hath bin told unto mee,
I am like your lordship, as ever may bee:
And if you will but lend me your gowne,
There is none shall knowe us at fair London towne."—

[376]

"Now horses and serving-men thou shalt have,
With sumptuous array most gallant and brave,
With crozier, and miter, and rochet, and cope,
Fit to appeare 'fore our Father the Pope."—

"Now welcome, sir Abbot," the King he did say,
" 'Tis well thou'rt come back to keepe thy day;
For and if thou canst answer my questions three,
Thy life and thy living both savéd shall bee.

"And first, when thou seest me here in this stead,
With my crown of golde so fair on my head,
Among all my liege-men so noble of birthe,
Tell me to one penny what I am worthe."—

"For thirty pence our Saviour was sold
Amonge the false Jewes, as I have bin told;
And twenty-nine is the worthe of thee,
For I thinke thou art one penny worser than hee."

The King he laughed, and swore by St. Bittel,
"I did not thinke I had been worthe so littel!
—Now secondly tell me, without any doubt,
How soone I may ride this whole world about."—

"You must rise with the sun, and ride with the same,
Until the next morning he riseth againe;
And then your Grace need not make any doubt,
But in twenty-four hours you'll ride it about."

[377]

The King he laughed, and swore by St. Jone,
"I did not think it could be gone so soone!
—Now from the third question thou must not shrinke,
But tell me here truly what I do thinke."—

"Yea, that shall I do, and make your Grace merry:
You thinke I'm the Abbot of Canterburye;
But I'm his poor shepheard, as plain you may see,
That am come to beg pardon for him and for mee."

The King he laughed, and swore by the Masse,
"I'll make thee Lord Abbot this day in his place!"—
"Now naye, my liege, be not in such speede,
For alacke I can neither write, ne reade."—

"Four nobles a weeke, then, I will give thee
For this merry jest thou hast showne unto mee;
And tell the old Abbot when thou comest home,
Thou hast brought him a pardon from good King John."

TRADITIONAL: ENGLISH

THE GLOVE AND THE LIONS

King Francis was a hearty king, and loved a royal sport,
And one day, as his lions fought, sat looking on the court.
The nobles filled the benches, with the ladies in their pride,
And 'mongst them sat the Count de Lorge, with one for
      whom he sighed:
And truly 'twas a gallant thing to see that crowning show,
Valor and love, and a king above, and the royal beasts below.

Ramped and roared the lions, with horrid laughing jaws;
They bit, they glared, gave blows like beams, a wind went
      with their paws;
With wallowing might and stifled roar they rolled on one
      another;
Till all the pit with sand and mane was in a thunderous
      smother;
The bloody foam above the bars came whisking through the
      air;
Said Francis then, "Faith, gentlemen, we're better here than
      there."

De Lorge's love o'erheard the King, a beauteous likely dame,
With smiling lips and sharp bright eyes, which always seemed
      the same;
She thought, The Count my lover is brave as brave can be;

He surely would do wondrous things to show his love of me;
King, ladies, lovers, all look on; the occasion is divine;
I'll drop my glove, to prove his love; great glory will be mine.

She dropped her glove, to prove his love, then looked at him
    and smiled;
He bowed, and in a moment leaped among the lions wild;
The leap was quick, return was quick, he has regained his
    place,
He threw the glove, but not with love, right in the lady's face.
"By Heaven," said Francis, "rightly done!" and he rose from
    where he sat;
"No love," quoth he, "but vanity, sets love a task like that."

LEIGH HUNT

THE LADY OF SHALOTT

On either side the river lie
Long fields of barley and of rye,
That clothe the wold and meet the sky;
And thro' the fields the road runs by
    To many-tower'd Camelot;
And up and down the people go,
Gazing where the lilies blow
Round an island there below,
    The island of Shalott.

Willows whiten, aspens quiver,
Little breezes dusk and shiver
Thro' the wave that runs for ever
By the island in the river
    Flowing down to Camelot.
Four gray walls, and four gray towers,
Overlook a space of flowers,
And the silent isle imbowers
    The Lady of Shalott.

By the margin, willow-veil'd,
Slide the heavy barges trail'd
By slow horses; and unhail'd

The shallop flitteth silken-sail'd
  Skimming down to Camelot:
But who hath seen her wave her hand?
Or at the casement seen her stand?
Or is she known in all the land,
  The Lady of Shalott?

Only reapers, reaping early
In among the bearded barley,
Hear a song that echoes cheerly
From the river winding clearly,
  Down to tower'd Camelot:
And by the moon the reaper weary,
Piling sheaves in uplands airy,
Listening, whispers " 'Tis the fairy
  Lady of Shalott."

PART II

There she weaves by night and day
A magic web with colors gay.
She has heard a whisper say,
A curse is on her if she stay
  To look down to Camelot.
She knows not what the curse may be,
And so she weaveth steadily,
And little other care hath she,
  The Lady of Shalott.

And moving thro' a mirror clear
That hangs before her all the year,

[382]

Shadows of the world appear.
There she sees the highway near
    Winding down to Camelot:
There the river eddy whirls,
And there the surly village-churls,
And the red cloaks of market girls,
    Pass onward from Shalott.

Sometimes a troup of damsels glad,
  An abbot on an ambling pad,
Sometimes a curly shepherd-lad,
Or long-hair'd page in crimson clad,
    Goes by to tower'd Camelot;
And sometimes through the mirror blue
The knights come riding two and two:
She hath no loyal knight and true,
    The Lady of Shalott.

But in her web she still delights
To weave the mirror's magic sights,
For often thro' the silent nights
A funeral, with plumes and lights,
    And music, went to Camelot:
Or when the moon was overhead,
Came two young lovers lately wed;
"I am half sick of shadows," said
    The Lady of Shalott.

[383]

PART III

A bow-shot from her bower-eaves,
He rode between the barley-sheaves,
The sun came dazzling thro' the leaves,
And flamed upon the brazen greaves
    Of bold Sir Lancelot.
A red-cross knight for ever kneel'd
To a lady in his shield,
That sparkled on the yellow field,
    Beside remote Shalott.

The gemmy bridle glitter'd free,
Like to some branch of stars we see
Hung in the golden Galaxy.
The bridle bells rang merrily
    As he rode down to Camelot:
And from his blazon'd baldric slung
A mighty silver bugle hung,
And as he rode his armor rung,
    Beside remote Shalott.

All in the blue unclouded weather
Thick-jewell'd shone the saddle-leather,
The helmet and the helmet-feather
Burn'd like one burning flame together,
    As he rode down to Camelot.
As often thro' the purple night,
Below the starry clusters bright,
Some bearded meteor, trailing light,
    Moves over still Shalott.

[384]

His broad clear brow in sunlight glow'd;
On burnish'd hooves his war-horse trode;
From underneath his helmet flow'd
His coal-black curls as on he rode,
    As he rode down to Camelot.
From the bank and from the river
He flash'd into the crystal mirror,
"Tirra lirra," by the river
    Sang Sir Lancelot.

She left the web, she left the loom,
She made three paces thro' the room,
She saw the water-lily bloom,
She saw the helmet and the plume,
    She look'd down to Camelot.
Out flew the web and floated wide;
The mirror crack'd from side to side;
"The curse is come upon me!" cried
    The Lady of Shalott.

PART IV

In the stormy east-wind straining,
The pale yellow woods were waning,
The broad stream in his banks complaining,
Heavily the low sky raining
    Over tower'd Camelot;
Down she came and found a boat
Beneath a willow left afloat,
And round about the prow she wrote
    The Lady of Shalott.

And down the river's dim expanse—
Like some bold seer in a trance,
Seeing all his own mischance—
With a glassy countenance
  Did she look to Camelot.
And at the closing of the day
She loosed the chain, and down she lay;
The broad stream bore her far away,
  The Lady of Shalott.

Lying, robed in snowy white
That loosely flew to left and right—
The leaves upon her falling light—
Thro' the noises of the night
  She floated down to Camelot:
And as the boat-head wound along
The willowy hills and fields among,
They heard her singing her last song,
  The Lady of Shalott.

Heard a carol, mournful, holy,
Chanted loudly, chanted lowly,
Till her blood was frozen slowly,
And her eyes were darken'd wholly,
  Turn'd to tower'd Camelot;
For ere she reach'd upon the tide
The first house by the water-side,
Singing in her song she died,
  The Lady of Shalott.

Under tower and balcony,
By garden-wall and gallery,
A gleaming shape she floated by,
Dead-pale between the houses high,
    Silent into Camelot.
Out upon the wharfs they came,
Knight and burgher, lord and dame,
And round the prow they read her name,
    The Lady of Shalott.

Who is this? and what is here?
And in the lighted palace near
Died the sound of royal cheer;
And they cross'd themselves for fear,
    All the knights at Camelot:
But Lancelot mused a little space;
He said, "She has a lovely face;
God in His mercy lend her grace,
    The Lady of Shalott."

ALFRED TENNYSON

POEMS ABOUT THE SEA

THE SANDS OF DEE

"O Mary, go and call the cattle home,
   And call the cattle home,
   And call the cattle home,
     Across the sands of Dee";
The western wind was wild and dank with foam,
     And all alone went she.

The western tide crept up along the sand,
   And o'er and o'er the sand,
   And round and round the sand,
     As far as eye could see.
The rolling mist came down and hid the land:
     And never home came she.

"O is it weed, or fish, or floating hair—
   A tress of golden hair,
   A drowned maiden's hair,
     Above the nets at sea?"
Was never salmon yet that shone so fair
     Among the stakes of Dee.

They rowed her in across the rolling foam,
   The cruel crawling foam,

The cruel hungry foam,
   To her grave beside the sea.
But still the boatmen hear her call the cattle home,
   Across the sands of Dee.

CHARLES KINGSLEY

THE GOLDEN VANITY

There was a gallant ship, and a gallant ship was she,
  Eck iddle du, and the Lowlands low;
And she was called the Goulden Vanitie.
  As she sailed to the Lowlands low.

She had not sailed a league, a league but only three,
When she came up with a French gallee.
  As she sailed to the Lowlands low.

Out spoke the little cabin-boy, out spoke he;
"What will you give me if I sink that French gallee?
  As ye sail to the Lowlands low."

"I'll give thee gold, and I'll give thee fee,
And my eldest daughter thy wife shall be
  If you sink her off the Lowlands low."

"Then row me up ticht in a black bull's skin,
And throw me oer deck-buird, sink I or swim.
  As ye sail to the Lowlands low."

So they've rowed him up ticht in a black bull's skin,
And have thrown him oer deck-buird, sink he or swim.
  As they sail to the Lowlands low.

About, and about, and about went he,
Until he came up with the French gallee.
  As they sailed to the Lowlands low.

O some were playing cards, and some were playing dice,
The boy he had an auger bored holes two at twice;
He let the water in, and it dazzled in their eyes,
  As they sailed to the Lowlands low.

Then some they ran with cloaks, and some they ran with
            caps,
To see if they could stap the saut-water draps.
  As they sailed to the Lowlands low.

About, and about, and about went he,
Until he cam back to the Goulden Vanitie.
  As they sailed to the Lowlands low.

"Now throw me oer a rope and pu me up on buird,
And prove unto me as guid as your word,
  As we sail to the Lowlands low."

"We'll no throw ye oer a rope, nor pu ye up on buird,
Nor prove unto you as guid as our word.
  As we sail to the Lowlands low."

"You promised me gold, and you promised me fee,
Your eldest daughter my wife she should be.
  As we sail to the Lowlands low."

[393]

"You shall have gold, and you shall have fee,
But my eldest daughter your wife shall never be.
  As we sail to the Lowlands low."

Out spoke the little cabin-boy, out spoke he;
"Then hang me, I'll sink ye as I sunk the French gallee.
  As ye sail to the Lowlands low."

The boy he swam round all by the starboard side,
  Eck iddle du, and the Lowlands low;
When they pu'd him up on buird it's there he soon died;
  Eck iddle du, and the Lowlands low;
They threw him oer deck-buird to go down with the tide,
  And sink off the Lowlands low.

TRADITIONAL: ENGLISH

ONE FRIDAY MORN

One Friday morn when we set sail,
  Not very far from land,
We there did espy a fair pretty maid
  With a comb and a glass in her hand, her hand, her hand,
  With a comb and a glass in her hand.
    While the raging seas did roar,
      And the stormy winds did blow,
    While we jolly sailor boys were up in the top,
      And the land-lubbers lying down below, below,
      below,
      And the land-lubbers lying down below.

Then up starts the captain of our gallant ship,
  And a brave young man was he:
"I've a wife and a child in fair Bristol town,
  But a widow I fear she will be."
    And the raging seas did roar,
      And the stormy winds did blow.

Then up starts the mate of our gallant ship,
  And a bold young man was he:
"Oh! I have a wife in fair Portsmouth town,
  But a widow I fear she will be."
    And the raging seas did roar,
      And the stormy winds did blow.

Then up starts the cook of our gallant ship,
    And a gruff old soul was he:
"Oh! I have a wife in fair Plymouth town,
    But a widow I fear she will be."
    And the raging seas did roar,
      And the stormy winds did blow.

And then up spoke the little cabin-boy,
    And a pretty little boy was he;
"Oh! I am more grieved for my daddy and my mammy
    Than you for your wives all three."
    And the raging seas did roar,
      And the stormy winds did blow.

Then three times round went our gallant ship,
    And three times round went she;
And three times round went our gallant ship,
    And she sank to the bottom of the sea. . . .
    And the raging seas did roar,
      And the stormy winds did blow.
    While we jolly sailor-boys were up into the top,
      And the land-lubbers lying down below, below,
      below,
      And the land-lubbers lying down below.

AUTHOR UNKNOWN

THE WRECK OF THE HESPERUS

It was the schooner Hesperus,
That sailed the wintry sea;
And the skipper had taken his little daughter,
To bear him company.

Blue were her eyes as the fairy flax,
Her cheeks like the dawn of day,
And her bosom white as the hawthorn buds
That ope in the month of May.

The skipper he stood beside the helm,
His pipe was in his mouth,
And he watched how the veering flaw did blow
The smoke now West, now South.

Then up and spake an old Sailor,
Had sailed to the Spanish Main,
"I pray thee, put into yonder port,
For I fear a hurricane.

"Last night the moon had a golden ring,
And tonight no moon we see!"
The skipper, he blew a whiff from his pipe,
And a scornful laugh laughed he.

Colder and louder blew the wind,
A gale from the Northeast;
The snow fell hissing in the brine,
And the billows frothed like yeast.

Down came the storm, and smote amain
The vessel in its strength;
She shuddered and paused, like a frightened steed,
Then leaped her cable's length.

"Come hither! come hither! my little daughter,
And do not tremble so;
For I can weather the roughest gale
That ever wind did blow."

He wrapped her warm in his seaman's coat
Against the stinging blast;
He cut a rope from a broken spar,
And bound her to the mast.

"O father! I hear the church-bells ring,
Oh say, what may it be?"
" 'Tis a fog-bell on a rock-bound coast!"
And he steered for the open sea.

"O father! I hear the sound of guns,
Oh say, what may it be?"
"Some ship in distress, that cannot live
In such an angry sea!"

"Oh father! I see a gleaming light,
Oh say, what may it be?"
But the father answered never a word,—
A frozen corpse was he.

Lashed to the helm, all stiff and stark,
With his face turned to the skies,
The lantern gleamed through the gleaming snow
On his fixed and glassy eyes.

Then the maiden clasped her hands and prayed
That saved she might be;
And she thought of Christ, who stilled the waves
On the Lake of Galilee.

And fast through the midnight dark and drear,
Through the whistling sleet and snow,
Like a sheeted ghost, the vessel swept
Towards the reef of Norman's Woe.

And ever the fitful gusts between
A sound came from the land;
It was the sound of the trampling surf,
On the rocks and the hard sea-sand.

The breakers were right beneath her bows,
She drifted a dreary wreck,
And a whooping billow swept the crew
Like icicles from her deck.

She struck where the white and fleecy waves
Looked soft as carded wool,
But the cruel rocks, they gored her side
Like the horns of an angry bull.

Her rattling shrouds, all sheathed in ice,
With the masts went by the board;
Like a vessel of glass, she stove and sank,
Ho! Ho! the breakers roared.

At daybreak, on the bleak sea-beach,
A fisherman stood aghast,
To see the form of a maiden fair,
Lashed close to a drifting mast!

The salt sea was frozen on her breast,
The salt tears in her eyes;
And he saw her hair, like the brown sea-weed,
On the billows fall and rise.

Such was the wreck of the Hesperus,
In the midnight and the snow!
Christ save us all from a death like this,
On the reef of Norman's Woe!

HENRY WADSWORTH LONGFELLOW

SIR PATRICK SPENS

The King sits in Dunfermline town,
   Drinking the blude-red wine:
"O whaur will I get a skeely skipper
   To sail this new ship o' mine?"

O up and spake an eldern knight,
   Sat at the King's right knee:
"Sir Patrick Spens is the best sailor
   That ever sailed the sea."

Our King has written a braid letter
   And sealed it wi' his hand,
And sent it to Sir Patrick Spens,
   Was walking on the strand.

"To Noroway, to Noroway,
   To Noroway o'er the faem;
The King's daughter to Noroway,
   'Tis thou maun bring her hame."

The first word that Sir Patrick read,
   Sae loud, loud lauchéd he;
The neist word that Sir Patrick read,
   The tear blinded his ee.

"O wha is this has done this deed,
    And tauld the King of me,
To send us out at this time o' year
    To sail upon the sea?

"Be it wind, be it weet, be it hail, be it sleet,
    Our ship must sail the faem;
The King's daughter to Noroway,
    'Tis we must bring her hame."

They hoysed their sails on Monday morn
    Wi' a' the speed they may;
They hae landed in Noroway
    Upon a Wodensday.

They hadna been a week, a week,
    In Noroway but twae,
When that the lords of Noroway
    Began aloud to say:

"Ye Scottishmen spend a' our King's goud
    And a' our Queenis fee."
"Ye lie, ye lie, ye liars loud,
    Fu' loud I hear ye lie!

"For I brought as mickle white monie
    As gane my men and me,
And I brought a half-fou o' gude red goud
    Out-o'er the sea wi' me.

Mak' ready, mak' ready, my merry men a'!
   Our gude ship sails the morn."
"Now ever alake, my master dear,
   I fear a deadly storm.

"I saw the new moon late yestreen
   Wi' the auld moon in her arm;
And if we gang to sea, master,
   I fear we'll come to harm."

They hadna sailed but a league, a league,
   A league but barely three,
When the lift grew dark, and the wind blew loud,
   And gurly grew the sea.

"O where will I get a gude sailor
   To tak' the helm in hand,
Till I gae up to the tall topmast
   To see if I can spy land?"

"O here am I, a sailor gude,
   To tak' the helm in hand,
Till you gae up to the tall topmast;
   But I fear you'll ne'er spy land."

He hadna gone a step, a step,
   A step but barely ane,
When a bolt flew out o' our goodly ship,
   And the salt sea it came in.

[403]

"Gae fetch a web o' the silken claith,
    Anither o' the twine,
And wap them into our ship's side,
    And letna the sea come in."

They fetched a web o' the silken claith,
    Anither o' the twine,
And they wapped them round that gude ship's side,
    But still the sea cam' in.

O laith, laith were our gude Scots lords
    To weet their milk-white hands;
But lang ere a' the play was ower
    They wat their gowden bands.

O laith, laith were our gude Scots lords
    To weet their cork-heeled shoon;
But lang ere a' the play was played
    They wat their hats aboon.

O lang, lang may the ladies sit
    Wi' their fans intill their hand,
Before they see Sir Patrick Spens
    Come sailing to the strand!

And lang, lang may the maidens sit
    Wi' their goud kames in their hair,
A' waiting for their ain dear loves!
    For them they'll see nae mair.

Half ower, half ower to Aberdour,
  It's fifty fathoms deep,
And there lies gude Sir Patrick Spens
  Wi' the Scots lords at his feet.

TRADITIONAL: SCOTS

THE INCHCAPE ROCK

No stir in the air, no stir in the sea,
The ship was as still as she could be;
Her sails from heaven received no motion,
Her keel was steady in the ocean.

Without either sign or sound of their shock,
The waves flow'd over the Inchcape Rock;
So little they rose, so little they fell,
They did not move the Inchcape bell.

The good Abbot of Aberbrothok
Had placed that bell on the Inchcape Rock;
On a buoy in the storm it floated and swung,
And over the waves its warning rung.

When the rock was hid by the surge's swell,
The mariners heard the warning bell:
And then they knew the perilous rock,
And blest the Abbot of Aberbrothok.

The sun in heaven was shining gay,
All things were joyful on that day;
The sea-birds scream'd as they wheel'd around,
And there was joyance in their sound.

The buoy of the Inchcape bell was seen,
A darker speck on the ocean green;
Sir Ralph the Rover walk'd his deck,
And he fixed his eye on the darker speck.

He felt the cheering power of spring,
It made him whistle, it made him sing;
His heart was mirthful to excess—
But the Rover's mirth was wickedness.

His eyes were on the Inchcape float:
Quoth he, "My men, put out the boat,
And row me to the Inchcape Rock,
And I'll plague the Abbot of Aberbrothok."

The boat is lower'd, the boatmen row,
And to the Inchcape Rock they go;
Sir Ralph bent over from the boat,
And he cut the bell from the Inchcape float.

Down sank the bell with a gurgling sound—
The bubbles rose and burst around;
Quoth Sir Ralph, "The next who comes to the Rock
Won't bless the Abbot of Aberbrothok."

Sir Ralph the Rover sail'd away;
He scoured the seas for many a day;
And, now grown rich with plunder'd store,
He steers his course for Scotland's shore.

So thick a haze o'erspreads the sky,
They cannot see the sun on high;
The wind hath blown a gale all day,
At evening it hath died away.

On the deck the Rover takes his stand,
So dark it is they see no land.
Quoth Sir Ralph, "It will be lighter soon,
For there is the dawn of the rising moon."

"Canst hear," said one, "the breakers roar?
For methinks we should be near the shore.
Now where we are I cannot tell,
But I wish I could hear the Inchcape bell."

They hear no sound—the swell is strong;
Though the wind hath fallen they drift along
Till the vessel strikes with a shivering shock—
"Mercy! it is the Inchcape Rock!"

Sir Ralph the Rover tore his hair,
And beat his breast in his despair:
The waves rush in on every side,
And the ship sinks down beneath the tide.

ROBERT SOUTHEY

THE COASTS OF HIGH BARBARY

Look ahead, look astern, look the weather and the lee.
    Blow high! Blow low! and so sailed we.
I see a wreck to windward and a lofty ship to lee,
    A-sailing down all on the coasts of High Barbary.

"Then hail her," our captain he called o'er the side,
    Blow high! Blow low! and so sailed we.
"O are you a pirate or a man-o'-war?" cried he.
    A-sailing down all on the coasts of High Barbary.

"O are you a pirate or a man-o'-war" cried we.
    Blow high! Blow low! and so sailed we.
"O no! I'm not a pirate, but a man-o'-war," cried he.
    A-sailing down all on the coasts of High Barbary.

"Then back up your topsails and heave your vessel to,"
    Blow high! Blow low! and so sailed we.
"For we have got some letters to be carried home by you."
    A-sailing down all on the coasts of High Barbary.

"We'll back up our topsails and heave our vessel to,"
    Blow high! Blow low! and so sailed we.
"But only in some harbor and along the side of you."
    A-sailing down all on the coasts of High Barbary.

For broadside, for broadside, they fought all on the main,
 Blow high! Blow low! and so sailed we.
Until at last the frigate shot the pirate's mast away.
 A-sailing down all on the coasts of High Barbary.

"For quarters, for quarters!" the saucy pirate cried,
 Blow high! Blow low! and so sailed we.
The quarters that we showed them was to sink them in the
   tide.
 A-sailing down all on the coasts of High Barbary.

With cutlass and with gun, O we fought for hours three;
 Blow high! Blow low! and so sailed we.
The ship it was their coffin, and their grave it was the sea.
 A-sailing down all on the coasts of High Barbary.

But, oh, it was a cruel sight, and grievéd us full sore,
 Blow high! Blow low! and so sailed we.
To see them all a-drowning as they tried to swim to shore,
 A-sailing down all on the coasts of High Barbary.

       TRADITIONAL: ENGLISH

SIR HUMPHREY GILBERT

Southward with fleet of ice
  Sailed the corsair Death;
Wild and fast blew the blast,
  And the east-wind was his breath.

His lordly ships of ice
  Glisten in the sun;
On each side, like pennons wide,
  Flashing crystal streamlets run.

His sails of white sea-mist
  Dripped with silver rain;
But where he passed there were cast
  Leaden shadows o'er the main.

Eastward from Campobello
  Sir Humphrey Gilbert sailed;
Three days or more seaward he bore,
  Then, alas! the land-wind failed.

Alas! the land-wind failed,
  And ice-cold grew the night;
And nevermore, on sea or shore,
  Should Sir Humphrey see the light.

He sat upon the deck,
   The Book was in his hand;
"Do not fear! Heaven is as near,"
   He said, "by water as by land!"

In the first watch of the night,
   Without a signal's sound,
Out of the sea, mysteriously,
   The fleet of Death rose all around.

The moon and the evening star
   Were hanging in the shrouds;
Every mast, as it passed,
   Seemed to rake the passing clouds.

They grappled with their prize,
   At midnight black and cold!
As of a rock was the shock;
   Heavily the ground-swell rolled.

Southward through day and dark,
   They drift in close embrace,
With mist and rain, o'er the open main,
   Yet there seems no change of pace.

Southward, forever southward,
   They drift through dark and day;
And like a dream, in the Gulf-Stream
   Sinking, vanish all away.

HENRY WADSWORTH LONGFELLOW

POEMS ABOUT ANIMALS

THE SPIDER AND THE FLY

"Will you walk into my parlor?" said the Spider to the Fly,
" 'Tis the prettiest little parlor that ever you did spy;
The way into my parlor is up a winding stair,
And I have many curious things to show when you are there."
"Oh no, no," said the little Fly, "to ask me is in vain;
For who goes up your winding stair can ne'er come down
      again."

"I'm sure you must be weary, dear, with soaring up so high;
Will you rest upon my little bed?" said the Spider to the Fly.
"There are pretty curtains drawn around, the sheets are fine
      and thin;
And if you like to rest awhile, I'll snugly tuck you in!"
"Oh no, no," said the little Fly, "for I've often heard it said
They never wake again, who sleep upon your bed!"

Said the cunning Spider to the Fly, "Dear friend, what can I
      do
To prove the warm affection I've always felt for you?
I have within my pantry, good store of all that's nice;
I'm sure you're very welcome—will you please to take a
      slice?"
"Oh no, no," said the little Fly, "kind sir, that cannot be,
I've heard what's in your pantry, and I do not wish to see!"

"Sweet creature," said the Spider, "you're witty and you're
      wise;
How handsome are your gauzy wings, how brilliant are your
      eyes!
I have a little looking-glass upon my parlor shelf;
If you'll step in one moment dear, you shall behold yourself."
"I thank you, gentle sir," she said, "for what you're pleased
      to say,
And bidding you good-morning now, I'll call another day."

The Spider turned him round about, and went into his den,
For well he knew the silly Fly would soon be back again;
So he wove a subtle web in a little corner sly,
And set his table ready to dine upon the Fly.
Then he came out to his door again, and merrily did sing,
"Come hither, hither, pretty Fly, with the pearl and silver
      wing;
Your robes are green and purple, there's a crest upon your
      head;
Your eyes are like the diamond bright, but mine are dull as
      lead."

Alas, alas! how very soon this silly little Fly,
Hearing his wily, flattering words, came slowly flitting by;
With buzzing wings she hung aloft, then near and nearer
      drew,—
Thinking only of her brilliant eyes, and green and purple hue;
Thinking only of her crested head—poor foolish thing! At
      last,

Up jumped the cunning Spider, and fiercely held her fast.
He dragged her up his winding stair, into his dismal den
Within his little parlor—but she ne'er came out again!

And now, dear little children, who may this story read,
To idle, silly, flattering words, I pray you ne'er give heed;
Unto an evil counsellor close heart, and ear, and eye,
And take a lesson from this tale of the Spider and the Fly.

MARY HOWITT

ON A FAVORITE CAT, DROWNED
IN A TUB OF GOLDFISHES

'Twas on a lofty vase's side,
Where China's gayest art had dyed
  The azure flowers that blow;
Demurest of the tabby kind,
The pensive Selima reclined,
  Gazed on the lake below.

Her conscious tail her joy declared;
The fair round face, the snowy beard,
  The velvet of her paws,
Her coat, that with the tortoise vies,
Her ears of jet, and emerald eyes,
  She saw; and purr'd applause.

Still had she gazed, but 'midst the tide
Two angel forms were seen to glide,
  The Genii of the stream:
Their scaly armor's Tyrian hue
Thro' richest purple to the view
  Betray'd a golden gleam.

The hapless Nymph with wonder saw:
A whisker first and then a claw,
  With many an ardent wish,

[417]

She stretch'd in vain to reach the prize.
What female heart can gold despise?
  What Cat's averse to fish?

Presumptuous Maid! with looks intent
Again she stretch'd, again she bent,
  Nor knew the gulf between.
(Malignant Fate sat by, and smiled.)
The slipp'ry verge her feet beguiled,
  She tumbled headlong in.

Eight times emerging from the flood
She mew'd to ev'ry wat'ry god,
  Some speedy aid to send.
No Dolphin came, no Nereid stirr'd:
Nor cruel *Tom*, nor *Susan* heard.
  A Fav'rite has no friend!

From hence, ye Beauties undeceived,
Know, one false step is ne'er retrieved,
  And be with caution bold.
Not all that tempts your wand'ring eyes
And heedless hearts, is lawful prize;
  Nor all that glisters, gold.

THOMAS GRAY

[418]

ELEGY ON THE DEATH
OF A MAD DOG

Good people all, of every sort,
    Give ear unto my song;
And if you find it wondrous short
    It cannot hold you long.

In Islington there was a man,
    Of whom the world might say,
That still a godly race he ran,
    Whene'er he went to pray.

A kind and gentle heart he had,
    To comfort friends and foes;
The naked every day he clad,
    When he put on his clothes.

And in that town a dog was found,
    As many dogs there be,
Both mongrel, puppy, whelp, and hound,
    And curs of low degree.

This dog and man at first were friends;
    But when a pique began,
The dog, to gain some private ends,
    Went mad and bit the man.

Around from all the neighboring streets
   The wond'ring neighbors ran,
And swore the dog had lost his wits,
   To bite so good a man.

The wound it seem'd both sore and sad
   To every Christian eye;
And while they swore the dog was mad,
   They swore the man would die.

But soon a wonder came to light,
   That show'd the rogues they lied:
The man recover'd of the bite,
   The dog it was that died.

OLIVER GOLDSMITH

GROWLTIGER'S LAST STAND

Growltiger was a Bravo Cat, who lived upon a barge:
In fact he was the roughest cat that ever roamed at large.
From Gravesend up to Oxford he pursued his evil aims,
Rejoicing in his title of "The Terror of the Thames."

His manners and appearance did not calculate to please;
His coat was torn and seedy, he was baggy at the knees;
One ear was somewhat missing, no need to tell you why,
And he scowled upon a hostile world from one forbidding
      eye.

The cottagers of Rotherhithe knew something of his fame,
At Hammersmith and Putney people shuddered at his name.
They would fortify the hen-house, lock up the silly goose,
When the rumor ran along the shore: GROWLTIGER'S
      ON THE LOOSE!

Woe to the weak canary, that fluttered from its cage;
Woe to the pampered Pekinese, that faced Growltiger's rage.
Woe to the bristly Bandicoot, that lurks on foreign ships,
And woe to any Cat with whom Growltiger came to grips!

But most to Cats of foreign race his hatred had been vowed;
To Cats of foreign name and race no quarter was allowed.

The Persian and the Siamese regarded him with fear—
Because it was a Siamese had mauled his missing ear.

Now on a peaceful summer night, all nature seemed at
    play,
The tender moon was shining bright, the barge at Molesey
    lay.
All in the balmy moonlight it lay rocking on the tide—
And Growltiger was disposed to show his sentimental side.

His bucko mate, GRUMBUSKIN, long since had disap-
    peared,
For to the Bell at Hampton he had gone to wet his beard;
And his bosun, TUMBLEBRUTUS, he too had stol'n
    away—
In the yard behind the Lion he was prowling for his prey.

In the forepeak of the vessel Growltiger sat alone,
Concentrating his attention on the Lady GRIDDLEBONE.
And his raffish crew were sleeping in their barrels and their
    bunks—
As the Siamese came creeping in their sampans and their
    junks.

Growltiger had no eye or ear for aught but Griddlebone,
And the Lady seemed enraptured by his manly baritone,
Disposed to relaxation, and awaiting no surprise—
But the moonlight shone reflected from a thousand bright
    blue eyes.

And closer still and closer the sampans circled round,
And yet from all the enemy there was not heard a sound.
The lovers sang their last duet, in danger of their lives—
For the foe was armed with toasting forks and cruel carving
    knives.

Then GILBERT gave the signal to his fierce Mongolian
    horde;
With a frightful burst of fireworks the Chinks they swarmed
    aboard.
Abandoning their sampans, and their pullaways and junks,
They battened down the hatches on the crew within their
    bunks.

Then Griddlebone she gave a screech, for she was badly
    skeered;
I am sorry to admit it, but she quickly disappeared.
She probably escaped with ease, I'm sure she was not
    drowned—
But a serried ring of flashing steel Growltiger did surround.

The ruthless foe pressed forward, in stubborn rank on rank;
Growltiger to his vast surprise was forced to walk the plank.
He who a hundred victims had driven to that drop,
At the end of all his crimes was forced to go ker-flip, ker-
    flop.

Oh there was joy in Wapping when the news flew through
      the land;
At Maidenhead and Henley there was dancing on the strand.
Rats were roasted whole at Brentford, and at Victoria Dock,
And a day of celebration was commanded at Bangkok.

T. S. Eliot

MARY AND HER LAMB

Mary had a little lamb,
Its fleece was white as snow,
And everywhere that Mary went
The lamb was sure to go;
He followed her to school one day—
That was against the rule.
It made the children laugh and play
To see a lamb at school.

And so the teacher turned him out,
But still he lingered near,
And waited patiently about
Till Mary did appear;
And then he ran to her, and laid
His head upon her arm,
As if he said, "I'm not afraid—
You'll keep me from all harm."

"What makes the lamb love Mary so?"
The eager children cry.
"Oh, Mary loves the lamb, you know,"
The teacher did reply;

"And you each gentle animal
In confidence may bind
And make them follow at your call,
If you are always kind."

SARAH JOSEPHA HALE

BETH GELERT

The spearman heard the bugle sound,
   And cheer'ly smiled the morn;
And many a brach, and many a hound,
   Attend Llewellyn's horn.

And still he blew a louder blast,
   And gave a louder cheer;
"Come, Gelert, why art thou the last
   Llewellyn's horn to hear?

"Oh, where does faithful Gelert roam,
   The flower of all his race.
So true, so brave—a lamb at home,
   A lion in the chase."

That day Llewellyn little loved
   The chase of hart or hare,
And scant and small the booty proved,
   For Gelert was not there.

Unpleased, Llewellyn homeward hied,
   When, near the portal seat,
His truant Gelert he espied,
   Bounding his lord to greet.

But when he gained the castle door,
   Aghast the chieftain stood;
The hound was smeared with gouts of gore,
   His lips and fangs ran blood!

Llewellyn gazed with wild surprise:
   Unused such looks to meet,
His favorite checked his joyful guise,
   And crouched, and licked his feet.

Onward in haste Llewellyn passed
   (And on went Gelert, too),
And still where'er his eyes were cast,
   Fresh blood-gouts shocked his view!

O'erturned his infant's bed he found,
   The bloodstained cover rent;
And all around the walls and ground
   With recent blood besprent.

He called his child—no voice replied;
   He searched with terror wild;
Blood! blood! he found on every side,
   But nowhere found his child!

"Hell-hound! by thee my child's devoured!"
   The frantic father cried;
And to the hilt his vengeful sword
   He plunged in Gelert's side.

[428]

His suppliant, as to earth he fell,
    No pity could impart;
But still his Gelert's dying yell,
    Passed heavy o'er his heart.

Aroused by Gelert's dying yell,
    Some slumberer wakened nigh;
What words the parent's joy can tell,
    To hear his infant cry!

Concealed beneath a mangled heap,
    His hurried search had missed,
All glowing from his rosy sleep,
    His cherub-boy he kissed!

Nor scratch had he, nor harm, nor dread,
    But the same couch beneath
Lay a great wolf, all torn and dead,
    Tremendous still in death!

Ah! what was then Llewellyn's pain!
    For now the truth was clear:
The gallant hound the wolf had slain,
    To save Llewellyn's heir.

Vain, vain was all Llewellyn's woe;
    "Best of any kind, adieu!
The frantic deed which laid thee low
    This heart shall ever rue!"

[429]

And now a gallant tomb they raised,
    With costly sculpture decked;
And marbles storied with his praise
    Poor Gelert's bones protect.

Here never could the spearman pass,
    Or forester, unmoved,
Here oft the tear-besprinkled grass
    Llewellyn's sorrow proved.

And here he hung his horn and spear,
    And oft, as evening fell,
In fancy's piercing sounds would hear
    Poor Gelert's dying yell.
                    WILLIAM ROBERT SPENCER

A RUNNABLE STAG

When the pods went pop in the broom, green broom,
  And apples began to be golden-skinned,
We harbored a stag in the Priory coomb,
  And we feathered his trail up-wind, up-wind,
  We feathered his trail up-wind—
    A stag of warrant, a stag, a stag,
    A runnable stag, a kingly crop,
    Brow, bay and tray and three on top,
    A stag, a runnable stag.

Then the huntsman's horn rang yap, yap, yap,
  And "Forwards" we heard the harborer shout;
But 'twas only a brocket that broke a gap
  In the beechen underwood, driven out,
  From the underwood antlered out
    By warrant and might of the stag, the stag,
    The runnable stag, whose lordly mind
    Was bent on sleep, though beamed and tined
    He stood, a runnable stag.

So we tufted the cover till afternoon
  With Tinkerman's Pup and Bell-of-the-North;
And hunters were sulky and hounds out of tune
  Before we tufted the right stag forth,

Before we tufted him forth,
  The stage of warrant, the wily stag,
  The runnable stag with his kingly crop,
  Brow, bay and tray and three on the top,
  The royal and runnable stag.

It was Bell-of-the-North and Tinkerman's Pup
  That stuck to the scent till the copse was drawn
"Tally ho! tally ho!" and the hunt was up,
  The tufters whipped and the pack laid on
  The resolute pack laid on,
    And the stag of warrant away at last,
    The runnable stag, the same, the same,
    His hoofs on fire, his horns like flame,
    A stag, a runnable stag.

"Let your gelding be: if you check or chide
  He stumbles at once and you're out of the hunt;
For three hundred gentlemen, able to ride
  On hunters accustomed to bear the brunt,
  Accustomed to bear the brunt,
    Are after the runnable stag, the stag,
    The runnable stag with his kingly crop,
    Brow, bay and tray and three on top,
    The right, the runnable stag."

By perilous paths in coomb and dell,
  The heather, the rocks, and the river-bed,
The pace grew hot, for the scent lay well,

And a runnable stag goes right ahead,
The quarry went right ahead—
 Ahead, ahead, and fast and far;
 His antlered crest, his cloven hoof,
 Brow, bay and tray and three aloof,
 The stag, the runnable stag.

For a matter of twenty miles and more,
 By the densest hedge and the highest wall,
Through herds of bullocks he baffled the lore
 Of harborer, huntsman, hounds and all,
 Of harborer, hounds and all—
  The stag of warrant, the wily stag,
  For twenty miles and five and five,
  He ran, and he never was caught alive,
  This stag, this runnable stag.

When he turned at bay in the leafy gloom,
 In the emerald gloom where the brook ran deep,
He heard in the distance the rollers boom,
 And he saw in a vision of peaceful sleep,
 In a wonderful vision of sleep,
  A stag of warrant, a stag, a stag,
  A runnable stag in a jeweled bed,
  Under the sheltering ocean dead,
  A stag, a runnable stag.

So a fateful hope lit up his eye,
 And he opened his nostrils wide again,

[433]

And he tossed his branching antlers high,
  As he headed the hunt down the Charlock glen,
  As he raced down the echoing glen
    For five miles more, the stag, the stag,
    For twenty miles, and five and five,
    Not to be caught now, dead or alive,
    The stag, the runnable stag.

Three hundred gentlemen, able to ride,
  Three hundred horses as gallant and free,
Beheld him escape on the evening tide,
  Far out till he sank in the Severn Sea,
  Till he sank in the depths of the sea—
    The stag, the buoyant stag, the stag
    That slept at last in a jeweled bed
    Under the sheltering ocean spread,
    The stag, the runnable stag.

JOHN DAVIDSON

WIDDECOMBE FAIR

"Tom Pearse, Tom Pearse, lend me your gray mare,"
All along, down along, out along, lee.
"For I want for to go to Widdecombe Fair,
Wi' Bill Brewer, Jan Stewer, Peter Gurncy, Peter Davy,
Dan'l Whiddon, Harry Hawk,
Old Uncle Tom Cobley and all."
Old Uncle Tom Cobley and all.

"And when shall I see again my gray mare?"
All along, down along, out along, lee.
"By Friday soon, or Saturday noon,
Wi' Bill Brewer, Jan Stewer, Peter Gurney, Peter Davy,
Dan'l Whiddon, Harry Hawk,
Old Uncle Tom Cobley and all."
Old Uncle Tom Cobley and all.

Then Friday came and Saturday noon,
All along, down along, out along, lee.
But Tom Pearse's old mare hath not trotted home,
Wi' Bill Brewer, Jan Stewer, Peter Gurney, Peter Davy,
Dan'l Whiddon, Harry Hawk,
Old Uncle Tom Cobley and all.
Old Uncle Tom Cobley and all.

So Tom Pearse he got up to the top o' the hill,
    All along, down along, out along, lee.
And he seed his old mare down a-making her will,
    Wi' Bill Brewer, Jan Stewer, Peter Gurney, Peter Davy,
    Dan'l Whiddon, Harry Hawk,
    Old Uncle Tom Cobley and all.
       Old Uncle Tom Cobley and all.

So Tom Pearse's old mare her took sick and her died,
    All along, down along, out along, lee.
And Tom he sat down on a stone, and he cried
    Wi' Bill Brewer, Jan Stewer, Peter Gurney, Peter Davy,
    Dan'l Whiddon, Harry Hawk,
    Old Uncle Tom Cobley and all.
       Old Uncle Tom Cobley and all.

But this isn't the end o' this shocking affair,
    All along, down along, out along, lee.
Nor, though they be dead, of the horrid career
    Of Bill Brewer, Jan Stewer, Peter Gurney, Peter Davy,
    Dan'l Whiddon, Harry Hawk,
    Old Uncle Tom Cobley and all.
       Old Uncle Tom Cobley and all.

When the wind whistles cold on the moor of a night,
    All along, down along, out along, lee.
Tom Pearse's old mare doth appear, ghastly white,
    Wi' Bill Brewer, Jan Stewer, Peter Gurney, Peter Davy,
    Dan'l Whiddon, Harry Hawk,

Old Uncle Tom Cobley and all.
Old Uncle Tom Cobley and all.

And all the long night he heard skirling and groans,
All along, down along, out along, lee.
From Tom Pearse's old mare in her rattling bones,
And from Bill Brewer, Jan Stewer, Peter Gurney, Peter
Davy,
Dan'l Whiddon, Harry Hawk,
Old Uncle Tom Cobley and all.
Old Uncle Tom Cobley and all.

TRADITIONAL: ENGLISH

HUMOROUS POEMS

SORROWS OF WERTHER

Werther had a love for Charlotte
 Such as words could never utter;
Would you know how first he met her?
 She was cutting bread and butter.

Charlotte was a married lady,
 And a moral man was Werther,
And for all the wealth of Indies
 Would do nothing for to hurt her.

So he sighed and pined and ogled,
 And his passion boiled and bubbled,
Till he blew his silly brains out,
 And no more by it was troubled.

Charlotte, having seen his body
 Borne before her on a shutter,
Like a well-conducted person,
 Went on cutting bread and butter.
   WILLIAM MAKEPEACE THACKERAY

A CODE OF MORALS

Now Jones had left his new-wed bride to keep his house in
        order
And hied away to the Hurrum Hills above the Afghan bor-
        der,
To sit on a rock with a heliograph; but ere he left he taught
His wife the working of the Code that sets the miles at
        naught.

And Love had made him very sage, as Nature made her fair;
So Cupid and Apollo linked, *per* heliograph, the pair.
At dawn, across the Hurrum Hills, he flashed her counsel
        wise—
At e'en, the dying sunset bore her husband's homilies.

He warned her 'gainst seductive youths in scarlet clad and
        gold,
As much as 'gainst the blandishments paternal of the old;
But kept his gravest warnings for (hereby the ditty hangs)
That snowy haired Lothario, Lieutenant-General Bangs.

'Twas General Bangs, with Aide and Staff, who tittupped on
        the way,
When they beheld a heliograph tempestuously at play.
They thought of Border risings, and of stations sacked and
        burnt—

So stopped to take the message down—and this is what they
      learnt—

"Dash dot dot, dot, dot dash, dot dash dot" twice. The Gen-
      eral swore.
"Was ever General Officer addressed as 'dear' before?
" 'My Love,' i' faith! 'My Duck,' Gadzooks! 'My darling
      popsy-wop!'
"Spirit of great Lord Wolseley, *who* is on that mountain-
      top?"

The artless Aide-de-camp was mute, the gilded Staff were
      still,
As, dumb with pent-up mirth, they booked that message
      from the hill;
For clear as summer lightning-flare, the husband's warning
      ran:—
"Don't dance or ride with General Bangs—a most immoral
      man."

(At dawn, across the Hurrum Hills, he flashed her counsel
      wise—
But, howsoever Love be blind, the world at large hath eyes.)
With damnatory dot and dash he heliographed his wife
Some interesting details of the General's private life.

The artless Aide-de-camp was mute, the shining Staff were
      still,
And red and ever redder grew the General's shaven gill.

[442]

And this is what he said at last (his feelings matter not):—
"I think we've tapped a private line. Hi! Threes about there!
    Trot!"

All honor unto Bangs, for ne'er did Jones thereafter know
By word or act official who read off that helio.
But the tale is on the Frontier, and from Michni to Mooltan
They know the worthy General as "that most immoral man."

                    RUDYARD KIPLING

JABBERWOCKY

'Twas brillig, and the slithy toves
   Did gyre and gimble in the wabe:
All mimsy were the borogroves,
   And the mome raths outgrabe.

"Beware the Jabberwock, my son!
   The jaws that bite, the claws that catch!
Beware the Jubjub bird, and shun
   The frumious Bandersnatch!"

He took his vorpal sword in hand:
   Long time the manxome foe he sought—
So rested he by the Tumtum tree,
   And stood awhile in thought.

And, as in uffish thought he stood,
   The Jabberwock, with eyes of flame,
Came whiffling through the tulgey wood,
   And burbled as it came!

One, two! One, two! And through and through
   The vorpal blade went snicker-snack!
He left it dead, and with its head
   He went galumphing back.

"And hast thou slain the Jabberwock?
  Come to my arms, my beamish boy!
O frabjous day! Callooh! Callay!"
  He chortled in his joy.

'Twas brillig, and the slithy toves
  Did gyre and gimble in the wabe:
All mimsy were the borogroves,
  And the mome raths out grabe.

LEWIS CARROLL

BALLAD

The auld wife sat at her ivied door,
   (*Butter and eggs and a pound of cheese*)
A thing she had frequently done before;
   And her spectacles lay on her apron'd knees.

The piper he piped on the hill-top high,
   (*Butter and eggs and a pound of cheese*)
Till the cow said "I die," and the goose ask'd "Why?"
   And the dog said nothing, but searched for fleas.

The farmer he strode through the square farmyard;
   (*Butter and eggs and a pound of cheese*)
His last brew of ale was a trifle hard—
   The connection of which with the plot one sees.

The farmer's daughter hath frank blue eyes;
   (*Butter and eggs and a pound of cheese*)
She hears the rooks caw in the windy skies,
   As she sits at her lattice and shells her peas.

The farmer's daughter hath ripe red lips;
   (*Butter and eggs and a pound of cheese*)
If you try to approach her, away she skips
   Over tables and chairs with apparent ease.

[446]

GENTLE ALICE BROWN

It was a robber's daughter, and her name was ALICE
    BROWN,
Her father was the terror of a small Italian town;
Her mother was a foolish, weak, but amiable old thing;
But it isn't of her parents that I'm going for to sing.

As ALICE was a-sitting at her window-sill one day
A beautiful young gentleman he chanced to pass that way;
She cast her eyes upon him, and he looked so good and true,
That she thought, "I could be happy with a gentleman like
    you!"

And every morning passed her house that cream of gentle-
    men,
She knew she might expect him at a quarter unto ten,
A sorter in the Custom-house, it was his daily road
(The Custom-house was fifteen minutes' walk from her
    abode).

But ALICE was a pious girl, who knew it wasn't wise
To look at strange young sorters with expressive purple eyes;
So she sought the village priest to whom her family con-
    fessed—
The priest by whom their little sins were carefully assessed.

"Oh, holy father," ALICE said, " 'twould grieve you, would
    it not?
To discover that I was a most disreputable lot!
Of all unhappy sinners I'm the most unhappy one!"
The padre said, "Whatever have you been and gone and
    done?"

"I have helped mamma to steal a little kiddy from its dad,
I've assisted dear papa in cutting up a little lad.
I've planned a little burglary and forged a little check,
And slain a little baby for the coral on its neck!"

The worthy pastor heaved a sigh, and dropped a silent tear—
And said, "You mustn't judge yourself too heavily, my dear—
It's wrong to murder babies, little corals for to fleece;
But sins like these one expiates at half-a-crown apiece.

"Girls will be girls—you're very young, and flighty in your
    mind;
Old heads upon young shoulders we must not expect to find:
We mustn't be too hard upon these little girlish tricks—
Let's see—five crimes at half-a-crown—exactly twelve-and-
    six."

"Oh, father," little ALICE cried, "your kindness makes me
    weep,
You do these little things for me so singularly cheap—
Your thoughtful liberality I never can forget;
But oh, there is another crime I haven't mentioned yet!

"A pleasant-looking gentleman, with pretty purple eyes,—
I've noticed at my window, as I've sat a-catching flies;
He passes by it every day as certain as can be—
I blush to say I've winked at him, and he has winked at me!"

"For shame," said FATHER PAUL, "my erring daughter!
  On my word
This is the most distressing news that I have ever heard.
Why, naughty girl, your excellent papa has pledged your
  hand
To a promising young robber, the lieutenant of his band!

"This dreadful piece of news will pain your worthy parents
  so!
They are the most remunerative customers I know;
For many, many years they've kept starvation from my doors,
I never knew so criminal a family as yours!

"The common country folk in this insipid neighborhood
Have nothing to confess, they're so ridiculously good;
And if you marry any one respectable at all,
Why, you'll reform, and what will then become of FA-
  THER PAUL?"

The worthy priest, he up and drew his cowl upon his crown,
And started off in haste to tell the news to ROBBER
  BROWN;
To tell him how his daughter, who was now for marriage fit,
Had winked upon a sorter, who reciprocated it.

[453]

Good ROBBER BROWN he muffled up his anger pretty
      well,
He said, "I have a notion, and that notion I will tell;
I will nab this gay young sorter, terrify him into fits,
And get my gentle wife to chop him into little bits.

"I've studied human nature, and I know a thing or two;
Though a girl may fondly love a living gent, as many do,
A feeling of disgust upon her senses there will fall
When she looks upon his body chopped particularly small."

He traced that gallant sorter to a still suburban square;
He watched his opportunity and seized him unaware;
He took a life-preserver and he hit him on the head,
And MRS. BROWN dissected him before she went to bed.

And pretty little ALICE grew more settled in her mind,
She never more was guilty of a weakness of the kind,
Until at length good ROBBER BROWN bestowed her
      pretty hand
On the promising young robber, the lieutenant of his band.

W. S. GILBERT

THE WALRUS AND THE CARPENTER

The sun was shining on the sea,
  Shining with all his might:
He did his very best to make
  The billows smooth and bright—
And this was odd, because it was
  The middle of the night.

The moon was shining sulkily,
  Because she thought the sun
Had got no business to be there
  After the day was done—
"It's very rude of him," she said,
  "To come and spoil the fun!"

The sea was wet as wet could be,
  The sands were dry as dry.
You could not see a cloud, because
  No cloud was in the sky:
No birds were flying overhead—
  There were no birds to fly.

The Walrus and the Carpenter
  Were walking close at hand:
They wept like anything to see
  Such quantities of sand:

"If this were only cleared away,"
  They said, "it *would* be grand!"

"If seven maids with seven mops
  Swept it for half a year,
Do you suppose," the Walrus said,
  "That they could get it clear?"
"I doubt it," said the Carpenter,
  And shed a bitter tear.

"O Oysters, come and walk with us!"
  The Walrus did beseech.
"A pleasant walk, a pleasant talk,
  Along the briny beach:
We cannot do with more than four,
  To give a hand to each."

The eldest Oyster looked at him,
  But never a word he said:
The eldest Oyster winked his eye,
  And shook his heavy head—
Meaning to say he did not choose
  To leave the oyster-bed.

But four young Oysters hurried up,
  All eager for the treat:
Their coats were brushed, their faces washed,
  Their shoes were clean and neat—
And this was odd, because, you know,
  They hadn't any feet.

[456]

Four other oysters followed them,
  And yet another four;
And thick and fast they came at last,
  And more, and more, and more—
All hopping through the frothy waves,
  And scrambling to the shore.

The Walrus and the Carpenter
  Walked a mile or so,
And then they rested on a rock
  Conveniently low:
And all the little Oysters stood
  And waited in a row.

"The time has come," the Walrus said,
  "To talk of many things:
Of shoes—and ships—and sealing-wax—
  Of cabbages—and kings—
And why the sea is boiling hot—
  And whether pigs have wings."

"But wait a bit," the Oysters cried,
  "Before we have our chat;
For some of us are out of breath,
  And all of us are fat!"
"No hurry!" said the Carpenter.
  They thanked him much for that.

"A loaf of bread," the Walrus said,
  "Is what we chiefly need:

[457]

Pepper and vinegar besides
    Are very good indeed—
Now, if you're ready, Oysters dear,
    We can begin to feed."

"But not on us!" the Oysters cried,
    Turning a little blue.
"After such kindness, that would be
    A dismal thing to do!"
"The night is fine," the Walrus said.
    "Do you admire the view?

"It was so kind of you to come!
    And you are very nice!"
The Carpenter said nothing but
    "Cut us another slice.
I wish you were not quite so deaf—
    I've had to ask you twice!"

"It seems a shame," the Walrus said,
    "To play them such a trick.
After we've brought them out so far,
    And made them trot so quick!"
The Carpenter said nothing but
    "The butter's spread too thick!"

"I weep for you," the Walrus said:
    "I deeply sympathize."
With sobs and tears he sorted out

Those of the largest size,
Holding his pocket-handkerchief
Before his streaming eyes.

"O Oysters," said the Carpenter,
"You've had a pleasant run!
Shall we be trotting home again?"
But answer came there none—
And this was scarcely odd, because
They'd eaten every one.

LEWIS CARROLL

LITTLE BILLEE

There were three sailors of Bristol city
   Who took a boat and went to sea.
But first with beef and captain's biscuits
   And pickled pork they loaded she.

There was gorging Jack and guzzling Jimmy,
   And the youngest he was little Billee,
Now when they got so far as the Equator
   They'd nothing left but one split pea.

Says gorging Jack to guzzling Jimmy,
   "With one another, we shouldn't agree!
There's little Bill, he's young and tender,
   We're old and tough, so let's eat he."

"Oh! Bill, we're going to kill and eat you,
   So undo the button of your chemie."
When Bill received this information
   He used his pocket-handkerchie.

"First let me say my catechism,
   Which my poor mammy taught to me."
"Make haste, make haste," says guzzling Jimmy
   While Jack pulled out his snickersnee.

So Billy went up to the main topgallant mast,
   And down he fell on his bended knee.
He scarce had come to the twelfth commandment
   When up he jumps, "There's land I see.

"Jerusalem and Madagascar,
   And North and South Amerikee:
There's the British flag a-riding at anchor,
   With Admiral Napier, K.C.B."

So when they got aboard of the Admiral's
   He hanged fat Jack and flogged Jimmee;
But as for little Bill, *he* made him
   The Captain of a Seventy-Three.

      WILLIAM MAKEPEACE THACKERAY

THE BALLAD OF THE OYSTERMAN

It was a tall young oysterman lived by the river-side,
His shop was just upon the bank, his boat was on the tide;
The daughter of a fisherman, that was so straight and slim,
Lived over on the other bank, right opposite to him.

It was the pensive oysterman that saw a lovely maid,
Upon a moonlight evening, a-sitting in the shade;
He saw her wave her handkerchief, as much as if to say,
"I'm wide awake, young oysterman, and all the folks away."

Then up arose the oysterman, and to himself said he,
"I guess I'll leave the skiff at home, for fear that folks should
            see;
I read it in the story-book, that, for to kiss his dear,
Leander swam the Hellespont,—and I will swim this here."

And he has leaped into the waves, and crossed the shining
            stream,
And he has clambered up the bank, all in the moonlight
            gleam;
Oh there were kisses sweet as dew, and words as soft as
            rain,—
But they have heard her father's steps, and in he leaps again!

Out spoke the ancient fisherman,—"Oh what was that, my
    daughter?"
" 'Twas nothing but a pebble, sir, I threw into the water."
"And what is that, pray tell me, love, that paddles off so
    fast?"
"It's nothing but a porpoise, sir, that's been a-swimming
    past."

Out spoke the ancient fisherman,—"Now bring me my har-
    poon!
I'll get into my fishing boat, and fix the fellow soon."
Down fell that pretty innocent, as falls a snow-white lamb,
Her hair drooped round her pallid cheeks, like seaweed on a
    clam.

Alas for those two loving ones! she waked not from her
    swound,
And he was taken with the cramp, and in the waves was
    drowned;
But Fate has metamorphosed them, in pity of their woe,
And now they keep an oyster-shop for mermaids down be-
    low.

OLIVER WENDELL HOLMES

SAVE THE TIGER!

When Lady Jane refused to be
The wife of Viscount Fiddledee
He rose abruptly from his knee
   And said, "Excuse this bungle—
I think I will not stay to dine,
There is a train at half-past nine;
Tomorrow by the fastest line
   I'm leaving for the jungle.

   "Ho, varlet, run and pack my gun,
   My passport pray discover;
I mean to shoot some savage brute
   To show how much I love her.
Far off in India's poisoned swamps
Some unsuspecting tiger romps,
   Condemned to die;
   And you know why—
'Cos you won't marry me.
Oh, ain't you got no heart, my gal?
Think of that dumb animal.
   Save that tiger,
   Poor dumb tiger,
   Save that tiger—marry me!

"I'll hunt him down on shiny nights
With cunning telescopic sights,
And if the creature turns and bites,
    As is his cruel fashion,
I'll lie content and let him chew,
A-thinking all the time of you;
For what's the worst that he can do
    Compared with hopeless passion?

    "Ho, varlet, run and pack my gun,
        My lovely one rejects me.
I kind of ache to shoot a snake,
        For that's how it affects me.
With battle-axe and blunderbuss
I'll kill the hippopotamus;
        Some buffalo
        Has got to go
    Because you won't be mine.
Heartless one, I'm better dead,
But think of that dumb quadruped;
        Save that python,
        Save that hippo,
    Save that buffalo—be mine!"

The Lady Jane began to cry;
The thought of hippopotami
Unnaturally doomed to die
    Had stirred her woman's pity.
She married him. And till this day,

Whenever he would have his way,
He only has to sing or say
   This moving little ditty:

    "Ho, pack my gun, you naughty one!
    Although I love you madly,
I'm off to shoot some savage brute,
   You do behave so badly.
I'd like to beat you, but you'd laugh,
I'll take it out of some giraffe,
    Some buffalo
    Has got to go
   Because you won't be good.
Ain't you got no heart, dear wife?
You can't approve of taking life—
    Then save that tiger,
    Poor dumb tiger,
   Save that buffalo—be good!"

A. P. HERBERT

THE OWL AND THE PUSSY-CAT

The Owl and the Pussy-Cat went to sea
   In a beautiful pea-green boat:
They took some honey, and plenty of money
   Wrapped up in a five-pound note.
The Owl looked up to the stars above,
   And sang to a small guitar,
   "O lovely Pussy, O Pussy, my love,
   What a beautiful Pussy you are,
      You are,
      You are!
   What a beautiful Pussy you are!"

Pussy said to the Owl, "You elegant fowl,
   How charmingly sweet you sing!
Oh! let us be married; too long we have tarried:
   But what shall we do for a ring?"
They sailed away, for a year and a day,
   To the land where the bong-tree grows;
And there in a wood a Piggy-wig stood,
   With a ring at the end of his nose.
      His nose,
      His nose,
   With a ring at the end of his nose.

"Dear Pig, are you willing to sell for one shilling
  Your ring?" Said the Piggy, "I will."
So they took it away, and were married next day
  By the Turkey who lives on the hill.
They dined on mince and slices of quince,
  Which they ate with a runcible spoon;
And hand in hand, on the edge of the sand
  They danced by the light of the moon,
      The moon,
      The moon,
  They danced by the light of the moon.

EDWARD LEAR

THE POBBLE WHO HAS NO TOES

The Pobble who has no toes
   Had once as many as we;
When they said, "Some day you may lose them all;"
   He replied, "Fish fiddle de-dee!"
And his Aunt Jobiska made him drink
Lavender water tinged with pink;
For she said, "The World in general knows
There's nothing so good for a Pobble's toes!"

The Pobble who has no toes,
   Swam across the Bristol Channel;
But before he set out he wrapped his nose
   In a piece of scarlet flannel.
For his Aunt Jobiska said, "No harm
Can come to his toes if his nose is warm;
And it's perfectly known that a Pobble's toes
Are safe—provided he minds his nose."

The Pobble swam fast and well,
   And when boats or ships came near him,
He tinkledy-binkledy-winkled a bell
   So that all the world could hear him.
And all the Sailors and Admirals cried,
When they saw him nearing the further side,—

"He has gone to fish for his Aunt Jobiska's
Runcible Cat with crimson whiskers!"

But before he touched the shore,—
    The shore of the Bristol Channel,
A sea-green Porpoise carried away
    His wrapper of scarlet flannel.
And when he came to observe his feet,
Formerly garnished with toes so neat,
His face at once became forlorn
On perceiving that all his toes were gone!

And nobody ever knew,
    From that dark day to the present,
Whoso had taken the Pobble's toes,
    In a manner so far from pleasant.
Whether the shrimps or crawfish grey,
Or crafty Mermaids stole them away,
Nobody knew; and nobody knows
How the Pobble was robbed of his twice five toes!

The Pobble who has no toes
    Was placed in a friendly bark,
And they rowed him back, and carried him up
    To his Aunt Jobiska's Park.
And she made him a feast, at his earnest wish,
Of eggs and buttercups fried with fish;
And she said, "It's a fact the whole world knows,
That Pobbles are happier without their toes."

                                    EDWARD LEAR

THE DUEL

The gingham dog and the calico cat
Side by side on the table sat;
'Twas half-past twelve, and (what do you think!)
Nor one nor t'other had slept a wink!
  The old Dutch clock and the Chinese plate
  Appeared to know as sure as fate
There was going to be a terrible spat.
  (I wasn't there; I simply state
  What was told to me by the Chinese plate!)

The gingham dog went "bow-wow-wow!"
And the calico cat replied "mee-ow!"
The air was littered, an hour or so,
With bits of gingham and calico,
  While the old Dutch clock in the chimney-place
  Up with its hands before its face,
For it always dreaded a family row!
  (Now mind: I'm only telling you
  What the old Dutch clock declares is true!)

The Chinese plate looked very blue,
And wailed, "Oh, Dear! what shall we do!"
But the gingham dog and the calico cat
Wallowed this way and tumbled that,

Employing every tooth and claw
In the awfullest way you ever saw—
And, oh! how the gingham and calico flew!
   (Don't fancy I exaggerate—
   I got my news from the Chinese plate!)

Next morning, where the two had sat
They found no trace of dog or cat;
And some folks think unto this day
That burglars stole that pair away!
   But the truth about the cat and pup
   Is this: they ate each other up!
Now what do you really think of that!
   (The old Dutch clock it told me so,
   And that is how I came to know.)

                EUGENE FIELD

THE DEACON'S MASTERPIECE

Have you heard of the wonderful one-hoss shay,
That was built in such a logical way
It ran a hundred years to a day,
And then, of a sudden, it—ah, but stay,
I'll tell you what happened without delay,
Scaring the parson into fits,
Frightening people out of their wits,—
Have you ever heard of that, I say?

Seventeen hundred and fifty-five.
Georgius Secundus was then alive,—
Snuffy old drone from the German hive.
That was the year when Lisbon-town
Saw the earth open and gulp her down,
And Braddock's army was done so brown,
Left without a scalp to its crown.
It was on the terrible earthquake-day
That the Deacon finished the one-hoss shay.

Now in building of chaises, I tell you what,
There is always *somewhere* a weaker spot,—
In hub, tire, felloe, in spring or thill,
In panel, or crossbar, or floor, or sill,
In screw, bolt, thoroughbrace,—lurking still,

Find it somewhere you must and will,—
Above or below, or within or without,—
And that's the reason, beyond a doubt,
A chaise *breaks down,* but doesn't *wear out.*

But the Deacon swore (as Deacons do),
With an "I dew vum," or an "I tell yeou,"
He would build one shay to beat the taown
'N' the keounty 'n' all the kentry raoun';
It should be so built that it *couldn'* break daown:
—"Fur," said the Deacon, " 'tis mighty plain
Thut the weakes' place mus' stan' the strain;
'N' the way t' fix it, uz I maintain,
    Is only jest
T' make that place uz strong uz the rest."

So the Deacon inquired of the village folk
Where he could find the strongest oak,
That couldn't be split nor bent nor broke,—
That was for spokes and floor and sills;
He sent for lancewood to make the thills;
The crossbars were ash, from the straightest trees,
The panels of white-wood, that cuts like cheese,
But lasts like iron for things like these;
The hubs of logs from the "Settler's ellum,"—
Last of its timber,—they couldn't sell 'em,
Never an axe had seen their chips,
And the wedges flew from between their lips,
Their blunt ends frizzled like celery tips;

[474]

Step and prop-iron, bolt and screw,
Spring, tire, axle, and linchpin too,
Steel of the finest, bright and blue;
Thoroughbrace bison-skin, thick and wide;
Boot, top, dasher, from tough old hide
Found in the pit when the tanner died.
That was the way he "put her through."—
"There!" said the Deacon, "naow she'll dew!"

Do! I tell you, I rather guess
She was a wonder, and nothing less!
Colts grew horses, beards turned gray,
Deacon and Deaconess dropped away,
Children and grandchildren—where were they?
But there stood the stout old one-hoss shay
As fresh as on Lisbon-earthquake-day!

EIGHTEEN HUNDRED;—it came and found
The Deacon's masterpiece strong and sound.
Eighteen hundred increased by ten;—
"Hahnsum kerridge" they called it then.
Eighteen hundred and twenty came;—
Running as usual; much the same.
Thirty and forty at last arrive,
And then come fifty, and FIFTY-FIVE.

Little of all we value here
Wakes on the morn of its hundredth year
Without both feeling and looking queer.

In fact, there's nothing that keeps its youth,
So far as I know, but a tree and truth.
(This is a moral that runs at large;
Take it.—You're welcome.—No extra charge.)
FIRST OF NOVEMBER—the Earthquake-day,—
There are traces of age in the one-hoss shay,
A general flavor of mild decay,
But nothing local, as one may say.
There couldn't be,—for the Deacon's art
Had made it so like in every part
That there wasn't a chance for one to start.
For the wheels were just as strong as the thills,
And the floor was just as strong as the sills,
And the panels just as strong as the floor,
And the whipple-tree neither less nor more,
And the back-cross bar as strong as the fore,
And spring and axle and hub *encore*.
And yet, as *a whole*, it is past a doubt
In another hour it will be *worn out!*

First of November, 'Fifty-five!
This morning the parson takes a drive.
Now, small boys, get out of the way!
Here comes the wonderful one-hoss shay,
Drawn by a rat-tailed, ewe-necked bay.
"Huddup!" said the parson. Off went they.
The parson was working his Sunday text,—
Had got to *fifthly*, and stopped perplexed
At what the—Moses—was coming next.

[476]

All at once the horse stood still,
Close by the meet'n'-house on the hill.
First a shiver, and then a thrill,
Then something decidedly like a spill,—
And the parson was sitting up on a rock,
At half-past nine by the meet'n'-house clock,—
Just the hour of the Earthquake shock!
—What do you think the parson found,
When he got up and stared around?
The poor old chaise in a heap or mound,
As if it had been to the mill and ground!
You see, of course, if you're not a dunce,
How it went to pieces all at once,—
All at once, and nothing first,—
Just as bubbles do when they burst.

End of the wonderful one-hoss shay,
Logic is logic. That's all I say.

OLIVER WENDELL HOLMES

THE FAMOUS BALLAD OF
THE JUBILEE CUP

You may lift me up in your arms, lad, and turn my face to
the sun,
For a last look back to the dear old track where the Jubilee
Cup was won;
And draw your chair to my side, lad—no, thank ye, I feel no
pain—
For I'm going out with the tide, lad; but I'll tell you the tale
again.

I'm seventy-nine or nearly, and my head it has long turned
gray,
But it all comes back as clearly as though it was yesterday—
The dust, and the bookies shouting around the clerk of the
scales,
And the clerk of the course, and the nobs in force, and 'Is
'Ighness the Pr**ce of W*les.

'Twas a nine-hole thresh to wind'ard (but none of us cared
for that),
With a straight run home to the service tee, and a finish
along the flat,
"Stiff?" ah, well you may say it! Spot barred, and at five stone
ten!

But at two and a bisque I'd ha' run the risk; for I was a green-
horn then.

So we stripped to the B.Race signal, the old red swallow-
tail—
There was young Ben Bolt and the Portland Colt, and Aston
Villa, and Yale;
And W.G., and Steinitz, Leander and The Saint,
And the G*rm*n Emp*r*r's Meteor, a-looking as fresh as
paint;

John Roberts (scratch), and Safety Match, The Lascar, and
Lorna Doone,
Oom Paul (a bye), and Romany Rye, and me upon Wooden
Spoon;
And some of us cut for partners, and some of us strung for
baulk,
And some of us tossed for stations— But there, what use to
talk?

Three-quarter-back on the Kingsclere crack was station
enough for me,
With a fresh jackyarder blowing and the Vicarage goal a-lee!
And I leaned and patted her center-bit and eased the quid in
her cheek,
With a "Soh my lass!" and a "Woa you brute!"—for she
could do all but speak.

She was geared a thought too high perhaps; she was trained a
trifle fine;

[479]

But she had the grand reach forward! I never saw such a line!
Smooth-bored, clean run, from her fiddle head with its dainty
    ear half-cock,
Hard-bit, *pur sang*, from her overhang to the heel of her off
    hind sock.

Sir Robert he walked beside me as I worked her down to the
    mark;
"There's money on this, my lad," said he, "and most of 'em's
    running dark;
But ease the sheet if you're bunkered, and pack the scrim-
    mages tight,
And use your slide at the distance, and we'll drink to your
    health tonight!"

But I bent and tightened my stretcher. Said I to myself, said
    I—
"John Jones, this here is the Jubilee Cup, and you'll have to
    do or die."
And the words weren't hardly spoken when the umpire
    shouted "Play!"
And we all kicked off from the Gasworks End with a
    "Yoicks!" and a "Gone Away!"

And first I thought of nothing, as the clay flew by in lumps,
But stuck to the old Ruy Lopez, and wondered who'd call
    for trumps,
And luffed her close to the cushion, and watched each one
    as it broke,

And in triple file up the Rowley Mile we went like a trail of
    smoke.

The Lascar made the running but he didn't amount to much,
For old Oom Paul was quick on the ball, and headed it back
    to touch;
And the whole first flight led off with the right as The Saint
    took up the pace,
And drove it clean to the putting green and trumped it there
    with an ace.

John Roberts had given a miss in baulk, but Villa cleared
    with a punt;
And keeping her service hard and low the Meteor forged to
    the front;
With Romany Rye to windward at dormy and two to play,
And Yale close up—but a Jubilee Cup isn't run for every day.

We laid our course for the Warner— I tell you the pace was
    hot!
And again off Tattenham Corner a blanket covered the lot.
Check side! Check side! now steer her wide! and barely an
    inch of room,
With The Lascar's tail over our lee rail and brushing Lean-
    der's boom.

We were running as strong as ever—eight knots—but it
    couldn't last;
For the spray and the bails were flying, the whole field tail-
    ing fast;

[481]

And the Portland Colt had shot his bolt, and Yale was
    bumped at the Doves,
And The Lascar resigned to Steinitz, stalemated in fifteen
    moves.

It was bellows to mend with Roberts—starred three for a
    penalty kick:
But he chalked his cue and gave 'em the butt, and Oom Paul
    marked the trick—
"Offside—No Ball—and at fourteen all! Mark Cock! and
    two for his nob!"
When W.G. ran clean through his lee and beat him twice
    with a lob.

He yorked him twice on a crumbling pitch and wiped his eye
    with a brace,
But his guy-rope split with the strain of it and he dropped
    back out of the race;
And I drew a bead on the Meteor's lead, and challenging
    none too soon,
Bent over and patted her garboard strake, and called upon
    Wooden Spoon.

She was all of a shiver forward, the spoondrift thick on her
    flanks,
But I'd brought her an easy gambit, and nursed her over the
    banks;
She answered her helm—the darling! and woke up now with
    a rush,

While the Meteor's jock, he sat like a rock—he knew we
    rode for his brush!

There was no one else left in it. The Saint was using his whip,
And Safety Match, with a lofting catch, was pocketed deep
    at slip;
And young Ben Bolt with his niblick took miss at Leander's
    lunge,
But topped the net with the ricochet, and Steinitz threw up
    the sponge.

But none of the lot could stop the rot—nay, don't ask *me*
    to stop!
The Villa had called for lemons, Oom Paul had taken his
    drop,
And both were kicking the referee. Poor fellow! he done his
    best;
But, being in doubt, he'd ruled them out—which he always
    did when pressed.

So, inch by inch, I tightened the winch, and chucked the
    sandbags out—
I heard the nursery cannons pop, I heard the bookies shout:
"The Meteor wins!" "No, Wooden Spoon!" "Check!"
    "Vantage!" "Leg Before!"
"Last Lap!" "Pass Nap!" At his saddle-flap I put up the
    helm and wore.

You may overlap at the saddle-flap, and yet be loo'ed on the
    tape:

And it all depends upon changing ends, how a seven-year-
old will shape;
It was tack and tack to the Lepe and back—a fair ding-dong
to the Ridge,
And he led by his forward canvas yet as we shot 'neath Hammersmith Bridge.

He led by his forward canvas—he led from his strongest
suit—
But along we went on a roaring scent, and at Fawley I gained
a foot.
He fisted off with his jigger, and gave me his wash—too late!
Deuce—Vantage—Check! By neck and neck we rounded
into the straight.

I could hear the "Conquering 'Ero" a-crashing on Godfrey's
band,
And my hopes fell sudden to zero, just there, with the race in
hand—
In sight of the Turf's Blue Ribbon, in sight of the umpire's
tape,
As I felt the tack of her spinnaker c-rack! as I heard the steam
escape!

Had I lost at that awful juncture my presence of mind? . . .
but no!
I leaned and felt for the puncture, and plugged it there with
my toe . . .
Hand over hand by the Members' Stand I lifted and eased
her up,

[484]

Shot—clean and fair—to the crossbar there, and landed the
      Jubilee Cup!

"The odd by a head, and leg before," so the Judge he gave
      the word:
And the umpire shouted "Over!" but I neither spoke nor
      stirred.
They crowded round: for there on the ground I lay in a dead-
      cold swoon,
Pitched neck and crop on the turf atop of my beautiful
      Wooden Spoon.

Her dewlap tire was punctured, her bearings all red hot;
She'd a lolling tongue, and her bowsprit sprung, and her run-
      ning gear in a knot;
And amid the sobs of her backers, Sir Robert loosened her
      girth
And led her away to the knacker's. She had raced her last
      on earth!

But I mind me well of the tear that fell from the eye of our
      noble Pr*nce,
And the things he said as he tucked me in bed—and I've laid
      there ever since;
Tho' it all gets mixed up queerly that happened before my
      spill,—
But I draw my thousand yearly; it'll pay for the doctor's bill.

I'm going out with the tide, lad—you'll dig me a numble
      grave,

And whiles you will bring your bride, lad, and your sons, if
    sons you have,

And there when the dews are weeping, and the echoes mur-
    mur "Peace!"

And the salt, salt tide comes creeping and covers the popping-
    crease;

In the hour when the ducks deposit their eggs with a boasted
    force,

They'll look and whisper "How was it?" and you'll take them
    over the course,

And your voice will break as you try to speak of the glorious
    first of June,

When the Jubilee Cup, with John Jones up, was won upon
    Wooden Spoon.

                ARTHUR T. QUILLER-COUCH

CASEY AT THE BAT

It looked extremely rocky for the Mudville nine that day;
The score stood two to four, with but one inning left to play.
So, when Cooney died at second, and Burrows did the same,
A pallor wreathed the features of the patrons of the game.

A straggling few got up to go, leaving there the rest,
With that hope which springs eternal within the human
        breast.
For they thought: "If only Casey could get a whack at that,"
They'd put even money now, with Casey at the bat.

But Flynn preceded Casey, and likewise so did Blake,
And the former was a pudd'n, and the latter was a fake.
So on that stricken multitude a deathlike silence sat;
For there seemed but little chance of Casey's getting to the
        bat.

But Flynn let drive a "single," to the wonderment of all.
And the much-despiséd Blakey "tore the cover off the ball."
And when the dust had lifted, and they saw what had oc-
        curred,
There was Blakey safe at second, and Flynn a-huggin' third.

Then from the gladdened multitude went up a joyous yell—
It rumbled in the mountaintops, it rattled in the dell;

It struck upon the hillside and rebounded on the flat;
For Casey, mighty Casey, was advancing to the bat.

There was ease in Casey's manner as he stepped into his
place;
There was pride in Casey's bearing and a smile on Casey's
face;
And when responding to the cheers he lightly doffed his hat,
No stranger in the crowd could doubt 'twas Casey at the bat.

Ten thousand eyes were on him as he rubbed his hands with
dirt,
Five thousand tongues applauded when he wiped them on
his shirt;
Then when the writhing pitcher ground the ball into his hip,
Defiance glanced in Casey's eye, a sneer curled Casey's lip.

And now the leather-covered sphere came hurtling through
the air,
And Casey stood a-watching it in haughty grandeur there.
Close by the sturdy batsman the ball unheeded sped;
"That ain't my style," said Casey. "Strike one," the umpire
said.

From the benches black with people, there went up a muffled roar,
Like the beating of the storm waves on the stern and distant
shore.
"Kill him! kill the umpire!" shouted someone on the stand;

[488]

And it's likely they'd have killed him had not Casey raised his
  hand.

With a smile of Christian charity great Casey's visage shone;
He stilled the rising tumult, he made the game go on;
He signaled to the pitcher, and once more the spheroid flew;
But Casey still ignored it, and the umpire said, "Strike two."

"Fraud!" cried the maddened thousands, and the echo answered "Fraud!"
But one scornful look from Casey, and the audience was
  awed;
They saw his face go stern and cold, they saw his muscles
  strain,
And they knew that Casey wouldn't let the ball go by again.

The sneer is gone from Casey's lips, his teeth are clenched in
  hate,
He pounds with cruel vengeance his bat upon the plate;
And now the pitcher holds the ball, and now he lets it go,
And now the air is shattered by the force of Casey's blow.

Oh, somewhere in this favored land the sun is shining bright,
The band is playing somewhere, and somewhere hearts are
  light;
And somewhere men are laughing, and somewhere children
  shout,
But there is no joy in Mudville—Mighty Casey has struck
  out.

ERNEST LAWRENCE THAYER

[489]

INDEX OF AUTHORS

[491]

INDEX OF TITLES

[493]

INDEX OF FIRST LINES

[497]